THE SECOND
BOOK OF THE
STRANGE

THE SECOND
BOOK OF THE
STRANGE

Laurence D. Gadd

and

The Editors of
THE WORLD ALMANAC®

WORLD ALMANAC PUBLICATIONS
NEW YORK

Cover design: Donald C. DeMaio

Paperback edition distributed in the United States by Ballantine Books, a
Division of Random House, Inc. and in Canada by Random House of
Canada, Ltd.

Hardcover edition published and distributed by Prometheus Books,
700 East Amherst St., Buffalo, New York 14215
Library of Congress Catalog Card Number (paperback edition) 80-65779
Library of Congress Catalog Card Number (hardcover edition) 81-82644
Newspaper Enterprise Association, Inc. ISBN 0-911818-20-0
Ballantine Books ISBN 0-345-29776-8
Prometheus Books ISBN 0-87975-170-3

Printed in the United States of America

Newspaper Enterprise Association, Inc.
World Almanac Publications
200 Park Avenue
New York, New York 10166

Contents

THE HUMAN BEING

MEDICINE AND HEALING

THE UNIVERSE ● 165

UNIDENTIFIED FLYING OBJECTS ● 179

STRANGE BELIEFS AND PRACTICES ● 221

CULTS ● 239

PSYCHIC PHENOMENA ● 267

PARAPSYCHOLOGY 279

STRANGE PEOPLE ● 307

LEGENDARY CREATURES ● 319

INDEX ● 334

THE HUMAN BEING

Curiosities of the Mind

U-Shaped Behavior

An odd characteristic of the learning process of children is known as U-shaped behavior. Very young children, even the newborn, have special abilities which they spontaneously seem to forget in middle childhood and have to "relearn" as they grow older. This behavior is termed U-shaped after the up-down-up form of the graph of the child's development.

Probably the most widely known U-shaped phenomenon is the ability to walk. Newborn infants can walk if properly supported, but this capacity disappears within a month or two of birth. It does not reappear again until the infant is about a year old. U-shaped behavior also is apparent in speaking. When children first begin to talk, they usually form plurals and past tenses correctly. Howard Gardner, a developmental psychologist at Harvard University, gave the following example of this (see *The New York Times,* September 25, 1979, p. C3): children will say, for instance, "the mice came." Months later, they will make mistakes, however, saying "the mouses came" or "the mice comed." Proper usage does not usually return until the age of 3 or 4.

U-shaped behavior has also been observed in problem-solving ability and in artistic capacity. Researchers have discovered, for instance, that children aged 4 or 5 do better at solving certain problems than older children. In one experiment (also reported by Gardner, a developmental psychologist at Harvard University, in *The New York Times* article) children of several ages were shown two identical beakers filled with sugar water. The water from the two beakers was then poured into a single larger container. Four- and five-year-olds responded when questioned that the sweetness of the water had remained the same. Older children, aged 6 to 9, however, thought that the water had become twice as sweet. This error was found to disappear after age 10.

In a related phenomenon, younger children often seem to display greater creative imagination and artistic ability than older children. Gardner reported, for instance, that preschool children have a high degree of metaphoric ability—they will say that a bald man has a "barefoot head" or that a foot falling asleep feels "fizzy." This sort of imaginative linguistic output appears to decline in school-age children and then to re-emerge in pre-adolescence.

A traditional tenet of human developmental psychology is that children get progressively better at what they do as they grow older. The phenomenon of U-shaped behavior contradicts this tenet. It appears then that human development is not as rigidly schematic as previously believed.

A possible explanation for U-shaped behavior is that the child's initial abilities are of a different order from later learning or ability: They may be instinctive rather than learned. As Gardner notes: "The neural structures that allow the newborn child to 'walk' and also to 'swim' and to imitate certain facial movements seem to be reflexive. Thus, they should be sharply distinguished from later more volitional forms of walking, swimming, or imitation." In a similar manner, the child's early language ability may be due merely to imitation or memorization: the child simply parrots the proper forms of "mouse" and "come." Later, when the child begins to learn that speech is governed by rules of grammar, he at first may misapply some of these rules, leading to errors such as "the mouse comed." Proper speech returns when the rules of language—including the exceptions—are completely mastered.

In the sugar water experiment, younger children are thought to get the right answer because they view the problem on a common-sense basis: they know from experience that if two glasses of a sweetened drink are combined, the sweetness remains constant. Older children in the early grades of school view the problem from a more complicated point of view. They are just learning that when quantities are added together, they become greater. They apply this knowledge in an unsophisticated manner, however, and mistakenly assume that the sweetened drink has become twice as sweet; they do not take into account the fact that the amount of water has also doubled. Only around age 10, when they have thoroughly mastered the principles of addition, do they again solve the problem correctly.

In a sense, then, the middle stage of U-shaped behavior may not actually represent a decline in the child's ability. It may instead merely reflect the child's temporary confusion as he attempts to master a more sophisticated way of doing things. Mistakes naturally occur, but they represent forward movement rather than backsliding.

According to Gardner, this has important educational implications: "If teachers and parents are alerted to the fact that apparently wrong answers may in fact signal increasing sophistication, if they become aware of errors of growth, they will not penalize youngsters simply for failing to utter the desired answer. They will learn to focus instead on the reasoning processes that underlie all judgments."

Holographic Memory

The theory of holographic memory explains a traditional scientific mystery: how the brain processes and stores information.

Memory is one of the brain's key functions. The actual mechanisms that account for memory are poorly understood. Memory researchers agree only on the fact that memory is a result of biochemical changes in the brain and that memory is recalled when electrochemically activated. It has been theorized, most notably by Karl Pribram, a neuropsychologist at Stanford University in California, that the brain processes information as holograms and that memory is a holographic function.

A hologram is a three-dimensional image produced from a two-dimensional object (see *Holography*, p. 160). Commercial holograms, for instance, are contained on flat plates which, when illuminated by polarized light, produce an uncannily realistic image that actually seems to change position when the viewer views it from different angles. The key characteristic of any hologram is that any portion of the holographic plate bears *all* the information contained in the whole hologram; even a small fragment of the hologram can reproduce the image stored in the entire original.

The holographic theory would help explain several classic paradoxes of memory.

Brain science has long been puzzled by the mystery of memory loss, or rather, lack of memory loss. Why, for instance, are not certain memories destroyed by brain accidents? If a person has a stroke, and half his brain is destroyed, he does *not* lose half his memory. There seems to be no correspondence between how much brain tissue is lost and how much memory is lost. Some sections of the brain can continue to function perfectly while retaining only 2 percent of their cells or fibers. (Any other organ in the body would be almost completely incapacitated after losing 98 percent of itself.) The brain's "spare reserve" seems to be almost limitless.

Another paradox concerns the way motor skills can be transferred from one part of the body to another. Thus, a right-handed person can, if necessary, write a legible sentence with his left hand. This is a greater mystery than may at first appear. In the normal right-handed person, writing ability is controlled by a particular portion of the opposite, or left, hemisphere of the brain. The left hand, conversely, is controlled by the right hemisphere of the brain, which does not possess a writing control center and has never "written" before. How then does the right hemisphere instruct the left hand to produce a legible sentence? Why doesn't the right hemisphere have to learn from scratch—as in the case of a young child—how to write?

Traditional views of brain function do not explain these conundrums. The dominant theory of memory states that any particular memory is stored in one particular brain cell or set of cells. Yet the brain seems to have some method of diffusing memory over many cells or of moving memories from one part of the brain to another; otherwise, strokes would result in heavy memory loss and right-handed people would have an impossible task in writing with their left hands.

The holographic theory explains these mysteries by proposing that the brain does not store memories as separate "bits"—one memory "bit" to each brain cell—but as holograms diffused over many brain cells. Thus, when the eye views, say, a tree, the brain would not store the memory as a collection of individual images of leaves, twigs, and branches, with each image relegated to one particular cell. Instead, the image of the tree would be spread over a number of brain cells, each of which would have the capacity, like a hologram, of reproducing the entire image. Such a system of holographic memory has been likened to an insect's eye, which contains many tiny lenses instead of one big lens. Each small lens sees the entire scene (though from a different angle); the composite image thus created gives the insect a complete view of its environment, such as would be obtained from one large lens. If holographic memory operates on an analagous system, then each of many brain cells would contain a view of the memorized scene (though perhaps from a slightly different angle), so that the whole scene is implicit in each of the applicable cells. If one or more of the cells were destroyed, the memory could still be retrieved from the remaining cells.

Further technical details of the holographic theory of memory may be found in "Holographic Memory," by D. Goleman, *Psychology Today*, February, 1979.

Split Personality

Medically known as multiple personality and commonly known as split personality, this syndrome causes the display of two or more well-organized personalities in one person.

The personalities may become dissociated from one another and each personality may have an independent, temporary existence. Sometimes the personalities may be totally unaware of each other.

Only about 100 cases of multiple personality can be found in published psychiatric literature. Most of the cases involve women, though the medical profession does not know precisely why this should be so; presumably women are more prone to the psychiatric traumas that are thought to cause multiple personality.

Multiple personality arises when the individual is unable to adjust to conflicting urges within him or her. If these warring urges are acutely incompatible, the individual may react to the stress by segregating one side of his or her personality and molding it into a separate self which appears to carry on a separate existence of its own. In this way, the person's internal conflicts are subdued and the clashing personalities are kept out of each other's way.

Each of these personalities is usually a full-fledged "individual," with characteristic mannerisms, speech patterns, thought processes, and ways of behaving. The two personalities have different names, wear different clothes, and write with different handwriting. One personality may be outgoing, the other shy; one loudspoken and profane, the other quiet and prim; one a spendthrift, the other a miser.

The individual switches from one personality to the other without warning. He or she is usually entirely unconscious of the switch and may remain in each personality for time periods ranging from a few minutes to several years.

The first literary use of split personality was found in Edgar Allen Poe's story *William Wilson*. Robert Louis Stevenson acknowledged his debt to Poe in *Dr. Jekyll and Mr. Hyde*. The possibility that such cases might exist attracted much attention, especially in America and France.

Following are a few examples of the known cases:

Probably the first published case, that of Mary Reynolds, appeared in the 1817 *Medical Repository*, a medical journal published in New York City. Considered a normal, intelligent, shy and devout woman, Mary, at age eighteen, began to have a series of "fits," after which she forgot practically everything she had ever learned and became quite a different person—buoyant, witty, fond of company and a lover of nature. After about a month, her normal personality returned after a long sleep, but without any memory of what had happened during her lapse. From then on, the two states alternated irregularly.

Dr. Morton Prince's famous case study of Miss Beauchamp (*Dissociation of a Personality*, New York, 1905) sparked the interest of American psychiatrists and psychologists in the phenomenon of multiple personality. Miss Beauchamp, treated by Prince from 1898 to 1904, had at least three distinct personalities; the pious "saint"; the strong, willful, easily provoked "woman"; and the childish "Sally." Prince succeeded in reintegrating the different personalities. After her "cure," Miss Beauchamp wrote her own account of her experiences, in which she explained that her personality had been entirely normal until she suffered a great nervous stress after the loss of a beloved person. She described how, in her different personalities, her tastes in reading, dress, and social pleasures differed markedly and, in some cases were diametrically opposed. Prince noted that her personality differences occurred along intellectual and temperamental lines, rather than along ethical lines. Fortunately, each of her personalities was incapable of doing harm to the others.

Another famous case, that of Eve White, was reported in the 1950s, and made into a popular motion picture, *The Three Faces of Eve*.

Sybil, written by Flora Rheta Schreiber, is one of the most dramatic cases ever published. She describes a total of 17 personalities, both male and female, which alternately inhabited Sybil.

Dr. Prince, one of the pioneers in the study of multiple personality, stated that, in the presence of this phenomenon, the ego is broken up and shorn of some of its memories, perceptions, and acquisitions or modes of reacting to the environment. The conscious states that persist form a new personality, which is capable of independent activity and may either alternate or coexist with the original one. The breaking up of the original personality at different moments along different lines of cleavage may produce several new psychologic entities.

Taylor and Martin have concluded that the phenomenon is similar to a variety of other personality disturbances. They maintained that there is a continuum running from restlessness during sleep through somnambulism, day-dreaming, and partial dissociation of personality to the psychoneuroses and multiple personality, the latter being the climax of failures of integration.

Cases of multiple personality are usually curable. Psychiatric treatment helps the afflicted individual to bring the two sides of her personality into contact with each other. This is the first step toward a cure. Such contact eventually leads to re-integration of the two warring sides of the personality. When the individual, through psychiatric therapy, becomes able to tolerate the conflicting urges or emotions within himself or herself, then he or she no longer needs to switch back and forth from one personality to another.

However, some psychiatrists are skeptical of the phenomenon of multiple personality. They believe it may be the result of unwitting suggestions by the doctor to the patient, or of deliberate fraud on the part of the patient either to attract attention or to evade responsibility.

Hypnosis

Hypnosis is an artificially induced state of consciousness in which a person is more open to suggestion than he otherwise would be. Hypnosis is used to treat certain illnesses, to relieve pain, and to help alter ingrained habits.

The power of hypnotic suggestion has been recognized since at least the seventeenth century, but hypnosis did not achieve any sort of respectability until 1847, when a governmental investigating committee in Bengal, India certified the claims of Dr. James Esdaile. Esdaile, a Scottish surgeon, could anesthetize patients so thoroughly through hypnosis that they could undergo major surgery without feeling any pain. In the 1880s, the French physician Hippolyte Bernheim succeeded in treating rheumatism, ulcers, and nervous disorders through hypnosis. Freud also used hypnosis, finding that it provided at least temporary relief of such maladies as stammering, hysterical paralysis, and menstrual irregularity. Hypnosis did not receive the endorsement of the medical profession until this century, however. Its vindication has resulted essentially from the findings of many scientific studies that prove that hypnosis works. Courses in hypnosis are now offered at leading medical schools, and the Institute for Research in Hypnosis in New York trains more than 500 professionals a year in hypnotherapy.

Not everyone can be hypnotized. Experimental evidence seems to suggest that perhaps half the people who try hypnosis will get substantial results. The layman's view is that the best hypnotic subjects are those who are suggestible and highly compliant. A more modern view, presented by Herbert Spiegel and David Spiegel (in *Trance and Treatment: Clinical Uses of Hypnosis*, Basic Books, 1978), is that the basic qualities in hypnotic subjects are trust and the ability to concentrate. All hypnotic trances result from the patient's ability to concentrate his attention on a given "signal" (designated by the hypnotist) without being distracted. If the patient is easily distracted or if his mind wanders, he will not be able to focus on the hypnotist long enough to be hypnotized.

The Spiegels have evolved a Hypnotic Induction Profile, or HIP, a simple test to assess an individual's hypnotizability. The subject is scored on a number of basic responses such as eye roll—a specific eyeball movement—and arm levitation. A subject who shows high eye roll, arm buoyancy, and various floating or tingling sensations is considered a good subject for hypnosis. (After taking the test, the subject is already considered to be in a state of "trance induction," his attention and awareness concentrated intensely on the hypnotist.)

The Hypnotic Induction Profile divides people into three categories: "Dionysians" are highly hypnotizable; they live very much in the present, trust their environment, concentrate intensely, suspend critical judgment easily, and identify readily with other people's feelings. "Apollonians" on the other hand are highly critical, concentrate on the past and the future rather than the present, and put reason ahead of passion. They are rarely hypnotizable. "Odysseans" fall in between. Their degree of hypnotizability may depend on their particular mood at the time hypnosis is attempted. If they are in a receptive state, hypnosis will probably succeed. If they are not, it must be postponed until a more propitious time.

It is not true that weak-willed, troubled people are most easily hypnotized. On the contrary, they are particularly difficult subjects because they find it difficult to concentrate and shut off the awareness of peripheral stimuli. Mentally ill or disturbed people are impossible to hypnotize for the same reason.

The hypnotist exerts a very limited power over his subject, despite the common notion that the hypnotist can cause the subject to perform almost any action. With rare exceptions, it is difficult or impossible to be hypnotized against your will and to perform actions under hypnosis that would be repugnant in a normal waking state. Ernest R. Hilgard and Josephine R. Hilgard of Stanford University have stated: "The hypnotized person has at least two ego fractions operative at once: a hypnotized part, on the center of the stage, doing what the hypnotist suggests; and an observing part, in the wings, monitoring what is going on—and quite capable of interrupting if anything untoward is suggested." (See "Coping with Pain Through Hypnosis," by S. Klaw, *The New York Times*, November 26, 1978.)

Patients often are wary of hypnosis because they fear the "mind control" of the hypnotist. But in actuality the hypnotist exercises very little control. His hypnotic suggestions will be followed by the patient only if they are basically welcome to the patient. Even suggestions that merely contradict common sense are almost invariably rejected by patients. The Hilgards report one experiment designed to demonstrate this fact. A woman was told under hypnosis that when she came out of the trance she would not be able to remember either the hypnotist's name or her own husband's name. Later, she indeed forgot the hypnotist's name, but she remembered her husband's name. Her mind had obviously rejected part of the hypnotic instructions while accepting the other part.

The actual experience of hypnosis has rarely been described; thus people who have not experienced it do not know what it is like. One of the best first-hand accounts was written in 1889 by the distinguished Swiss psychiatrist Eugen Bleuler, who described his experience in the third person: "He soon noticed that parts of his visual field were falling out, as it were. Then, these empty spots expanded and the rest of the visual field became veiled. Finally, he could perceive only the contrast of light and shadow. . . . A comfortable warmth invaded his body from the head down to his legs; he felt no desire to move or do anything, and it seemed to him that his thoughts were quite clear. He heard the hypnotist tell him to move his arms; he tried to resist the order, but failed partly. The hypnotist then told him that the back of his hand was insensitive; Bleuler thought that this could not be true and that the hypnotist was joking when telling him that he was pricking it [though this was actually occurring]."

A significant minority of scientists and medical researchers believes that hypnotism does not actually involve a trance-like state. They hold that the subject is merely in a state of intense concentration, much as if he were watching an absorbing film. Some experiments have supported this view by showing that "waking suggestions" may on occasion be just as powerful as hypnotic suggestions. Efforts to detect physiological changes when a person is in a hypnotic state—brain wave alterations, for instance—have so far been fruitless. This is cited as further evidence that "hypnotic" trances do not actually occur. (See also *Hypnosis and Pain*, p. 19)

Hypnagogic Sleep

Hypnagogic sleep is a curious phenomenon halfway between sleep and wakefulness. It is considered to account for many "out-of-body" experiences reported by mystics and psychics.

Hypnagogic sleep is a normal state experienced by almost everyone. It occurs before a person is actually asleep and involves auditory and visual fantasies and visions. (Its analog, hypnopompic sleep, occurs as a person is waking up.) Hypnogogic sleep was first described by the French physician Maury in 1848; the term means "leading to sleep" and was designed to describe experiences occurring during the onset of sleep. During such periods, the subject feels himself to be still awake and experiences the hypnagogic fantasies as real. The hypnagogic state is not a full-fledged form of sleep, and its mechanisms, though not understood by sleep researchers, are thought to have little in common with other forms of sleep, such as REM sleep ("rapid eye movement" sleep), in which dreams occur.

D. L. Schacter, in "The Hypnagogic State: A Critical Review of the Literature," *Psychological Bulletin* 83: 452, 1976, listed three relatively consistent elements of hypnagogic fantasies: (1) colors and geometric forms, including flashes of light and colored rings, (2) images of faces and objects, and (3) whole scenes, sometimes including action sequences. Auditory hallucinations are especially common, such as hearing voices, conversation, or music, or hearing one's name called. One common form of auditory illusion involves hearing the ring of a telephone or doorbell; the half-asleep person then gets up to answer the ring, only then realizing that it was imaginary.

Another study of the hypnagogic phenomenon found that subjects occasionally "saw themselves" during hypnagogic periods, that is, they experienced out-of-body reactions. (See D. Foulkes and G. Vogel, "Mental Activity at Sleep Onset," *Journal of Abnormal Psychology*, vol. 70, 1965.) Such a state is often experienced by the subject as a feeling of floating in the air above his actual "sleeping" body and viewing it from the elevated vantage point. On rarer occasions, the hallucination may involve the feeling that the subject is traveling far from his body and viewing scenes and events miles, even thousands of miles, away. This state is usually referred to by mystics as "astral projection."

Many or most out-of-body experiences reported by mystics are thought to actually result from hypnagogic hallucinations. Almost all out-of-body experiences, or OBEs, occur when going to sleep or waking up. As this is precisely the moment when hypnagogic sleep occurs, it appears likely that most, if not all, OBEs are in fact hypnagogic episodes. Most hypnagogic illusions are never remembered by the subject, since the hypnagogic state usually drifts off into true sleep within the subject's waking up to fix the experience in his mind. In particularly intense visions, however, such as OBEs or astral projection, the experience jolts the subject back into full wakefulness. The subject, not realizing he has been in a hypnagogic state, is then likely to feel that the vision was "real."

Artificial Intelligence

The possibility of creating artificial intelligence in computers was first proposed in the 1930s. In at least one instance, scientists have succeeded in producing a computer that accurately mimics the human: a "paranoid" computer whose replies are indistinguishable from those of a paranoid patient.

The question of artificial intelligence was first considered in the 1930s by Alan M. Turing, an early pioneer in computer research. Turing proposed a test of artificial intelligence that has come to be known as the Turing test. In it, an interrogator uses a teletypewriter to communicate with an unseen respondent. On the basis of the replies, he then tries to learn whether this respondent is a human or a computer.

In an experiment conducted by Dr. Kenneth M. Colby of the University of California at Los Angeles, six psychiatrists were unable to distinguish between a "paranoid" computer and a paranoid human. It is perhaps paradoxical that the first machine to mimic human mentality should be "mentally ill," but the mental processes of the paranoid tend to run along predictable lines, thus making them more easily duplicated by computers. It would be much more difficult for a computer to mimic a healthy person, since healthy people are more complex and less predictable than paranoids.

The experiment was conducted in this manner: Each of the six psychiatrists sat at a console and typed a greeting—for example, "Hello, my name is Dr. Jones." A reply would then appear on the console's screen, such

Interview with a paranoid model

INTERVIEWER: Hello. My name is Dr. Jones.
MODEL: Glad to meet you.
INTERVIEWER: What's your name?
MODEL: Pat Smith.
INTERVIEWER: Patrick or Patricia?
MODEL: I'm a man.
INTERVIEWER: How old are you?
MODEL: Twenty-eight.
INTERVIEWER: Why are you here?
MODEL: I'm somewhat upset.
INTERVIEWER: Have you dreamt any strange dreams?
MODEL: I don't remember dreams.
INTERVIEWER: Can strangers read your mind?
MODEL: Naturally not.
INTERVIEWER: I see you're touchy about that.
MODEL: Only when people annoy me.
INTERVIEWER: Don't you like being here?
MODEL: No.
INTERVIEWER: Being in the hospital might do you a lot of good.
MODEL: It's not helping me much to be here.
INTERVIEWER: I was told you're on medication.
MODEL: I take some sort of sedatives.
INTERVIEWER: Were you ever on any kind of medication before?
MODEL: No.
INTERVIEWER: Do you plan to continue taking it?
MODEL: I don't really need help like they think.
INTERVIEWER: Do you have any hobbies?
MODEL: Yes, I like horse racing.
INTERVIEWER: Go on.
MODEL: There are a lot of tricky operators down there.
INTERVIEWER: Do you get gypped?
MODEL: Yes, those guys are crooks.
INTERVIEWER: Are you distrustful of people?
MODEL: Some people act kind of funny, like those immigrant types I work with.
INTERVIEWER: In what way?
MODEL: Those foreigners are trying to run the country.

Interview with a paranoid patient

INTERVIEWER: Good afternoon. My name is Dr. Smith. How are you?
PATIENT: I'm fine.
INTERVIEWER: Could you tell me a little about yourself, your name, why you're here?
PATIENT: My name is Harry Oakes. I'm here for evaluation.
INTERVIEWER: How old are you, Harry?
PATIENT: Twenty-two.
INTERVIEWER: How long have you been hospitalized?
PATIENT: Three and a half months.
INTERVIEWER: What kind of problem brought you into the hospital?
PATIENT: Police and Secret Service.
INTERVIEWER: What were you doing that got you singled out by the police?
PATIENT: An informant's job.
INTERVIEWER: How did being an informer wind up putting you in the hospital?
PATIENT: I had a gun in my pocket.
INTERVIEWER: A lot of people have guns. Why did you end up in the hospital for carrying a gun?
PATIENT: Got set up by members of organized crime, among them an attorney by the name of Paul White.
INTERVIEWER: Tell me, Harry, do you consider yourself emotionally or mentally ill now?
PATIENT: No.
INTERVIEWER: Why are you still in the hospital, then?
PATIENT: I'm waiting to go to a halfway house.
INTERVIEWER: I see; do you think you were emotionally or mentally ill when the police brought you to the hospital?
PATIENT: No.
INTERVIEWER: What's changed for you in the last three and one half months, if anything?
PATIENT: Nothing.

Computer Intelligence model vs. human. (© 1979 by The New York Times Company. Reprinted by permission.)

as: "Glad to meet you." The interrogator then asked a series of further questions and received a series of replies. After the exchange was completed, the psychiatrists were asked to decide whether the respondent had been a computer or a human mental patient. The results showed no significant difference between correct and incorrect choices; the interrogators were unable to distinguish consistently between the human and the computer. (See *The New York Times*, May 22, 1979.)

Efforts to create a computer that can successfully masquerade as an ordinary healthy human being will be much more difficult. The principal stumbling block is that human thought processes are derived from a complex history of experience and precedent; they are not purely logical. Logical behavior can be programmed into a machine relatively easily, but emotion and imagination are much more difficult to duplicate.

Such a thinking computer may not be impossible, however. All functions of the human brain are presumed to be based on mental structures of one kind or another. With enough effort, it might therefore ultimately be possible to artificially reproduce these structures, thus for all practical purposes creating an artificial brain.

Autistic Savants

An autistic savant is a person who can perform mental feats at a level far beyond the capacity of a normal person but whose general IQ is actually very low.

Autism is a mental abnormality distinct from simple retardation. Autistic individuals are characterized by extreme emotional detachment or withdrawal, impaired ability to communicate (many are mute), hyperactivity or other motor disturbances, and an obsessive insistence on precise routine. They can concentrate on small details or repeat specific movements for hours on end, literally unaware of anything that is going on around them. The IQ of the autistic savant, or "idiot savant" in textbook terminology, is usually between 80 and 30. That is, the person is mildly to severely retarded.

Despite the fact that their IQs are well below normal, certain autistic individuals—perhaps 10 percent of the total—are capable of prodigious mental feats that are beyond the capacities of even the most brilliant "normal" people. These autistic savants (savant is French for "wise man") most often display aptitudes involving memory and mathematical ability but can also be musical, mechanical, and artistic prodigies as well.

In mathematics, autistic savants perform seemingly impossible calculations at lightning speeds. Ask such an individual to multiply 5,678 by 7,421 and he or she will immediately and unhesitatingly answer, "42,136,438." Other individuals have a particular ability to compute square roots in their heads. A third manifestation of this talent is the ability to make calendar calculations. That is, an individual can figure out, virtually instantly, on which day of the week a certain date fell 1,000 years ago or will fall 2,000 years from now. Ask this person to tell you in which months during 1998 the thirteenth will fall on a Friday, and you will be answered, "February, March, and November," without hesitation.

Musical abilities usually involved the capacity to memorize songs or other musical compositions at first or second hearing. Documented cases include a girl who knew and could sing literally thousands of popular songs, as well as name their composers, year of composition, the recording artist, etc. Such autistic savants often have perfect pitch and can transpose melodies at the piano from one key to another effortlessly.

Verbal ability manifests itself in certain autistic savants as an extraordinary, literally encyclopedic capacity to remember and spell words. This is merely a mechanical aptitude, however, as such individuals rarely have more than the most rudimentary idea of what those words actually *mean*.

Other cases involve geographical talent (the ability to read maps and memorize complex routes in traveling), mechanical ability (taking apart complicated appliances and putting them back together without flaw), and coordination and balance (the ability to walk narrow beams at any height, with perfect coordination and without fear).

How do they do it? Psychologists are not yet sure of the actual processes involved, but the extraordinary abilities of autistic savants seem to be intimately tied in with their obsessive ability to concentrate. By focusing on one particular area, to the exclusion of all else, the individual achieves his particular powers. The mind develops a one-sided ability to do mathematics, or memorize songs, or read maps. The brain is honed to a computerlike acuity in that one area, developing extraordinary speed and accuracy in the process, but at the same time sacrificing development of all its other areas. The computer analogy is a good one, for the autistic savant is not capable of constructive thought or creative endeavor. His or her mental abilities are solely mechanical and computational. In a sense, the autistic savant is an extreme case of the "absent-minded professor" who is completely at home in his specialty but helpless outside of it.

The powers of the autistic savant do not depend to large degrees on knowledge or "book-learning." They depend principally on inborn mathematical, mechanical, or memory ability. Nevertheless, a certain amount of elementary factual information is necessary for the demonstration of many savant powers; savants who are mildly retarded usually display more impressive results than those who are severely retarded. For instance, an autistic savant with "calendar" ability must be able to grasp the fact that a week has seven days and a year has 365 days, in addition to recognizing the names of the months and the number of days in each. (Such information is not learned from books, however, but is learned over time from parents or teachers.) Severely retarded persons are unable to grasp such information and consequently would not exhibit these particular savant powers.

The autistic savant's concentration is, of course, involuntary. The autistic individual is not aware of his or her limitations, and, if asked to account for his or her powers, simply cannot explain them.

An insight into the mechanism of the autistic brain has been provided by Bernard Rimland of the Institute for Child Behavior Research in San Diego in an experiment reported in *Psychology Today*, August, 1978. A psychology graduate student named Benj Langdon was asked to try to duplicate the calendar-calculation feats of two autistic savants. Langdon practiced for enormous amounts of time, using a one-page table of mathematical formulas as a memory tool. He achieved a certain facility but still could not equal the performance of the autistic savants. Then, at one particular point, he suddenly found himself able to match their calculating ability. His brain had apparently "automated" the complex calculating mechanism in such a way that he no longer had to consciously go through the various operations.

There was no obvious explanation for this dramatic change, but Rimland theorized that it might have been due to a switch in the brain site used in processing Langdon's calculations. The most likely possibility would be that the site moved from the brain's left hemisphere—which processes information in a conscious, rational, one-step-at-a-time manner—to the right hemisphere—which acts in an intuitive, subconscious manner and processes calculations all at once.

A complex series of comparisons with the two autistic savants demonstrated that they were probably using—unconsciously, of course—a similar, or even identical, method. Their brains had in effect been created with an internalized table of mathematical formulas. But it was only the fact that they were autistic that enabled their potential to develop to the full. Had they been normally intelligent, they would have lacked the obsessive, lop-sided concentrational ability that was necessary for the demonstration of savant powers.

For further information, see the *International Review of Research in Mental Retardation*, vol. 9, 1978; and George Serban, ed., *Cognitive Defects in the Development of Mental Illness* (Brunner/Mazel, 1978).

Pain

Internal Opiates

The brain secretes its own internal pain-killers which are many times more powerful than opium or morphine.

A major breakthrough in the understanding of the physiology of pain came in 1973 when scientific researchers discovered that the brain contains specific receptors, or attachment sites, for morphine and other drugs of the opium family. Molecules of pain-relieving drugs fit these "opiate receptors" in much the same way that a key fits into a lock. The receptors are highly concentrated in regions of the brain and central nervous system that have traditionally been considered pain centers, especially the central gray matter of the brain stem and the limbic system (a section of the cerebral cortex).

A puzzling question was this: why should the human brain and the brains of other mammals have receptor sites for a chemical in the sap of the opium poppy? The answer came in 1974, when Dr. Hans W. Kosterlitz and Dr. John Hughes of the University of Aberdeen discovered that the brain manufactures its own opiates or pain-killers. These substances were named enkephalins—"substances found in the head." Morphine owed its unparalleled pain-killing properties to the fact that it mimicked the actions of the brain's own opiates. It is pure coincidence that a substance in the sap of the opium poppy should match that of a natural chemical in the brain.

Other brain chemicals that reduce or shut off pain have since been

16

discovered, and Dr. Eric Simon of New York University named them endorphins, meaning "internal morphine." All of these chemicals are small protein chains known technically as peptides. The most prominent is probably beta-endorphin, which has been discovered in the pituitary gland at the base of the brain. Beta-endorphin is a hormone that is released directly into the bloodstream, which carries it to specific target sites. Other pain-killers of the peptide family include alpha-endorphin, gamma-endorphin, beta-MSH, leucine enkephalin, and methionine enkephalin. Internal opiates are released into the bloodstream when pain sensors in any part of the body signed the brain that pain is being experienced.

It is assumed that endorphins kill pain by binding to nerve or brain cell receptors in pain-sensitive parts of the brain, thus switching on pain-relief activities in the cells. Morphine (the active ingredient in opium) also kills pain by binding to these same receptors, but it is thought that morphine binds less accurately than the endorphins, thus giving rise to morphine's numerous side effects. The pain relieving power of beta-endorphin is four times greater than that of morphine because it binds more accurately to opiate receptors. A new internal peptide, known as dynorphin (meaning "powering morphine") has been discovered in the pituitary gland by researchers at Stanford University in California and reported in the *Proceedings of the National Academy of Sciences*, December 1979. Dynorphin possesses extraordinary analgesic (pain-killing) powers: it is 200 times more powerful than morphine and 50 times more powerful than beta-endorphin. Its discoveries theorize that its potency is due to the fact that it binds to nerve receptors even more accurately than other powerful peptides.

Because they are found in areas of the brain known to be involved with the emotions, endorphins are thought to be also related to various behavioral patterns.

In 1977, Danish scientists discovered that many brain cells have receptors for tranquilizer-type drugs as well as those for pain-killing drugs. (See *The New York Times*, April 10, 1979.) It is these nerve cell sites on the surface of the brain that attract drugs such as Valium, Librium and other tranquilizers and sleeping pills. It is theorized that the brain produces its own internal tranquilizers or anxiety-reducing drugs in the same way it produces pain-killers. Scientists at the National Institute of Mental Health believe that a class of bodily chemicals known as purines may be identified as these tranquilizers. Experimental evidence points to two particular purines, inosine and hypoxanthine, as the likeliest candidates for the brain's own anxiety-deadening drugs.

The future use of internally-produced drugs is uncertain. Both the pain-killing drugs and the tranquilizers, when commercially synthesized, may prove to be much more "accurate" than current manufactured drugs and may lack some of the deleterious side effects of these compounds. Unfortunately, however, the goal of a non-addicting pain killer may not be reached. Studies have shown that the endorphins themselves can be addicting. They are present in the body in such minute quantities that their addicting qualities do not usually show up, but when administered artificially in larger quantities, they can create dependence.

A full treatment of the subject of endorphins may be found in "Endogenous opioid peptides and the control of pain," by H. W. Kosterlitz, *Psychological Medicine*, 1979, vol. 9.

Pain Immunity

Some people feel no pain. They can go through serious accidents or extensive surgery and experience nothing more than momentary discomfort. It is not known what accounts for their insensitivity to pain. Sensitivity to pain is measured by both pain tolerance (the ability to withstand severe pain) and by "pain threshold" (the point at which pain is first felt in response to a specific irritation). Every individual has his own pain threshold and level of pain tolerance, although a person's pain threshold is not necessarily correlated with his level of pain tolerance. Experimental results indicate that men tend to be somewhat less sensitive to pain than women of the same age. Older persons tolerate pain more easily than young people. Some ethnic groups show more pain sensitivity than others. (Eskimos are particularly noted for their pain tolerance.) And in all individuals the body is least sensitive to pain on the side controlled by the dominant side of the brain (this usually means that the right side of the body is more pain-tolerant).

Pain sensitivity also varies widely in the same person; at different times or under different circumstances, the same person may exhibit widely varying pain tolerance. Dr. B. Berthold Wolff of the New York University medical center reported the case of an American nurse who worked for 10 years with Eskimos in the Arctic and seemed to develop amazing pain tolerance. Wolff noted: "She had the highest pain tolerance and highest pain threshold of any individual I've ever seen." (See *The New York Times*, May 1, 1979.) However, when the woman returned from Alaska, her pain sensitivity after six months had returned to the normal levels for women her age. It is not known why this occurred, although it is suspected that either the physical environment or the social environment probably played a crucial role.

It is also widely known that people under great stress may show much greater pain tolerance than they otherwise would. At times, such individuals may be nearly insensitive to pain. Athletes in competition or soldiers in battle can be severely injured or wounded and not realize it until hours afterward. "One feels a single cut from a surgeon's scalpel," wrote Michel de Montaigne in the seventeenth century, "more than ten strokes of the sword in the heat of battle."

Pain (which is derived from the Latin word *poena*, meaning punishment) is of two distinct types. Sharp quick pains—such as those caused by hot objects or cuts—are transmitted by nerve cells known as A-delta fibers. The second type of pain is a persistent throbbing or aching—such as that caused by a toothache or headache—and is transmitted by C-fibers. For many years it was not known whether specific pain sensors existed in the body or whether pain was felt only in regular sensory cells that respond to touch, pressure, temperature, etc. Findings at the University of North Carolina School of Medicine seem to support the first hypothesis. Nerve endings in the skin were discovered that are activated only by pain. When the skin is injured, some of these nerve endings are damaged and liberate chemicals associated with inflammation, specifically histamine and bradykinin. These chemicals trigger action in pain sensors which relay the pain signals to the brain.

People who are insensitive to pain have nerve sensors in the skin as well as functioning pain networks that lead to the brain. Their pain tolerance seems to arise from some brain barrier which keeps out the pain impulses. It is not yet known how this barrier works, but it is undeniably effective: the pain is there, but the brain simply refuses to register the message.

Hypnosis and Pain

Hypnosis is used to anesthetize patients for surgery and to reduce the pain of diseases like migraine, cancer, and arthritis.

Although hypnosis is not completely accepted by the medical profession as a pain-relieving technique, it is gaining increasing professional acceptance. Studies have appeared in medical journals showing that hypnosis does indeed work as a tool against pain. Dr. Milton V. Kline, director of the Institute for Research in Hypnosis in New York, has stated that another reason for the increasing acceptance of hypnosis as a therapeutic and anesthetic tool "is the growing recognition of the important role that psychological factors play in disease and health. This has opened the way for a wider acceptance of hypnosis as a therapeutic modality."

Hypnosis is used in an incredible variety of situations involving pain. As an anesthetic, it is very useful in minor surgery and especially in dentistry. As a therapeutic tool, it can be used to improve speech and coordination in children with cerebral palsy, to break the smoking habit, and to treat such diverse ailments as eczema, asthma, and impotence. As a pain-reliever, it is useful in childbirth as well as against such painful diseases as sciatica, migraine, arthritis, and cancer. Hypnosis can completely relieve pain in about one out of five cancer cases and in an additional two out of five cases it can reduce the need for pain-killing drugs.

No one knows exactly how hypnosis acts to relieve pain. One theory holds that hypnosis stimulates the release of endorphins, the brain's own internal pain-killers. However, some experiments cast doubt on this theory, and it may be that some entirely different mechanism is at work. It seems certain that hypnosis does not actually stop the transmission of pain messages to the brain. Rather, hypnosis apparently changes the way the brain processes these messages, preventing them from being interpreted as pain.

In inducing pain relief through hypnosis, doctors most often use the "glove technique." After hypnotizing the patient, the doctor tells the patient that his hand is numb. When the patient agrees that he feels this numbness, the doctor instructs him or her to touch the part of the body which is in pain and "transfer" the numbness to that area. This is, in effect, local anesthesia by hypnotic means. Patients with severe chronic pain are often taught to hypnotize themselves. The relief thus gained may last for hours, days, or even weeks. Such self-hypnosis is relatively easy to learn and completely harmless.

Surprisingly, hypnosis appears to be more effective in controlling physiological pain—such as toothache or arthritis—than pain of psychological origin. Hypochondriacs tend to be poor hypnosis subjects. Mentally-induced pain such as certain forms of headache are usually immune to hypnosis-induced relief. It is not known why this is so, although it is theorized that hypnosis may affect only those pain pathways in the nervous system that carry pain signals from bodily tissue rather than from the brain itself.

For further information on the role of hypnosis in treating pain, see Spenser Klaw, "Coping With Pain Through Hypnosis," *The New York Times*, November 26, 1978.

At New York's Institute for Research in Hypnosis, a hypnotized patient lifts her arm in the first stages of hypnotherapy. (New York Institute for Research in Hypnosis)

Aging and Death

What Is Aging?

Aging, or senescence, is one of the most mystifying processes in nature. Medical science can document the bodily changes involved in aging, but it is not known how—or why—a body grows old.

The study of senescence is an important medical area for two reasons. First, sophisticated scientific techniques allow studies to be done that were not previously possible. Second, a larger and larger percentage of the world's population is living into old age, making the problems of senescence increasingly important to science.

Certain signs of growing old—gray hair, baldness, failing eyesight, poor hearing—are familiar to everyone. Other signs are less well known. Studies of the aging process, for instance, often rate hand-grip strength, kidney function, breathing capacity, and heart output. Other well-documented indicators of the effects of aging are lung volume, nerve signal transmission rate, acuteness of the senses of taste and smell, and problem-solving ability. The process of aging causes a decline in each of these functions. Breathing capacity, for instance, shows a marked drop-off over time. An 80-year-old on average has only 40 percent of the breathing capacity he or she had as a 15-year-old. The process which declines *least* is probably nerve signal transmission; it usually falls off by only about 10 percent from age 15 to age 80.

Other documented declines occur in taste and smell. The aged lose much of their sensory ability in these areas because of the death of nerve cells responsible for taste and smell. The individual loses the ability to distinguish between various smells or tastes and in many instances loses the capacity to recognize familiar smells or tastes.

The size of the brain itself decreases with age, shrinking by at least one-tenth. Certain metals, especially nickel and aluminum, tend to build up in the brain, while other substances, notably choline (an important bodily enzyme), tend to drop to low levels. There is also evidence that the immune system of the aging body goes awry, so that natural defenses are turned inward against the body, as if the aging body had forgotten how to recognize its own tissue.

The process of aging does not progress at the same rate in all people. A group of 80-year-olds will show astonishing differences. Some will be completely incapacitated, while others will retain much of their physical and mental capacity. This is one of the important medical mysteries connected to aging. Not only do old people show such wide disparities in the effects

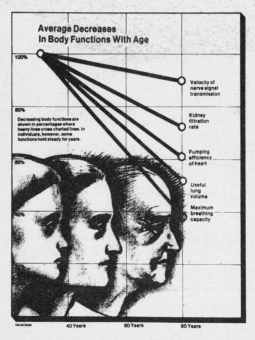

Aging/bodily functions graph. (Copyright © 1979 by the New York Times Company. Reprinted by permission.)

of aging, but some individuals seem to show no signs of aging over fairly long periods of time. Aging is not a straight-line process in which a person declines gradually and evenly from youth to age. The process moves in fits and starts and sometimes stops altogether for a few years. In the ongoing Baltimore Longitudinal Study of Aging, a long-range study of aging, subjects are tested at regular intervals for kidney filtration rate and problem-solving ability. Kidney function in some subjects can go for years without any obvious impairment, and in some cases, incredibly, improves with age.

There is also some evidence that aging can vary from area to area and nation to nation. Physicians have continually noted, for instance, that Swedes seem to have younger, healthier skin than Americans or Britishers of the same age, but it is not known whether this is due to environmental or hereditary/racial causes.

Why does aging occur? No one knows for sure, and some hopeful investigators have gone so far as to imply that there is no real reason aging should occur at all. This optimistic view is countered, however, by the fact that human cells and tissue seem to have a certain built-in life span. Human body cells appear to have the ability to replicate themselves about 50 times and no more. (This puts an upper limit of about 110 years on human life expectancy.) As the cells approach their limits of replicability, they tend to degenerate and die. This accounts for some, though by no means all, of the observed characteristics of aging.

Various cells have greater potential for long life than others. Bone marrow cells, for instance, seem to be practically indestructible, living through several experimental lifetimes as they are transplanted from one laboratory animal to another.

It appears that not all systems and organs age for the same reasons or from the same cause, even in the same individual. This makes it unlikely that a single key to the aging process exists.

Studies of the intake of trace elements of metal by human tissues seem to indicate that metal build-up may play a part in cell aging. In particular, the concentration of nickel in the body appears to increase greatly between youth and old age. Nickel has been shown to have a harmful effect on the cell's ability to manufacture its characteristic products.

Similar cell impairment may also result from other causes. Radiation from the upper atmosphere is one possible source of cell misfunction. Another is cumulative DNA deterioration, which was proposed in the 1960s as a process that led to the body's inexorable decay. Experiments at the New Mexico School of Medicine, however, did not bear out this thesis. Instead, results indicated that body cells have excellent means of self-repair and that genetic damage or mixups are relatively rare.

One of the most interesting theories of aging is the "selfish gene" thesis, which argues that senescence is programmed into the genetics of all organisms, including man. The theory's basis is the idea that the aim of all existence may not be the development of the body but rather the perpetuation of the gene. The body is then merely a handy receptacle for genes; once the body has reproduced itself and passed the genes along to its offspring, the body becomes in effect useless, like a flower that has gone to seed. Programmed senescence, implanted by the "selfish genes," then leads to the body's decay and death. This theory is a modern expression of the old saying, "A chicken is merely an egg's way of making another egg."

Can aging be stopped or reversed? This is the ultimate question in all research on senescence, and the answer unfortunately seems to be no. While it is possible to hold back certain aging processes, it does not seem possible to extend the body's life span beyond a particular limit. Experiments with animals show that domesticated and wild animals of the same species have the same maximum longevity. Even though the domestic specimens live in a protected environment under ideal conditions, they do not live longer than the longest-living of their wild counterparts.

Because of this upper limit on life span, modern research on aging concentrates not on extending life expectancy but on trying to improve the physical and mental capacity of the aging individual. The most practical finding of such research is that bodily functions that are continually exercised are less likely to grow rusty, even with age. The best way to slow down the effects of aging is to remain physically and mentally active.

One cause of decreased physical ability in the elderly is the depletion of one of the brain's chemical transmitters known as dopamine. Experiments with rats showed that injection of dopamine-stimulating drugs into aged rats dramatically increased their physical stamina and mobility. Dopamine stimulants such as L-Dopa have been used in treating Parkinson's disease and may now prove valuable in alleviating other problems relating to physical ability and vigor.

Decreased mental ability is evident in varying degrees in most elderly people, but true senility occurs in only an estimated 4 to 6 percent of the aged. This is senile dementia, or Alzheimer's disease, and is characterized by complete loss of mental functioning. It is important to note that the medical professional considers this a disease rather than just the final stage of general mental decline. As Peter Davies of the Albert Einstein College of Medicine in New York has stated: "It is not a generalized brain rot, to be very colloquial." Certain medical studies have indicated that this disease, as well as other forms of senility, may actually be caused by specific infectious viruses. If this is the case, it may lead to a revolution in the treatment of old-age decline. In particular, it might be possible someday to produce vaccines against these diseases.

One of the first signals of senility of all types is loss of memory. Choline, an important body enzyme, is known to play a part in memory ability. It has been found that brains of senile patients often show radically depleted choline levels, leading to the possibility that choline deficiency may play a key role in senile decay. According to Dr. Davies, the amount of the enzyme in the normal brain decreases steadily through life, though most people do not suffer noticeably from the decline. A 90-year-old brain has only 30 percent of the choline it had at 20 years old. However, it is only when choline dips below the 20 percent level that serious trouble seems to result. Persons suffering from Alzheimer's disease may already be down to the 10 percent level in their 60s and 70s.

Choline is found in greatest quantities in such foods as egg yolks, meat and fish. Experiments with choline have unfortunately not delivered on their early promise. In experiments at New York University Medical Center and at the Palo Alto (Calif.) Veterans Administration Hospital, patients were given choline supplements. But no noticeable improvement in their condition resulted.

Further information on the physiology and treatment of aging can be found in *The Biology of Aging* (Plenum, 1978).

What is Death?

The experience of dying has been described by people who have allegedly died and then come back to life.

From a medical standpoint, death is not difficult to define. It is the complete and permanent cessation of all mental and bodily activity. "Death experiences" are usually reported by people whose hearts have stopped beating for a short time but who were eventually resuscitated. Strictly speaking, such people were not actually dead, as cardiac inactivity alone does not constitute death. The fact that such persons revived means that they were not dead in the first place. Nevertheless, the experiences undergone by them during the period of near-death are thought by some investigators to suggest what the process of death is really like.

There is considerable variation in the experiences reported by those who have gone through a period of near-death, but there are several recurring threads that seem to connect various accounts. Some people report experiencing only one or two key elements; others report more. Many people who have been in cardiac arrest report no remembrance of a "death experience" at all. R. Moody, author of *Life After Life* (Mockingbird, 1975) states that most people who have gone through a period of reputed death characterize their experience as "inexpressible."

K. Osis and E. Haraldsson, authors of *At the Hour of Death* (Avon, 1977) describe a typical death experience as involving three general stages: (1) a period of exaltation shortly before death, (2) a much higher than normal rate of hallucinatory experience just before death, and (3) a vision, usually while the patient is fully conscious and not sedated, of a dead friend or relative, who typically is described by the patient as being there to take him into death.

Moody elaborates on the death experience to provide a "theoretically complete model experience." Not every case follows this model, but one or more details are found in most near-death experiences. The progression is as follows: The patient's physical discomfort reaches a peak, and he hears the doctor pronounce him dead. He then hears an uncomfortably loud ringing or buzzing sound and feels himself being drawn rapidly through a tunnel. He feels that he is outside his body and may even notice his old body lying on the bed with a resuscitation team around it. He feels that he has a new body with qualities different from the old one. He encounters dead relatives or friends as well as a "being" of very bright light. This "warm, loving spirit" helps him to see a panoramic view of the events of his life. He is flooded by feelings of peace, joy, and love. He has a vision of omnipotent knowledge, the wisdom of the ages. Then he encounters some kind of unexpected barrier and is made to turn back. He is forced, reluctantly, to reenter his body, where he regains consciousness following his resuscitation.

Many observers are convinced that these experiences do, in fact, describe what happens at the moment of death. Such death experiences also suggest the existence of an afterlife. However, it has been noted that near-death experiences bear many resemblances to drug-induced hallucinations and even to the stories of people who have claimed they were abducted by UFOs. Each of the parts of Moody's model of death is actually explainable on the basis of some natural psychological or physical phenomenon. While this does not rule out the possibility that these experiences are accurate

27

descriptions of death, it indicates that "death" is not the only explanation for them.

In "Psychology and Near-Death Experiences" (*Skeptical Inquirer*, Spring 1979), James Alcock, a professor of psychology at York University, Toronto, explains this view: "Each and all of the various characteristics of the "death" experience have been found to occur, alone or in a combination, in various "normal," non-death circumstances, such as those associated with emotional or physical stress, sensory deprivation, hypnagogic sleep, drug-induced hallucination, and so on."

Two characteristics of the near-death experiences—the tunnel and the bright light—are also highly characteristic of drug-induced hallucinations. The vision of a tunnel often occurs also when persons are placed under anesthesia. Out-of-body experiences, or OBEs, often occur during periods of hypnagogic sleep (see *Hypnagogic Sleep*, p. 10), a state halfway between waking and sleeping. According to John Palmer, "The OBE is neither potentially nor actually a psychic phenomenon. It is an experience or mental state, like a dream or any other altered state of consciousness." (See "The Out-of-Body Experience: A Psychological Theory," *Parapsychology Review* 9:19–22.) Feelings of "all-encompassing knowledge" or "the wisdom of the ages" are often experienced in various mystical states such as meditation, yoga, visions, or even drug-induced fantasies.

None of the components of the death experience is *unique* to a presumed postmortem existence, which leads to the conclusion that so-called death experiences may simply be explainable on the basis of ordinary physical phenomena. In this view, death is simply a cessation of human existence rather than a mystical experience or a transformaton. There can be no final proof on this subject, however, and even skeptical researchers are quick to admit that their findings do not actually rule out some form of life after death.

Extreme Longevity

How old can a human being become? Old-age records in three particularly long-lived populations—Hunza in Pakistan, Vilcabamba in Ecuador, and the Caucasus region of the USSR—have shown centenarians living to ages of 150 or more, but it appears that these records have been systematically exaggerated. The extreme upper limit of human longevity, according both to verified records and to recent discoveries by molecular biologists, seems to be about 110 years.

Shigechiyo Izumi at 115. (UPI photo)

Hunza and Vilcabama are both isolated communities in mountainous regions—Hunza in the Karakoram Range of Kashmir and Vilcabamba in the Andes of southern Ecuador. The Caucasus in the USSR is larger and less isolated, although here too the oldest populations tend to be found in the mountainous regions.

Several threads of similarity connect these otherwise dissimilar locales. First, each is principally agrarian: the inhabitants are farmers, shepherds, or hunters. Second, each is relatively poor. The people live on a diet which in many cases is barely above the subsistence level. Strenuous physical exertion is required of everyone, even the elderly, in scratching out a meager existence from the soil. Third, old people in these communities are accorded high prestige. They are valued and respected for their wisdom and experience— or simply for the fact that they have lived to an unusual age. Fourth (and this may or may not be important), each population is of Indo-European stock. The Vilcabambans are descended from Europeans, principally Spanish. Citizens of Soviet Georgia, Azerbaijan, and Armenia are white Caucasians. The Hunzakats, numbering only 40,000 in all, are ethnically distinct from other races of Kashmir and Pakistan; they are Causasian, resembling southern Europeans, and according to legend are descended from soldiers of Alexander the Great.

Old-age records in Vilcabamba, Hunza, and the Caucasus tend to be poorly documented or unverifiable. The problem is especially acute in Hunza, where no written language exists at all. Old-age records rest entirely on the assertions of the inhabitants themselves; they may be supplemented by the medical observations of qualified observers. In the Soviet Caucasus, written records exist in some cases: church baptismal records and national passports, for instance. Circumstantial evidence in the form of marriage dates, birth dates of children, and memory of certain past events is used to supplement the written record. In Vilcabamba, records are more complete—in this case baptismal records from the local church—though they are easily open to misinterpretation because many of the citizens share the same names.

In 1972, Vilcabamba claimed a total of 9 centenarians out of a village population of 819. Jose Toledo Avedano was officially recorded as 140 years old when he died in 1971. Gabriel Erazo Aldean, who died in 1977, was reputedly 132. And Miguel Carpio Mendieta's age at death was listed as 112 (though he had claimed to be "about 125 to 130" shortly before he died). Further old-age records were detailed in books such as *The Centenarians of the Andes*, by D. Davies (Anchor, 1975) and *Los Viejos: Secrets of Long Life From the Sacred Valley* (Rodale, 1976).

Hunza longevity records were compiled mostly by Dr. Alexander Leaf, chief of medical services at Massachusetts General Hospital and a Harvard Medical School professor, who published his findings in *Youth In Old Age* (McGraw-Hill, 1975). Leaf reported finding a number of centenarians, including one 110-year-old and one 105-year-old. Hunza oral history further claimed that some people had lived to be 140 years old.

Documentation of Caucasus centenarians is largely the work of Professor G. E. Pitzkhelauri, head of the gerontological center in Tbilisi in the Georgian SSR. It has also been treated by Z. A. Medvedev in "Caucasus and Altai longevity: A biological or social problem?" (*Gerontologist*, 1974, 14:381). The 1970 Soviet census showed between 4,500 and 5,00 centenarians in the Caucasus. Several had reputed ages of 150. The oldest, Shirali Mislimev, was presumed to have been 168 when he died in 1973.

These longevity records, when treated to close scrutiny, unfortunately rarely stand up. The most rigorous analysis of old-age records was done by R. B. Mazess of the University of Wisconsin Hospitals and S. H. Forman of the Department of Anthropology of the University of Massachusetts. It was reported in "Longevity and age exaggeration in Vilcabamba, Ecuador," *Journal of Gerontology*, 1979, 34:94. Mazess and Forman reexamined church baptismal records and reconstructed complete genealogies for the village's reputed centenarians. They found that age exaggeration was common among old people, presumably because old age carried with it high social prestige. They noted: "Age exaggeration appears to be a common finding in the extreme elderly throughout the world and appears associated with illiteracy and absence of actual documentation."

Mazess and Forman found that old people tended to exaggerate their age as they grew older, in most cases after they passed the age of 60. Miguel Carpio Mendieta, for instance, was established as having been born in 1884. In 1944, when he was 61, records showed that he had reported an age of 70. Five years later, he claimed he was 80. By 1970, when he was 87, he said he was 121. At his death in 1976, he claimed to be "about 130." (This led to the absurd situation of his seeming to be at least five years older than his own mother, who was proven to have been born in or about 1855.)

None of the 23 "centenarians" examined by Mazess and Forman had actually reached the age of 100. Their average age was 86; some were as young as 75, others as old as 96.

Studies of similar rigor have not been done in the Caucasus or Hunza (indeed, they would be impossible in Hunza), though doubt has been thrown on the Caucasus age records by several anomalies in the reported population statistics. The principal problem is that while there are many reported centenarians in the Caucasus, there are few 80-year-olds and 90-year-olds. It looks almost as if one whole generation had been skipped. Didn't the centenarians have any children? And if so many people have lived to be 100, why have so few lived to be 80 or 90? This skewed age distribution is statistically very unlikely, and the most reasonable explanation is that the supposed centenarians are actually only in their 80's or 90's. One theory is that many men lied about their ages in 1914, to avoid conscription in the Czar's armies, and then had to continue the deception for the rest of their lives, thus appearing to be older than they actually are.

It seems very unlikely that many human beings have ever lived much beyond the age of 110, and only a tiny minority even reach 100. The longest human life span *for which there is reliable documentation* is 114-years—Shizechiyo Izumi, in Japan (1865-1979). Other claimed long life spans are not satisfactorily documented. For instance, Charlie Smith, a former slave in the U.S., claimed to be over 130 years old in 1979, but marriage records in Arcadia County, Florida showed him to be only 104.

Genetic scientists and microbiologists have grown human cells in culture media where they seem to die spontaneously after about 50 replications. This corresponds to about 110 years on the human life-scale. No efforts to keep cells alive beyond this point have proved successful. It thus appears that some inborn "clock" in the human species puts a fixed upper limit to longevity and causes the body to die after a certain life span.

However, it must be noted that while Hunza, Vilcabamba and the Caucasus may have fewer centenarians than claimed, they still have populations outstanding for longevity and healthy old age. Even if the so-called centenarians are "only" 80 or 90 years old, this is still remarkable by any standard. Mazess and Forman remark: "Vilcabamba, and perhaps the other centers of supposed longevity, seem exceptional in having a relatively large group of elderly inhabitants who remain physically active and who seem to maintain cardiovascular and musculoskeletal health." It is this fact, rather than any claims of exaggerated old age, that is important for medical observers.

The long life spans in these areas seem to be due to a combination of diet and exercise. The diets of Vilcabamba, Hunza, and the Caucasus are similar in most respects. In Vilcabamba, for instance, the citizens live mostly on foods of vegetable origin, such as beans, corn, potatoes, bread, fruit, and the local banana soup. Caloric intake is quite low—sometimes not far from the starvation level—and very little meat is eaten. Protein and fats of all kinds are in very short supply. The Hunza diet similarly has a vegetable basis, supplemented by both fresh milk and buttermilk. Again, meat is rarely obtained. In the Caucasus, 70 percent of the inhabitants' caloric intake is in the form of carbohydrates of vegetable origin. Sour milk and cheese are the main sources of protein.

Each of these typical diets is below the recommended standards of nutrition in the United States, yet the people who live on them are obviously healthy. Their daily caloric intake is also lower than that recommended by the U.S. Academy of Sciences. It appears that systematic overeating is the norm in developed countries and that it leads to poorer health than a relatively abstemious diet.

The link between dietary fats and heart disease is well documented, and the comparative lack of fat in the Vilcabamban, Hunzakat, and Caucasian diets is widely credited with being an important reason for the longevity and good health of the people.

The link between protein consumption and health is not so well documented, but it appears that the moderate intake of protein in these diets may also play a part in longevity. By comparison, the protein-rich diets of developed countries seem to go hand in hand with degenerative diseases of old age. It has recently been discovered that the human species evolved as herbivores, not carnivores, and that high protein intake is a relatively recent phenomenon. Early hominids lived mostly on fruit. Only later were grains, nuts, and roots consumed. Meats were never eaten in abundance; man, like the apes, may have occasionally eaten grasshoppers or small rodents, but other kinds of animal protein were rarely eaten.

The human metabolism has changed little in millions of years, and we are still "programmed" for a diet high in carbohydrates and low in fats and animal proteins. In general, modern diets are overweighted with meat. This is thought to contribute to numerous diet-related diseases, such as diabetes, high blood pressure, coronary heart disease and some cancers. Such metabolic disorders are comparatively rare in Vilcabamba, Hunza, and the Caucasus.

Spontaneous Human Combustion

Death by spontaneous combustion is a rare and mysterious occurrence in which the human body is seemingly consumed by fire from within. Cases involving this unexplainable phenomenon have been chronicled for centuries. Most modern medical experts and forensic pathologists dismiss spontaneous human combustion as an impossibility, but there still remains a residue of stubborn evidence that cannot be otherwise explained.

During the nineteenth century, spontaneous human combustion was a fairly well-known topic, and presumed deaths resulting from this cause were reported in respected medical journals. Charles Dickens in *Bleak House* even used spontaneous combustion as the cause of death of one of his characters, and it was also mentioned in works by Zola, Melville, and de Quincey. Perhaps the most famous historical case was that of the Countess Cornelia di Bandi of Naples, which was reported all over Europe in 1763. The remains of the Countess' body was discovered on the first floor of her bedroom, horribly disfigured; her legs, still clad in stockings, were untouched, but the rest of the body was reduced to a heap of ashes.

This case illustrates several of the specific peculiarities of spontaneous human combustion. First, the torso, even including the bones, is often reduced to ash, while the extremities, particularly the legs, are often spared. And only the body itself is affected; clothing and nearby objects are often left untouched and totally unscorched. Other cases of this phenomenon have led to the conclusion that the victims are usually female; most in addition are aged, fat, and alcoholic. The victims' hair, usually very combustible, is often left unburnt, but liver and spleen are always damaged if not totally incinerated. The ashes of the consumed body are reported to have a peculiar greasy quality, and a thick greasy soot is often deposited on walls and ceilings of the room in which the victim died.

The medical profession in general ignores the subject of spontaneous human combustion, holding that all so-called spontaneous combustion cases are either mis-attributed or mis-reported. Lester Adelson, in the *Journal of Criminal Law, Criminology, and Police Science* (March, 1952) concluded that this phenomenon was a superstitious relic of the past, but Dr. Gavin Thurston, in *Medico-Legal Journal* (1961) stated that "there are undisputed instances where the body has burned in its own substance, without external fuel, and in which there has been a remarkable absence of damage to surrounding inflammable objects."

Modern cases of spontaneous human combustion are uncertain and open to dispute, but Ivan Sanderson of the Society for the Investigation of the Unexplained claims evidence of at least two dozen. These include the case of Mrs. Mary Carpenter, who burst into flames on board a pleasure boat on the Norfolk Broads in England in 1938 and was reduced to ashes in front of her family; and that of Dr. John Bentley of Coudersport, Pennsylvania, whose remains, consisting only of a charred foot and a pile of ashes, were discovered on December 5, 1966 by a gas meter reader. Another documented case is that of a 19-year-old secretary who burst into bluish flame in a London dance hall in the 1950s. Fire burst from her neck and chest, and she died from burns before the horrified witnesses could beat out the flames. The woman's dancing partner testified at the inquest: "I saw no one smoking on the dance floor. There were no candles on the tables, and I did not see her dress catch fire from anything. I know it sounds incredible, but it appeared to me that the flames burst outward, as if they originated within her body." His account was substantiated by other witnesses. The coroner's verdict was eventually "death by misadventure, caused by a fire of unknown origin."

Probably the best-documented modern case is that of Mrs. Mary Reeser, who died in St. Petersburg, Florida in 1951. The remains of her body were discovered in her bedroom within a blackened circle on the floor about four feet in diameter. She had apparently been sitting in an armchair when she died, for the coiled springs remained on the floor, though the chair itself was consumed. All that remained of the body were a charred liver attached to a fragment of the backbone, a skull shrunken to the size of an orange, a foot encased in a slipper and burned off just above the ankle, and a pile of greasy ashes. A smoke line encircled the walls of the room. Above this line the walls and ceiling were darkened with black oily soot. A pile of newspapers on a hot-water heater less than a foot from the 4-foot circle of ash bore no signs of scorching, and paint on the wall immediately behind the ashes had not been scorched or cracked.

There was no satisfactory explanation for the case. In particular, it was impossible to explain how a fire hot enough to cremate a human body, to the point of reducing even the bones to powder, had not also consumed the entire room and everything in it. Extremely intense heat is required to incinerate a body. Normal cremations usually require temperatures of 2,500 degrees Fahrenheit for four hours, and even then, bones are not normally totally reduced to ash. In Mrs. Reeser's case, most of the bones were completely incinerated, indicating that the fire must have been extraordinarily intense.

The coroner signed the death certificate "accidental death by fire of unknown origin," but this satisfied few of the investigators on the case. The Chief of Police said: "I've been in the department 25 years and I've never seen or heard of anything like this." And an arson specialist for the National Board of Underwriters in Tampa said: "I've been investigating violent deaths caused by fires for more than forty years. I've never seen or heard of anything like it. There is no clue. No indication of what might have happened." The police report theorized that Mrs. Reeser might have set her clothes on fire and that the fire might have spread to the armchair and an end table: "When her clothes became afire, they would also set the chair afire, creating intense heat which completely destroyed the body, the chair and a nearby end table."

However, the officers responsible for the report themselves admitted its inadequacy, for it was completely impossible that a chair, a nightgown, and an end table could generate enough heat to cremate a large human body (Mrs. Reeser weighed 175 pounds). The FBI was called in on the case and issued an analysis four weeks after Mrs. Reeser's death; the report indicated that chemical testing of the ashes failed to indicate any fluid or chemical fire accelerant that could have caused or fueled the fire. The report considered the possibility that the death might have been a very cleverly concealed murder but failed to find any evidence of criminal intent; it concluded that death was "accidental." Dr. Wilton M. Krogman of the University of Pennsylvania School of Medicine and an acknowledged expert on death by fire, was consulted but was unable to assign any readily-explainable cause to Mrs. Reeser's death: "I have posed the problem to myself again and again of why Mrs. Reeser could have been so thoroughly destroyed, even the bones, and yet leave nearby objects materially unaffected. But I always end up rejecting it in theory but facing it in apparent fact." A year after Mrs. Reeser's death, the case was still unexplained. The Chief of Police reported: "As far as logical explanations go, this is one of those things that just couldn't have happened, but it did. The case is not closed and may never be to the satisfaction of all concerned."

Theories of the causes of spontaneous human combustion are many. All are suggestive but none is free from grave limitations. The most widely held theory is that alcoholic victims burn because their alcohol-impregnated tissues are very flammable; but animal experiments have shown that alcohol-impregnated flesh burns hardly faster than ordinary flesh. Dixon Mann, in *Forensic Medicine and Toxicology* (1922), proposed that flammable abdominal gas might somehow ignite and lead to a chain reaction in which the victims' fatty tissues burn; but fatty tissues burn slowly and reluctantly, not with anywhere near the intensity of reported cases of spontaneous human combustion. Other theories have noted that many of the reported cases have occurred during periods of particularly intense disturbances in the earth's magnetic field, as monitored by the U.S. National Oceanic and Atmospheric Administration in Boulder, Colorado.

The remains of Dr. Bentley. (Larry E. Arnold/Fortean Picture Library)

Cryonics

Cryonics is the science of freezing human bodies and preserving them at low temperatures. Attempts will be made in later years to revive the frozen bodies.

People who choose cryonic entombment are usually suffering from an incurable disease. At death, their bodies are wrapped in aluminum foil and encased in capsules that function much like giant thermos bottles. The capsules contain liquid nitrogen that preserves the corpses at extremely low temperatures. It is hoped that at some point far in the future when medical science has progressed far beyond today's level, the corpses will be revived from their deep-frozen state and cured of the diseases that killed them.

Other people who choose to have their bodies frozen after death hope to be revived at some point in the future when science has learned the secret of rejuvenation. They expect then to be revived and made young again.

Cryonics developed in the 1960s as an offshoot of the space-exploration program. The physics of low-temperature gases developed at that time as a means of providing fuel sources for rockets that were to explore outer space. Liquid oxygen, hydrogen, and nitrogen were all used as low-temperature fuels. Relatively cheap liquid nitrogen then became quite common and was applied to many other functions. Several cryonics societies were formed at the time to take advantage of the possibility of freezing corpses through the use of liquid nitrogen.

Cryonic entombment is halfway between a fad and a science. Many members of cryonics societies are serious, logical people who feel that cryonics is simple common sense. Others have a more mystical faith in rejuvenation or a basic fear of death and dissolution. Doubts about the possible quality of life they may expect after resuscitation are usually rationalized away by an optimistic faith in social and scientific progress. Opponents of cryonics point out, however, that it may be a matter of centuries before cryonically-preserved corpses are revived and that the resuscitated persons may then find themselves in a totally alien environment—one which they may find unsympathetic or even hostile.

Current scientific opinion is that the chance of actually cheating death is slim. The process of freezing a corpse results in the inevitable destruction of some or all of the brain cells and other delicate tissue. Thus, even if the corpse were resuscitated at some date far in the future, essential elements of the person's personality, such as memory and self-identity, might be missing.

The actual cost of cryonic interment is high. Initial preparation and freezing, plus the cost of the capsule, usually exceed $50,000. Yearly maintenance fees for indefinite storage in the capsule—called a "Forever Flask" by cryonics societies—are also high.

More information about cryonics may be found in R. C. Ettinger, *Man Into Superman* (St. Martin's, 1972). Information on low-temperature science in general is found in D. Wilson, *The Colder the Better* (Atheneum, 1980).

Body frozen in cryocapsule for possible later revival. (Henry Groskinsky, LIFE Magazine, © 1967 TIME, INC.)

MEDICINE AND HEALING

Strange Diseases

Delirium Tremens

Delirium tremens—or the DT's, as they are often called—is the most serious complication of alcoholic withdrawal. It is accompanied by violent hallucinations and disconnected speech and is potentially fatal. About 5 to 15 percent of those who go into the DT's die, usually of the complications of shock and fever that can reach 107 degrees.

The DT's have been present since antiquity but became common only when the technique of distillation was discovered and high-proof spirits came into general use. Symptoms of the DT's were first systematically described in the late 18th century. The most prominent victim of the DT's was Edgar Allen Poe, who lay undiagnosed in a Baltimore hospital for four days before his death in 1849. Doctors' reports describe Poe as having been wildly delirious and incoherent, talking nonstop with imaginary objects on the walls. He answered questions nonsensically, his arms and legs trembled, and he was drenched in sweat from fever.

Withdrawal from alcohol causes a wide variety of symptoms. The commonest and mildest is the hangover. Muscle tremors and malaise may occur after more serious drinking bouts, and seizures called "rum fits" can occur in some cases. Delirium tremens usually occurs only when a confirmed alcoholic undergoes sudden withdrawal from alcohol. (Somewhat similar symptoms may occur when a heroin addict goes without a fix.)

Drunks with little chance to reform ended up with "incurable" delirium tremens. (The Bettman Archive.)

Dr. Lawrence K. Altman described a typical case of the DT's in *The New York Times*, August 21, 1979. A middle-aged businessman, admitted to a hospital in San Francisco for routine hip surgery, became agitated, restless, and unable to sleep on his first night in the hospital. He began to hallucinate, describing spiders and bugs crawling on the walls. The diagnosis was one of obvious delirium tremens, though the man had denied, in his medical report, that he drank more than an "occasional cocktail." Lawrence describes his other reactions: "His arms were shaking as he picked at his sheets in the mistaken belief that he was counting dollar bills . . . The content of his conversation was garbled. Yet he turned his head to listen to the people with whom he thought he was conversing. Clearly, he was misinterpreting the meaning of the sounds and shadows in his hospital room. In his disorientation, he thought he was on the street . . . When he stopped talking and seemed lucid for a moment, I did a simple test. My hands were held apart as if an imaginary string were being pulled taut. I asked him what color the string was. Blue, he responded. When I handed him an imaginary bottle of beer, he went through the motions of opening it. Then, holding it up, he 'drank' it."

The precise cause of the DT's is unknown. Autopsied brains of people who died from delirium tremens show no apparent difference from healthy brains. Presumably the DT's are a biochemical disorder the specific type of which is obscure. Part of the problem is caused by the critical drop in the level of body magnesium that occurs when an alcoholic is withdrawn from the drug.

Treatment of the DT's consists of replacing the lost magnesium—along with other electrolytes such as sodium and potassium—through intravenous feeding. Large amounts of fluid, sometimes as much as seven quarts per day, are also administered to replace water lost through sweating and fever. Drugs are given to combat body trembling and other symptoms; Librium, Valium, Thorazine, Compazine, and especially paraldehyde are the most common. DT patients are often placed on "cooling mattresses" to combat fever. Glucose, the usual intravenous food, is not administered because alcoholics often lack the necessary B vitamins in the blood to digest the glucose. Excess glucose can lead to Wernicke's disease, which has dangerous physical and psychological symptoms and is characterized by paralysis of the eye muscles and a staggering gait.

The DT's usually end as abruptly as they began, within two days of the onset of the attack. The patient wakes up exhausted, lucid, and uncomfortable but with no actual memory of having had the DT's. This often complicates rehabilitation, for the affected person often denies his alcoholism and refuses to believe that he could have had the DT's at all.

"Thrifty-Gene" Diabetes

Diabetes is one of the least-understood diseases of modern man. It is actually thought to represent several diseases of different causes. Heredity, viral infection, and malfunction of the body's immune system have all been implicated in diabetes. The latest theory postulates a genetic basis, the "thrifty-gene" syndrome.

Diabetes in all its forms involves a bodily failure to produce adequate or timely supplies of insulin. Insulin is necessary to the metabolizing of sugar in the blood; without the necessary insulin, the individual experiences a variety of symptoms and may even go into shock. Both juvenile and adult forms of diabetes are known. The adult form is the less serious; it can often be controlled by limiting dietary intake of sugar. Juvenile diabetes is more dangerous. It cannot be treated by dietary modifications alone, and the individual usually requires daily injections of insulin.

Diabetes is diagnosed by means of a medical procedure known as a glucose tolerance test. This measures the body's insulin activity. The procedure is full of pitfalls, however, and in some cases even leads to misdiagnosis of the disease. For instance, insulin levels in the blood are highly sensitive to adrenalin, and even a small increase in the amount of adrenalin released into the bloodstream can cause a dramatic decrease in the insulin level. In some patients, the ordinary stress caused by a medical examination is enough to cause the release of adrenalin. These patients then often show distorted results in the glucose tolerance test, simply because their bodies have produced temporary excesses of insulin under the influence of the adrenalin. Cases are on record of individuals being diagnosed as diabetic when in fact they are not. One recorded instance is the case of a 4-year-old boy who was diagnosed as having juvenile diabetes; he took regular insulin injections for 20 years before another test revealed that he was not actually diabetic at all. (*The New York Times*, May 22, 1979.)

Diabetes seems to have several interrelated causes. Heredity is the most widely recognized. In particular, the juvenile form of the disease tends to run in families. Diabetics have been found to have a specific blood factor, controlled by the sixth chromosome of the human chromosomal chain. A team of Harvard researchers reported (in *The Lancet*, June 9, 1979) that this blood factor—Bf F1 of properdin factor B—is found in nearly 25 percent of diabetics but in just 2 percent of the general population. It is not known exactly how this blood factor is inherited, but it provides a valuable "marker" or means of tracing the disease from generation to generation.

Juvenile diabetes also appears to be linked to both viral causes and autoimmune causes. Researchers at the National Institutes of Health and the National Naval Medical Center in Bethesda, Maryland discovered a virus known as Coxsackie B4 in the tissues of a 10-year-old boy who died from diabetes, thus providing strong evidence for a viral implication in diabetes. The actual mechanisms of the infection are not known, for Coxsackie B4 is a common, usually harmless virus.

The basis for the autoimmune theory of diabetes comes from several medical studies, the most important of which are the University of Massachusetts studies (see *Science*, December 21, 1979) and the McGill University studies (see *Nature*, December 6, 1979). It was discovered that diabetic rats could be cured by injections of a specific antiserum. The implication is that the disease results from the failure of the body to produce adequate amounts of this antiserum. It was also found that blood vessels in the brain have receptors that bind to insulin. If these receptors were absent or damaged, it might account for the lack of "useful" insulin in the diabetic's bloodstream.

The most interesting theory of diabetes is the "thrifty gene" model,

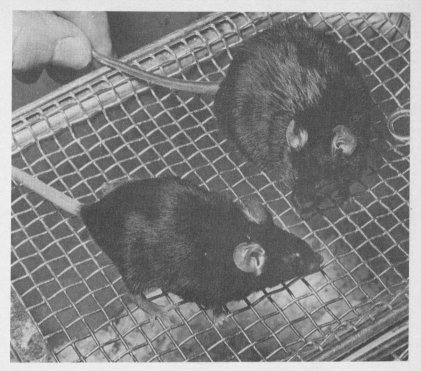

Laboratory mice used in "thrifty-gene" diabetes experiments. (Jackson Laboratory, Bar Harbor, Maine.)

proposed by James Neel of the University of Michigan. (See *Science News*, February 24, 1979.) The gene is apparently an evolutionary "leftover" that helped primitive man and others avoid starvation. The gene is still found in many populations today. People with the "thrifty" gene can make more efficient use of food supplies, thus enabling them to withstand prolonged fasts. Laboratory mice with a comparable gene withstand starvation diets much longer than mice without the gene. In human populations, the gene would have survival value for tribes that faced uncertain food supplies. In today's world, however, where starvation conditions are less common, the gene is relatively useless. Indeed, it may prove a liability, for it may process food too efficiently, leading to increased blood sugar. This strains the body's ability to produce insulin, thus setting the stage for the development of diabetes. Primitive tribes all over the world rarely contract diabetes, but when these people are shifted into more affluent conditions, 10 to 20 percent of them contract diabetes.

Epilepsy

Epilepsy is a poorly understood disease that can lead to lapses of consciousness, violent seizures, and other strange and compulsive behavior. In the past, epilepsy has been equated with mental illness, mental retardation, violence, and even possession by the devil. Modern drug treatments can control epileptic symptoms but cannot actually cure the disease.

There are many types of epileptic seizure, but the three most common are called grand mal, petit mal, and psychomotor seizures. Grand mal seizures are the classic epileptic fits characterized by blackouts and violent agitation of the body, often accompanied by gasping breath and foaming at the mouth. Petit mal seizures are simply lapses of consciousness lasting 10 to 20 seconds. They occur most often in children and are frequently mistaken for daydreaming. Psychomotor seizures result in some sort of compulsive movement, such as continuous chewing, unbuttoning clothes, or reciting phrases over and over.

Contrary to popular belief, epilepsy is not considered a primarily hereditary disease. It is more often caused by infections, head injuries, prenatal or post-natal brain damage, brain tumors, or nutritional disorders. Often the cause is sufficiently obscure that it cannot be traced with any certainty. No two cases of epilepsy are alike.

The mechanisms involved in epilepsy are better understood than the causes of the disease itself. Epilepsy is a central nervous system disorder in which certain brain cells are electrically abnormal. These damaged cells send out abnormal electrical signals to the body, thus producing seizures. It is not known how epileptic cells become abnormal or how the electrical signals they generate spread throughout the body via normal nerve cells. It is suspected that epileptic cells lack a bodily chemical that is instrumental in controlling electrical activity. This chemical is gamma-aminobutyric acid, or GABA for short. Researchers at the City of Hope National Medical Center in California discovered that epileptic cells have a reduced capacity to produce GABA, which thus leads to their electrical hypersensitivity. (See *The New York Times*, August 28, 1979.)

Treatment of epilepsy normally involves special drugs but can also include surgery to remove a specific injured area of the brain. Sophisticated diagnostic equipment is used to provide mappings of the brain's electrical activity; these electroencephalograms help pinpoint the nature and location of the epileptic cells. Treatment of the disorder normally consists of administration of an anticonvulsant drug such as valproic acid. This drug in some cases causes impaired liver function but is still considered superior to previous drugs which were derived from barbiturates. Dosages are carefully calculated to provide just enough of the drug to minimize side effects while also suppressing seizures. The epileptic's blood levels are continally monitored by GLC/EMIT techniques (short for Gas Liquid Chromatography of the anticonvulsant drug and Enzyme Multiple Immunoassay Technique); when the dosage of the anticonvulsant drug falls below the critical level, additional quantities are administered.

Drug therapy controls or eliminates 80 percent of all epileptic seizures but is powerless against the other 20 percent. At least 100,000 new cases of epilepsy occur in the United States each year. At least one-fifth of these result from head injuries sustained in auto accidents. Other cases could be minimized by early diagnosis and treatment, but public ignorance and prejudice unfortunately often prevent this.

More details on modern medical finding relating to epilepsy may be found in *The New York Times*, August 28, 1979, p. C3.

Polydipsia

Psychogenic polydipsia is a self-induced disease characterized by drinking too much water. It is a manifestation of psychiatric illness and can lead to coma and death.

The patient typically complains of feeling "dirty" or "unclean." Such feeling can arise from several neurotic causes. (In this respect, polydipsia is similar to anorexia nervosa, a neurotic disease in which the patient literally starves himself or herself under the delusion that he or she is "fat".) In some cases, the sufferer believes that his or her system is being corrupted or poisoned by contaminants in food, medicine, air or any other material that is ingested into the body. More often he or she will harbor guilt feelings of one sort or another that lead to the belief that he or she is sinfully corrupt or lacking in purity. In either case, the afflicted person sets out to "cure" himself or herself by drinking large quantities of water. This water guzzling is often combined with fasting.

In extreme cases, this obsessive overconsumption of water can lead to potentially fatal conditions. Excess water in the system leads to depletion of sodium in the blood, and, in some instances, to convulsions and coma. Drs. Marc Rendell, Daniel McGrane, and Manuel Cuesta reported two fatal cases of polydipsia in the *Journal of the American Medical Association*, December 1, 1978. One patient, a 29-year-old woman, went on a one-month "water fast" to cleanse herself of guilt feelings associated with sexual activity. After losing an inordinate amount of weight, she was treated in a Miami hospital, where her blood showed depleted sodium levels. Taken off her self-induced water diet, she recovered quickly and her blood sodium level returned to normal with surprising speed. A week after being released, however, she was brought into another hospital in a coma. Friends reported she had again been drinking enormous quantities of water. Despite infusions of saline solution to raise her blood sodium level, she entered cardiac arrest and died without regaining consciousness.

Doctors stress that treatment of psychogenic polydipsia must deal with the patient's underlying neurotic condition before a cure can be definitely effected. Treatment of the patient with psychoactive drugs, though often effective, can be risky, because such drugs often inhibit urination and can contribute to the retention of water in the body.

For additional information, see *The Sciences*, April, 1979, p. 4.

Autoimmune Diseases

Autoimmunity is a poorly understood condition in which the body's natural disease-fighters—antibodies and white blood cells—turn inward and attack various part of the body itself. This can lead to disability, paralysis, and even death. Many diseases, even common ones such as rheumatoid arthritis, are suspected of being autoimmune diseases.

In myasthenia gravis, a rare but serious disease of the nervous system, antibodies attack the sites where nerve cells connect with muscle cells. This destroys communication between nerves and muscles and leads at first to poor coordination and then progressively to complete paralysis. In rheumatoid arthritis, white blood cells known as leucocytes mistakenly sense "foreign" substances in the joints and converge at these sites to fight the presumed "infection." In mild cases, this causes chronic inflammation. In more severe cases, the leucocytes may actually eat away at cartilage tissue and bone tissue, leading to eventual deformity. Lupus erythematosus is a somewhat similar

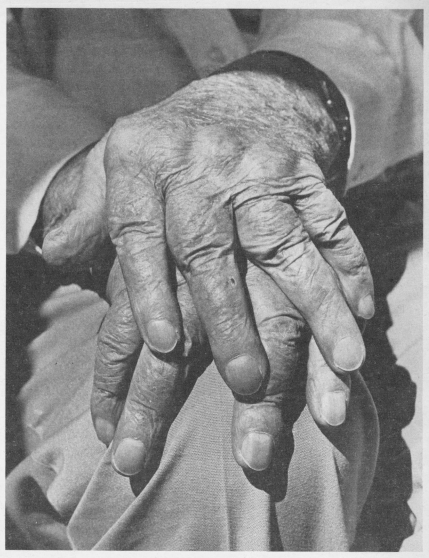

Arthritic hands. (Buddy Mays/Black Star)

disease in which the leucocytes attack red blood cells, platelets, and other white blood cells, as well as large quantities of worn-out DNA. Inflammation is the first symptom, then anemia, low white-blood cell count, and kidney damage. Fifty percent of sufferers from the disease die within 6 years of the disease's onset. Polymyositis, another suspected autoimmune disease, produces progressive muscle disability that may eventually lead to death through cardiorespiratory failure. It also leads to cancer in approximately 10 percent of cases.

Strangely, these autoimmune diseases strike women much more often than men, particularly young women in the 20-to-40 age group. Female victims of myasthenia and polymyositis outnumber male victims 2 to 1, while in lupus they outnumber males 9 to 1.

Since autoimmune diseases usually appear in adults, it has been hypothesized that the diseases result from the reappearance of immune system cells that were incompletely suppressed during the early years of life. These cells—leucocytes, for instance—are thought to go haywire when and if they reappear in the adult. (See *Proceedings of the National Academy of Sciences*, January, 1979.) Drs. Daniel Wallace, James Klinenberg and Dennis Goldfinger of the Cedars-Sinai Medical Center in Los Angeles have reported finding that other substances in the blood—not just leucocytes—may also contribute to autoimmune diseases, particularly to arthritis. (See *Time*, July 9, 1979.) It is not known yet exactly what these substances are. According to Klinenberg: "If we can identify the troublesome factors in the white cells or [blood] plasma, maybe we can do something to provide lasting relief or even a cure."

At the present time, treatment of autoimmune diseases is chancy and unreliable. Sufferers from rheumatoid arthritis may get relief from a new blood-filtration technique known as lymphapheresis, in which the rampaging leucocytes are removed from the victim's blood. Stiffness and deformation in the joints often disappear for periods up to several months after such treatments.

Other cases of arthritis, as well as those of lupus erythematosus, may involve immune system cells other than leucocytes, specifically those known as "suppressor-T" cells. The diseases can sometimes be permanently or temporarily halted when these disordered cells are removed from the body either by drainage through the thoracic duct or by radiation treatments of lymph tissue. (See *Science News*, November 24, 1979 for more details on suppressor-T treatment.)

Strange Drugs

Placebo

A placebo is an inert substance prescribed to satisfy a patient's demand for medication. Though it has no actual medical value, the placebo in many cases leads to real alleviation of the patient's symptoms.

The most common placebo is the "sugar pill," but other non-medical substances, such as vitamins and plain salt-water injections, are also common. The term has been extended today to cover any medication or medical procedure that serves no specific medical function and is used primarily for its psychological or psychophysiological effect. X-rays, antibiotics, even certain forms of surgery are employed for their placebo effects.

The patient, believing the placebo is actually a potent drug or other medication, in many cases experiences an actual reduction in the symptoms that had been troubling him. A large number of studies have shown that placebos can be effective against such diverse complaints as headache, arthritis, angina pectoris, post-operative pain, high blood pressure, colds, coughs, seasickness, ulcers, vertigo, and hay fever. In almost all of these studies, the proportion of patients responding to placebos is about 30 to 40 percent.

It is a common misconception that placebos are most effective on patients who are chronic complainers or hypochondriacs. On the contrary, however, these patients are poor placebo candidates. Placebos give their greatest effect in the cases of patients who are suffering from real, severe pain. The typical placebo responder is anxious and emotionally unstable, though not, as might be expected, gullible. Studies on the placebo have failed to establish any relationship between the placebo's effectiveness and the patient's gullibility or suggestibility.

Until recently it was assumed that the placebo effect was "all in the mind," i.e., that the placebo worked by changing the patient's reaction to pain rather than by altering the pain itself. It appears, however, that placebos may act directly to affect the biochemical processes involved with pain itself.

The brain is known to have its own internal pain-killers, small protein-like substances known as endorphins. (See *Internal Opiates*, p. 16.) Pain is suppressed when these endorphins are activated in the brain. This endorphin response is triggered by the brain itself under a wide variety of conditions. For instance, when the body is under severe stress, endorphin may be released to mask pain. (This is the reason soldiers in battle often do not realize they have been wounded.) The brain's electrochemical impulses activate the endorphin sites, which results in a blocking of pain impulses. A research study at the University of California at San Francisco (see Levine et al, "Mechanisms of placebo analgesia," *Lancet*, 1978, II, p. 654) concluded that placebos induce a psychological response that triggers the activation of the endorphin system, thus leading to a genuine reduction in pain.

Placebos may also stimulate certain other of the body's self-healing mechanisms besides endorphins. Interferon, for instance, which fights viral infections, may be responsible for the placebo's observed effectiveness against colds. And steroids, which counter inflammation, could account for the arthritis relief that placebos engender. The wide effectiveness of placebos implies to some observers that the mind and the body are intimately interconnected in the suppression of pain and that the two cannot be treated separately. This view offers support for the "holistic" view of the human organism. (See *Holistic Healing*, p. 55.)

Interferon

Interferon is a naturally-produced drug that appears to be the body's first line of defense against virus attacks. It also interferes with cell division and shows amazing abilities to control some forms of cancer. The interferon system can sometimes go awry, however, and interferon malfunction has been implicated in diseases as widely different as severe asthma and rheumatoid arthritis.

Interferon was first discovered in England in 1957 and has proved to be a far more complex substance than was first suspected. Interferon is produced in the body in infinitesimal amounts, usually under the stimulus of a viral infection. Almost all body cells can produce interferon, and the interferon produced by one cell can "warn" or protect adjoining cells against the spread of the virus. Interferon is a complex protein compound, and at least three forms of it have been discovered. One type is produced by white blood cells, another by connective cells between skin and other organs, a third by T lymphocytes, special immune cells that are especially active against viral or bacterial invaders. Each form of interferon seems to have its own specialization, working best to protect cells similar to those that produced it.

Interferon in its various forms seem to be a broad-spectrum anti-viral agent. It attacks nearly all sorts of virus indiscriminately and produces a curious biological phenomenon known as viral interference. A person with a viral infection almost never comes down with another viral disease at the same time. It appears that the first virus is "interfering" with the second, but what is actually happening is that the interferon produced under the stimulus of the first attack is repelling the second. The strength of this ability of interferon to control viral infections has led to its being characterized as a wonder drug that would be as effective against viruses as penicillin is against bacteria. Interferon has been used successfully to combat such maladies as shingles, chicken pox, "pink eye" (a contagious and incapacitating infection), and the common cold.

Interferon is produced in such tiny quantities that current studies of its disease-fighting effectiveness must necessarily be small-scale. Interferon is extracted from the white blood cells of donated human blood. The entire world output of the drug in 1979 was little more than 1/100th of an ounce; it took 90,000 pints of blood to produce even this infinitesimal amount.

Spectacular new techniques of interferon production, however, have recently been discovered. The most dramatic is known as recombinant-DNA technology. Such techniques involves splicing a human interferon-producing gene into the chromosomes of a harmless form of laboratory bacteria. The bacteria, then begin turning out human interferon. As such bacteria, usually *E. coli,* can be raised in huge quantities in the laboratory, this technique holds out the possibility of greatly increased interferon production.

Interferon's alleged cancer-fighting abilities are due to its inhibiting effect on cell division: the action of the drug seems to halt the division of proliferating cancer cells. (It also inhabits the growth of healthy cells.) An American Cancer Society program has shown that interferon seems to have positive effects against cancer of the breast, bone marrow, skin, and lymph system. (See *Time,* March 31, 1980.) The medical establishment has been slow in accepting the reliability of results in interferon studies, charging that certain early studies in the mid-1970s had inadequate safeguards and controls. But a $2 million American Cancer Society grant for interferon research, in 1978 (the biggest single research grant in the organization's history), has given a badge of respectability to interferon's use in cancer treatment. A 1980 study, conducted at 10 U.S. medical centers with the American Cancer Society funds, has shown encouraging results. Of 16 cases of breast cancer that were no longer responding to conventional treatment, 7 showed noticeable improvement under interferon treatment. Similar noticeable results occurred in 3 of 11 cases of myeloma (cancer of the bone marrow), and encouraging (though not conclusive) results have been observed against melanoma (skin cancer) and lymphoma (cancer of the lymph system).

Such results, though suggestive, are not conclusive, and cancer researchers are quick to point out that interferon's role and effectiveness in cancer treatment will not be known with certainty for many years. Many questions remain to be ironed out, the biggest of which is how interferon, an anti-viral agent, acts against cancer, which in most cases is not caused by viruses.

When the body's interferon system malfunctions, various ailments can result. Asthma can be produced by the excessive release of histimines. And build-ups of an interferon variety known as Immune Interferon have been implicated in such exotic diseases as lupus erythematosus, (an inflammation of the connective tissue), scleroderma (swelling and atrophying of the skin), and Sjögren's syndrome insufficient secretion of tears and saliva). Immune Interferon was also present in over half of the rheumatoid arthritis patients examined in a National Institutes of Health survey (see *The New York Times,* May 8, 1979). It is suspected that Immune Interferon may also play a part in other autoimmune diseases. Researchers are not sure whether Immune Interferon is a cause, or only a consequence, of these diseases. But the drug is found only rarely in individuals not suffering from such diseases. Though it may not actually cause the diseases, researchers believe that it is a factor in determining the course and severity of the illness.

Strange Treatments

Holistic Healing

Holistic (or wholistic) medicine is a system of health care that treats the "whole" person. It concentrates less on disease and more on "wellness" and prevention than traditional medicine. The holistic philosophy embraces a galaxy of various therapies and methods, some of which are medically acceptable and others of which are based on mysticism or outright quackery.

The president of the American Holistic Medical Association, C. Norman Shealy, defines holistic medicine as a system of health care which assists individuals in harmonizing mind, body and spirit. Holistic healers criticize regular doctors for concentrating too narrowly on disease rather than on the larger question of the patient's overall health. In general, the holistic movement emphasizes treating the individual as a whole rather than as a collection of parts. Noting the inseparability of mind and body, holistic healers also stress the importance of the individual as a self-healer and the necessity of creating a way of life that is conductive to health.

Traditional Western medicine has always preached the necessity of treating the "whole patient," but most conventional physicians nevertheless concentrate on treating the symptoms of one particular disease. Michael Halberstam, editor of *Modern Medicine,* explains this: "To most American doctors, illness is more interesting, more exciting, than health." (*Psychology Today,* August 1978.) Many modern physicians are, however, adapting certain holistic practices, particularly the "back-to-basics" philosophy of preventive medicine.

Most reputable forms of holistic medicine, according to the American Holistic Medical Association, rely on seven basic therapies. The first three, termed the "holy trinity of health, more important than anything else," are: good nutrition, physical exercise, and self-regulation techniques such as relaxation and biofeedback. The other four therapies are acupuncture, neuromuscular integration, environmental medicine, and spiritual awareness. These areas are important but less easily controlled as the first three. Spiritual awareness, according to Shealy, requires that a person live in accordance with his or her ideals. If this area is neglected, Shealy says, "it's hard to be completely well."

Numerous sub-groups and sub-therapies exist under the holistic umbrella, some of them preaching questionable practices whose relation to good health is unproved. The East/West Center for Holistic Health in New York City, for instance, refuses to hire occult or psychic healers because "so many of them are quacks." Licensing requirements for holistic practitioners vary from state to state, with some states, such as California, requiring no license at all. Persons seeking holistic treatment are well advised to check the licensing laws of their state.

In the subject of holistic medicine are many faddish or outlandish therapies. *Radionics* preaches that examination of one particular part of the patient—a urine sample, for instance—is enough for a full diagnosis of the individual's problem; the practitioner relies principally on instinct in making his assessment. *"One-cause/one-cure"* systems are based on the notion that all health problems arise from one particular cause and can be cured by attacking that cause. Diet is often indicated as the culprit, and certain Oriental methods, for instance, say that health can be achieved simply by cutting out "yin" foods and concentrating on "yang" foods. In extreme forms, such as rice diets, these restricted dietary therapies can lead to malnutrition or even starvation. *Iridology* is a system based on the idea that every organ of the body corresponds to a section of the iris, and all disease can be diagnosed by examining the eye. *Chiropractic* considers many diseases and maladies to be caused by "subluxation" of the spine, a condition in which the vertebrae supposedly squeeze the spinal cord and cut off the flow of nerve impulse. *Foot reflexology* is akin to iridology in claiming that bodily parts are reflected in a particular organ, in this case the foot; diseases are said to be treatable by manipulating the proper segment of the sole.

Scientific studies of these methods have not shown them to have any positive value beyond the power of suggestion. In a study of iridology, for instance, three California researchers found no basis for its claim: "Iridology was neither selective nor specific, and the likelihood of correct detection was statistically no better than chance." (*Science News,* December 15, 1979.) In

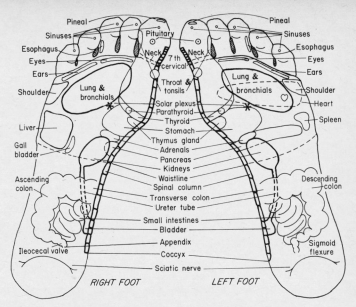

Foot reflexology chart. (M. Aymann, HOLISTIC HEALTH HANDBOOK)

a 1973 Yale University study of chiropractic, it was found that subluxation of the vertebrae, as described by chiropractic, simply did not exist.

Most of these therapies are harmless in themselves, but they can lead to dangerous situations through mis-diagnosis or lack of treatment. The practitioner may fail to diagnose diseases such as cancer or meningitis which would have been treatable under conventional medical practice.

Reputable holistic methods are particularly effective in combatting maladies which do not have a specific medical cure. In this category are depression, anxiety, stress, hysterical paralysis, and high blood pressure. These problems are all highly correlated with the patient's mental state and thus particularly amenable to the "whole person" approach. In treating hypertension, conventional medicine prescribes drugs that help reduce blood pressure. Holistic methods, on the other hand, stress relaxation and/or biofeedback techniques which often lead to a more lasting cure.

Acupuncture

The acupuncture technique of inserting needles in the skin has been used in Chinese medicine since at least 2,000 B.C. for the treatment of disease and the relief of pain. Neither Chinese nor Western scientists have yet ascertained conclusively how acupuncture works.

Acupuncture is based on ancient Chinese texts that devised a system of 900 acupuncture points ranging over the body surface. The points are spaced along 12 meridians and each corresponds to a specific bodily organ. Fine needles are inserted at the appropriate points during acupuncture treatment. The needles are connected to an electrical stimulator which applies a 10-volt current to the acupuncture point. (This is sensed by the patient only as a slight feeling of pressure at the site of the needle.) This technique of "electroacupuncture" has been in use only since the 1960s. Before that date, manual stimulus was applied to the acupuncture point by relays of nurses who twisted the needles by hand.

Acupuncture is used as an anesthetic in operations as widely varied as Caesarian sections and brain surgery. Test needlings are usually done before surgery to determine a patient's adaptability to acupuncture. Acupuncture requires alertness in the patient, and patients who are comatose, deaf, mute, or mentally retarded are not good prospects. Usually acupuncture is used in conjunction with sedatives. Tranquillizers such as sodium phenobarbitol, scopalamine, or atropine are given to most acupuncture patients an hour before surgery. The patient, however, remains fully conscious through the operation. Sedatives are readministered during the operation if necessary, and, in cases where the patient feels severe pain, a regular chemical anesthetic is immediately given.

The Chinese claim that acupuncture anesthesia, in addition to its anti-pain effect, also has anti-shock and anti-infection qualities. Acupuncture, unlike conventional anesthesia, does not affect blood pressure, pulse rate, and respiration; this helps guard patients against the shock of a normal operation and is especially valuable in the case of patients who are old, chronically ill, or who have weak hearts. Chinese studies seem to indicate that acupuncture's anti-infection effect results from a stimulation of production of white blood cells. In one experimental group of pulmonary patients, complications occurred among 10.5 percent of the patients who had undergone conventional anaesthesia, compared to only 2.8 percent among the acupuncture patients.

Apart from its value as an anesthetic, acupuncture is also used to treat disease and various physiological problems. Acupuncture has been described in Chinese texts as being effective against over 300 diseases. Today it is used in the treatment of malaria, appendicitis, ulcers, asthma, bronchitis, and arthritis, among others, but its most valuable application may be to various forms of heart ailments: angina pectoris, myocardial infarction, and hyper-

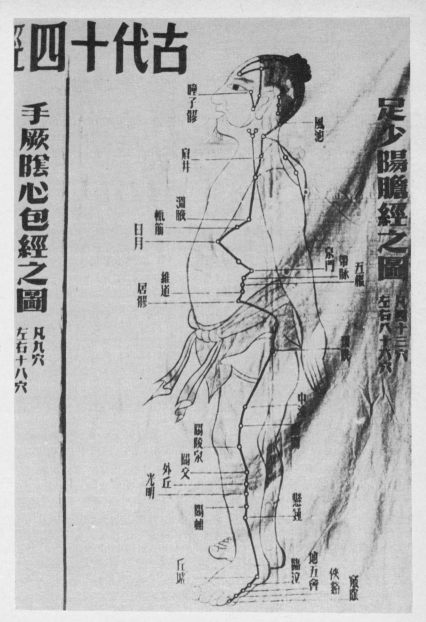

Diagram of the human body used by the Institute of Medicine in Peking to illustrate the critical points for acupuncture treatment. (UPI photo)

tension. In one Chinese study, many heart patients who had failed to respond to traditional Chinese herbal medicine or to Western techniques found relief through acupuncture treatment. One course of treatment consists of 10 applications of the acupuncture needles on a daily or alternate-day basis. Acupuncture treatment for the pain of cancer consists of regular insertion of needles (along with electrical stimulation) for 3 to 5 minutes; this treatment, according to Chinese doctors, brings from 5 to 10 hours of pain relief.

How and why does acupuncture work? Chinese researchers are exploring the hypothesis that acupuncture stimulates the production of endorphins, the brain's own internal pain-killers, thus acupuncture will very often lead to a real reduction in pain. This theory is suggested by the fact that patients with severed spinal cords are impervious to acupuncture when the acupuncture needles are applied *below* the point of severence. When needles are applied above the point of severence, pain relief results. It seems likely that the acupuncture needles transmit a stimulus to local nerve cells which is relayed along the spinal cord to the brain, where it stimulates the brain to release endorphins. Chinese scientists seem to have pinpointed the area of the brain that receives the neural impulses that lead to the endorphin response; it is the caudate nucleus in the cerebral hemisphere near the thalamus. Further research in Canada has also suggested that acupuncture may also stimulate the pituitary gland and other brain structures to release endorphins. Experimental measurement of the endorphin to levels in the spinal fluid during acupuncture treatment indicates that the level of the morphine-like substances increased by over one third after acupuncture needling.

If the endorphin hypothesis is true, then acupuncture would be akin to placebos, the "sugar pill" of Western medicine, which also seem to be connected to the endorphin response. A University of Florida study seemed to support this conclusion. Two hundred patients were given acupuncture treatment. Half were needled at the traditional acupuncture points along the 12 meridians. The other half had needles inserted at random in the skin. *Both* groups reported an equal amount of pain relief. This implies that acupuncture *does* work but that it is the stimulation of the brain itself, not the individual placement of the needles, that really matters.

Acupuncture has not found a significant role in Western medical practice, and doctors in the U.S. and Europe, while not denying its undoubted effects, feel that it does not have a great future except in underdeveloped countries where more reliable anesthetics and procedures are not available. Many factors seem to be involved in successful acupuncture analgesia, perhaps including cultural conditioning. Most Chinese patients, for instance, receive several days of indoctrination before undergoing acupuncture surgery.

Western doctors consider regular chemical anesthetics to be more reliable than acupuncture in surgery. The one area where acupuncture is admitted to have a possible application is with patients with heart conditions who cannot safely undergo conventional anesthesia. In the area of general pain relief and disease treatment, Western doctors in general prefer conventional drug treatments because of their greater reliability. Also, a pain therapy known as transcutaneous nerve stimulation has been in use in the United States since the late 1960s. It works on the same principal as acupuncture but does not break the skin; it is considered safer and easier than acupuncture and produces the same levels of pain relief.

Further information on recent acupuncture research may be found in *Science News,* October 27, 1979, p. 200 and p. 296.

Ionization

A shortage of charged atmospheric particles called air ions causes deleterious effects in humans, according to some researchers. Shortage of ions is caused by pollution and is especially prevalent in smoggy areas, traffic jams, and smoky rooms.

Ions are unstable atoms and molecules which have either more or fewer electrons than normal. Ions are formed most commonly in the soil, where trace elements of radioactive potassium, radon, and uranium initiate the ion reaction. An atom of oxygen hit by a radioactive ray immediately links up with four to six molecules of water vapor to form an ion. Ions also form in the air when oxygen atoms are hit by cosmic rays or light rays. Because water is a necessary part of all ions, they are most common during and following rainfalls and showers.

Scientific evidence for an ionic effect upon human beings is as yet inconclusive, though it is suggestive. Depletion of air ions has been linked to fatigue and disease-susceptibility in both animals and man. Alfred P. Krueger, researcher of the University of California at Berkeley, conducted experiments with mice raised in a de-ionized environment and discovered that they were twice as prone to influenza as normal mice. De-ionization has also been implicated in lethargy, fatigue, and certain kinds of headaches in humans. Such reactions are most common in polluted environments. An experiment in Hungary (reported in *Saturday Review,* April 28, 1973) illustrated the effects of pollution on air ionization. An ordinary business office was tested in the morning, before employees arrived, for its ionization level; it contained 2,000 ions per cubic centimeter. After occupation for six hours by four employees, several of whom smoked, the room was found to contain no ions at all.

Ions are either positive or negative. Negative ions bear an extra electron, while positive ions are missing an electron. Experiments with ionization seem to indicate that negative ions are beneficial while positive ions are the opposite. Researchers at the University of California at Berkeley, the Multorgan Research Center in Lugano, Switzerland, and the Hebrew University in Jerusalem, among others, have documented that increases in positive air ions lead to a corresponding increase in bodily production of a hormone called serotonin. This leads to "serotonin irritation syndrome," which is characterized by constriction of blood vessels and an increase in hypertension. An excess of positive air ions is connected with certain weather conditions, especially the presence of dry winds such as the Santa Ana of California, the sharav of the Near East, the foehn of sourthern Europe, and the sirocco of Africa and Sicily.

These and other ion-related symptoms can be treated by negative ion therapy, i.e., artificially producing beneficial negative ions in a laboratory by the use of postively and negatively charged metal plates.

A complete discussion of ionization may be found in *The Ion Effect*, by Fred Soyka (Dutton, 1977).

THE NATURAL WORLD

Genetics

Viral Genes and Gene Splicing

Some viruses are believed to be nothing more than free-floating genes. In some cases, these viral genes may actually merge with genes of a host species to produce mutations.

Traditionally, the only method of gene transfer that takes place in nature is that from parent to child. The theory of viral gene transfer was proposed in 1975 by a team of researchers at the National Cancer Institute. (See the *Proceedings of the National Academy of Sciences,* October 1975.) Dr. George J. Todaro, Dr. Raoul E. Beneveniste, and their associates hypothesized that under some circumstances genes might turn into viruses and vice versa.

Genes from one animal could thus be transferred to another animal by means of a virus. In essence, genes of the donor animal would turn into viruses, then infect another animal, where they would change back into genes. If these genes were incorporated into the second animal's genetic makeup— perhaps through attaching themselves to DNA in the animal's cells—they could then be passed along to the animal's offspring. This offspring would have some of the qualities of the donor animal. The gene transfer would not necessarily have to occur between animals of the same species; a gene of a dog, for instance, could conceivably be transferred to a cow.

Such gene transfer may actually have played an important part in the evolution of the animals which today inhabit the world. The National Cancer

Institute researchers hypothesize that evidence exists for such gene transfer in at least three instances in the distant past. In each case, genes of one species are believed to have infected a second species after being transformed into type-C viruses. About three million years ago, for instance, genes from a species of primate were probably transferred to a species which was the ancestor of today's domestic cat. In a second case—probably happening between five and 10 million years ago—genes from a species ancestral to the modern mouse were transferred to a species ancestral to the domestic pig. The third transfer involved genes from an ancestral rat being transferred to the forerunner of the cat.

Evidence for such gene transfers is derived by comparing genes of living species with those of other species and also with viruses. Molecule-by-molecule chemical analysis of the genetic material involved showed the similarity between such genes and led to the conclusion that they originally derived from the same animal. The viral gene constitutes only a very small portion of the genetic makeup of the host animal, and it has not been discovered exactly what changes were induced by the gene in the host animal. According to Dr. Todaro, however, "Since these viral genes have persisted in the animals for millions of years, it is presumed that they serve some useful purpose in the species that adopted them."

Experimental evidence for the transfer of genes by means of viral infection has not yet been observed under natural conditions. Critics of the theory maintain that the presence of two similar genes in different species is not necessarily conclusive proof of viral transfer: such similarities could be due merely to coincidence.

If the hypothesis is correct, however, it would provide a potential means of reconstructing some of the genes of extinct animals. For example, the gene transferred from the ancestor of the mouse to that of the pig is still present in modified form in the modern mouse and the modern pig. Since pigs bear offspring at a later age than mice, there have been fewer generations of pigs than mice. As a result, pigs have changed less since the gene transfer; the gene in the modern pig is closer to the original. Thus, if the basic hypothesis is correct, a study of the gene of the pig would provide information about the same gene in the ancestor of the mouse. (For additional information, see Harold M. Schmeck, Jr., *The New York Times*, November 27, 1975.)

Genetic scientists have recently succeeded in transferring genes from one species to another through chemical and mechanical means. This radical process, known as gene-splicing or recombinant DNA technology, has resulted in human genes being transferred to bacteria and viral genes being transferred to mice.

Gene splicing is a delicate and complicated technique. It involves disrupting the process of cell division in such a way that individual genes can be liberated and then transferred into cells of other species. Genes are stripped from strands of DNA (the master molecule of heredity) by the use of special enzymes. Then they are injected into new cells using a miniaturized needle known as a micropipette.

Gene splicing has very practical applications. When the gene for human insulin is transplanted into bacteria, the bacteria start producing insulin identical to that produced in the human body. This provides a cheap source of insulin, which is used in the treatment of diabetes.

Bacteria are also being used in a similar manner to produce human growth hormone. According to genetic scientists, this is one of the most important substances to be snythesized through genetic engineering. Growth hormone is the only treatment for pituitary dwarfism, which afflicts 20,000 people in the United States alone. The only source for growth hormone— aside from bacterial synthesis—is the pituitary glands of cadavers; it takes 50 cadavers to provide enough hormone to treat one child for a year. Mass production of the growth hormone through the use of bacteria would be a major step forward in the treatment of the malady.

A third hormone, somatostatin, which is normally produced by the brain, has also been artifically produced through gene splicing. Somatostatin is used primarily in laboratory research, and its production by bacteria is not as urgent as that of insulin and growth hormone.

Further information on gene splicing may be found in *The New York Times,* July 17, 1979, p. C-1; and *Science News,* October 20, 1979, p. 260.

Clones

Cloning is a non-sexual form of reproduction. A clone is produced from a portion, sometimes just a single cell, of an adult being and grows into an exact genetic duplication—a twin—of that adult. Cloning is common in plants but much rarer in animals. Theoretically at least, any living thing can be cloned, but so far no adult mammal has been successfully cloned, much less a human being.

Cloning is a standard technique for the reproduction of plants. A cutting of a house plant rooted in a jar of water on a kitchen window sill is perhaps the commonest example of plant cloning. Commercial growers of plants use cloning techniques to reproduce particularly outstanding plant varieties. Besides using cuttings, growers also employ budding and layering, techniques familiar to most gardeners. Almost all commercially available rose bushes, for example, are clones of original parent plants reproduced by budding small portions of the parent onto the roots of a "host" plant.

Cloning in the animal kingdom is neither so easy nor so widespread. Natural cloning appears only among invertebrates. Starfish cut into pieces can regenerate the lost limbs to create complete new creatures. Less highly developed species are even more spectacular cloners. The planetarian worm, a small aquatic worm, can regrow a new body from a minute piece of the old. If the planetarian's tail is cut off, it grows a new one. If its head is removed, it replaces it. If it is cut into many small pieces, each piece grows the necessary body parts to make a complete new worm.

Among vertebrates, cloning is much more problematical. Frogs have been successfully cloned since the early 1960s, but the cloning is of a specialized sort involving highly complex surgical techniques. In most cases, the nucleus of a cell from an immature frog embryo is surgically inserted into a frog egg that has had its nucleus removed. The new egg then grows into an adult genetically identical to the cell that provided the implanted nucleus. Researchers are divided on the question of whether this should be considered a full-fledged case of cloning, since it was only an embryo that was cloned, not an actual adult frog. There are a few claimed instances of adult nuclei having been used to successfully clone frogs, but they are inadequately documented and the subject of scientific dispute.

The only mammal to have been successfully cloned is the mouse. In 1979, experimenters at the University of Geneva succeeded in creating cloned mice by roughly the same technique used to clone frogs. A nucleus from the cell of a mouse blastocyte (a very early embryonic stage), was inserted by microscopic pipette into a recently fertilized mouse ovum. A mild treatment with a chemical relaxant allowed the cell's wall to be pierced without damage. The same pipette was then used to remove the egg's own nucleus. The egg with its new nucleus was then implanted in a mouse foster mother, where it completed its embryonic development. A number of mice born of this procedure have grown to maturity.

Human cloning is a much more controversial subject. Several researchers have claimed varying degrees of success with cloning procedures, but none have been scientifically confirmed or replicated. In an experiment reported in the *American Journal of Obstetrics and Gynecology* (January 15, 1979) one researcher claimed to have inserted nuclei from male sperm cells into unfertilized female ova. The ova were then reported to have grown and divided normally to the blastocyst stage (the point at which an egg fertilized the usual way would leave the Fallopian tubes and become implanted in the uterus). The experimental embryos were not carried beyond this point, although the researcher noted that "there was every indication that each specimen was developing normally and could readily have been transferred into a womb "to develop as a normal baby."

This experiment has aroused much doubt among scientific observers, who question, for instance, how an unfertilized egg, even with a new nucleus, could grow and divide at all.

The most spectacular report of human cloning was contained in the 1978 book *In His Image, the Cloning of a Man* (Lippincott, 1978) by writer David Rorvik. Rorvik claimed to be reporting a successful cloning experiment in which an aging millionaire "father" donated cells that were used to create the clone. A nucleus from one of these donor cells was inserted into a denucleated egg. The egg grew successfully and was implanted in a surrogate mother where the embryo was carried to term. The resulting baby, reportedly born in December, 1976, would have been an exact copy of the "father." (Actually the clone would literally be the identical *twin* of the donor, not the "son.")

The scientific community was skeptical of Rorvik's claim, especially since he offered no tangible substantiation. None of the participants in the experiment was identified by name. According to the book's publisher, this was to protect the child from harmful publicity and the medical participants from unpleasant controversy. Rorvik claimed that all the techniques for human cloning existed at the time of the experiment but that no one had yet actually "put them together." He said that the successful cloning required only a refinement of existing cell-fusion techniques.

This case has spawned a number of related controversies, even including several public-interest lawsuits to determine whether governmental agencies such as the National Science Foundation and the National Institute of Health are providing grants to support cloning research. Human cloning is a controversial subject that has led the suit-filers to say (see *Science,* March 1978, p. 1316): "All our values would be upset if we could Xerox life. We need to be responsible enough to divide good science from that which is dangerous."

Further information on the scientific processes involved in cloning are to be found in *Science News,* February 17 and July 28, 1979; and *Science,* March 1978. A good general treatment of the subject is to be found in R. C. McKinnell, *Cloning: A Biologist Reports* (University of Minnesota Press, 1979).

Evolution

Origin of Life

Life began on earth 3 to 3.5 billion years ago, but science has not yet been able to explain how life arose spontaneously from the chemical compounds that composed the earth at that time.

The most likely scenario is that as the earth cooled from its original fiery state, water condensed to form the salty oceans. The oceans harbored a host of elements and compounds, some of which eventually (perhaps energized by lightning) combined to form the first amino acids, the building blocks of life. This theory receives credence from the fact that even today blood bears a very close resemblance to salt water.

The actual mechanisms of life's beginning are less clear. It is possible that certain forms of clay played a prominent role. It is well known that clay plays a catalytic role in the formation of certain organic polymers from monomers. Researchers at the Laboratory of Chemical Evolution at the University of Maryland theorize that clay may have provided a sort of "scaffolding" for building larger and larger organic molecules. (See *Science News*, September 22, 1979.) If certain types of clay had affinities for certain amino acids, these clays may have originally determined which amino acids went into the make-up of living things.

Examination of 3.83-billion-year-old graphite rock from Greenland (the oldest rock on earth) has shown evidence of organic substances. University of Maryland researchers found organic hydrocarbon molecules in the rock, specifically benzene-like compounds and napthalene-like compounds. (See *Science News,* September 15, 1979.) There is some evidence that they may have been created by elementary forms of life, though it is just as possible that they themselves formed the building blocks of future elementary forms. So far, actual microfossils have not been discovered in rock of this age, but if they were, it would absolutely confirm the biological origin of those hydrocarbons.

The first form of "organized" life was probably a simple gene, merely a chain of amino acids in a specific order. Manfred Eigen, a Nobel prize winning chemist and member of the Max Planck Institute in Germany, has proposed that the first gene was RNA. Eigen theorized that the original gene would have had to be relatively short, with only 50 to 100 segments, or nucleotides; and that it would have to be capable of reproducing itself without the help of enzymes. A form of RNA known as transfer-RNA (or tRNA) is the closest living analog to this presumed primordial gene. Eigen's theory postulates that tRNA was fixed in early time and that all of the various modern forms of RNA evolved from it by simple mutation.

If the theory is correct, RNA probably represents the first true life form on earth.

Aside from the difficulties in pinning down the actual mechanism that led to the formation of life, there is also a further theoretical problem involved with the origin of life. Life has followed an upward progression, evolving toward higher forms and greater complexity; it seems to be governed by an inexorable forward urge. However, the Second Law of Thermodynamics, one of the bedrocks of physics, states in effect that all systems basically run "downhill," in much the same way that mountains are eroded or heat is dissipated from a fire. How then did life—a very complicated, ever-evolving phenomenon—ever originate in the face of the Second Law of Thermodynamics? This is one of the basic conundrums of science.

A possible answer may have been provided by Ilya Prigogine, a Belgian Nobel prize chemist, who has discovered a loophole in the Second Law. Prigogine has pointed out that in some cases a small system within a large system can utilize the decay of the large system to provide energy for its own growth. It thus moves "uphill" against the general "downhill" tide. In terms of life on earth, the smaller system—life—would have used the decay of the larger system—the Earth and the Sun—to provide the impetus for its upward course. According to Prigogine, this "is totally against the classical thermodynamic view that information must always degrade. It is, if you will, something profoundly optimistic." (See *The New York Times,* May 29, 1979.)

The Missing Link

The "missing link" is a presumed anthropoid ancestor that links man to the apes. Man and ape are assumed to have sprung from a common ancestor which has not yet been found in fossil form. There are several theories as to what this species looked like: a heavy orangutan-like creature; a light tree-swinging animal like today's gibbon; or a ground-walking form like an Old World monkey. But recent statistical research in body form and proportion shows that neither the orangutan, the gibbon, nor the chimpanzee is a logical candidate for the missing link, since all are too highly evolved—with strengthened or lengthened arms and small legs—to have provided the genetic material that also led to man. Only one present-day primate, the Howlever monkey, stands out as a possible candidate for the missing link. The Howlever has relatively short forelimbs and well developed hind limbs. An early primate akin to this monkey could have diversified into forms that led both to man and to all species of apes.

Aegyptopithecus. (Steven Kimbrough/Duke University)

The oldest ancestor of the missing link—if not the missing link itself—is a recently discovered primate that roamed Africa 30 million years ago. Named Aegyptopithecus because the principal fossil remains were found in Egypt, this small monkeylike animal, no bigger than today's house cat, was the most advanced form of life on earth at its time.*

Aegyptopithecus lived during the Oligocene Period and had a skull capacity of about 30 cubic centimeters, which was greater in relation to its body size than that of any other Oligocene mammal. Aegyptopithecus had evolved a complex social organization similar to that found in species of present day monkeys. Examination of fossils revealed that males had large, fanglike canine teeth whereas females had relatively small canines. This indicated that Aegyptopithecus had evolved specialized roles for the sexes. In particular, the males fought one another for mates and also used their well-developed fangs in defense of the tribe. This type of behavior required the animals to be aggressive, inventive, and fearless. Such a stressful existence is usually considered by evolutionary scientists to be conducive to the development of larger brains; species that led more sedentary, placid lives did not develop the large complex brains characteristic of the primates.

Considerations of brain size, social organization, and physical characteristics put Aegyptopithecus in the direct line of man's ancestors that may also include Ramapithecus, Paranthropus and Australopithecus.

Hominids

One of the great debates of human evolution revolves around the question of which fossil species belong to the line of development that led to man. Somewhere between three and four million years ago, the evolutionary line that led to man separated from the line that led to apes. Members of the human line are known as hominids.

Up until recently, the most widely accepted view of human evolution was that man diverged from the apes 20 to 25 million years ago. The distinctly hominid line was thought to contain various man-like species such as Ramapithecus, Paranthropus and Australopithecus, which gave rise several

*It was a common ancestor of man and apes, the oldest such man/ape link yet discovered. (See *The New York Times*, February 7, 1980.)

million years ago to the genus *Homo,* to which man belongs. Separate lines leading to today's apes—the gorilla, chimpanzee, orangutan, and gibbon—presumably developed alongside the hominid line.

This view of human development has been challenged by a theory based on the new science of molecular anthropology. Molecular anthropology is the study of the protein structure of primates. A basic tenet of the science—not totally accepted by traditional paleontologists—is that evolutionary mutations take place at a fairly constant rate. This tenet is supported by research on the molecular basis of mutation. If the theory is correct, then the molecular mutation rate can serve as a sort of evolutionary "clock." Heretofore, the only way to unravel the evolutionary lines that led to man was to compare the various fossil remains. According to molecular anthropology, a better way is to compare the protein structures of the living descendents of those fossil species.

As an example, molecular anthropologists have compared the proteins of man and the apes. The outcome was surprising. The protein structure of humans and apes is remarkably similar, as close as that between grizzly bears and brown bears, for instance. Such a result indicates that man and the apes are very closely related on the evolutionary scale—more closely than paleontologists had imagined. It seems unlikely, for instance, that man and the apes diverged from a common line 20 to 25 million years ago, for if that were so, the present protein structures of the two lines would be considerably more different than they are.

It appears then that man and the apes diverged only 3 to 4 million years ago. Thus many supposed hominids would not actually be hominids at all. They would instead be common ancestors of *both* man and apes. Ramapithecus, which existed from 10 to 15 million years ago, bears a close physical resemblance to man but would nevertheless not belong to man's own line. Vincent Sarich, a molecular anthropologist at the University of California, stated: "Ramapithecus cannot be a hominid, no matter what it looks like." (*Science News,* December 1, 1979.) Paranthropus and Australopithecus (3.5 million years ago would also be excluded from the hominid line on this basis. The genus *Homo* itself appeared about 3 million years ago, including such species as Homo erectus, Homo neadertalensis, and Homo cro-magnon.

The earliest footprints of a manlike creature were unearthed in Kenya in 1979. They are believed to have been made by Homo erectus. The Yale University expedition that uncovered the footprints estimated that they were made by an individual 5 to 5½ feet tall and weighing about 120 pounds. (See *The New York Times,* November 19, 1979.)

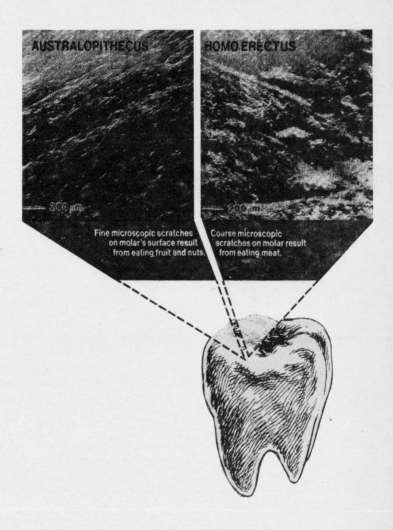

Magnifications of the molars of Australopithecus and Homo Erectus. (© 1979 by The New York Times Company. Reprinted by permission.)

Further differences between members of the genus Homo and pre-hominids such as Australopithecus have been theorized by examining the teeth of fossils. Microscopic examination of teeth by a research team at Johns Hopkins University in 1979 gave clues to diet. Every tooth examined from 12-million-year period, for instance, showed very little surface scratching and thus indicated that the individuals had lived almost solely on fruit. Every tooth of the later Homo erectus showed deep, coarse scratches; this indicated that the species ate meat, nuts, and roots as well as fruit. (See *The New York Times*, May 15, 1979.)

It would appear, then, that man's ancestors did not become omnivorous until relatively recently on the evolutionary scale. The older pre-hominids such as Australopithecus seem to have been strict herbivores, probably leading forest existences much like today's chimpanzees. The emergence of the omnivorous Homo erectus would have signaled the beginning of man's existence as a hunter/gatherer on the open plains.

Reverse Evolution

In certain cases, it is possible to recreate extinct animals through careful breeding of present-day species. In the future, it may even be possible to recreate long-extinct specimens, such as woolly mammoths or dinosaurs, by using genetic material contained in fossils.

Two species that have been successfully recreated are the tarpan and the aurochs. The first is a type of wild horse which was the ancestor of many modern breeds but which died out sometime in the 19th century. The aurochs was a prototypical form of cattle that died out in Europe during the 1600s.

The tarpan was a small horse, about the size of a large pony, mouse gray in color. Also called the forest horse, it ranged over much of the wooded area of Europe until recent times and is presumed to have been extant in small numbers in the Ukraine as late as the first half of the 19th century. It was a genuine wild species, on a par taxonomically with the zebra, although, unlike the zebra, it played a part in the derivation of domesticated breeds of horse. The tarpan had the bristly mane of all wild horse species (domestic horses have long flowing manes) and hooves much tougher than those of any modern horse. Zoologists in Europe reasoned that, since the tarpan had been one of the original wild species that had produced the domestic horse, some of its genes must still run in the bloodlines of various breeds of modern-day horses and ponies. As one of the zoologists explained: "We proceeded from the principle that no animal can be extinct whose heritable constitution still exists. This constitution may be crossed with other species of animals, it may have suffered changes through race formations, but if it still lives, with the aid of our present-day knowledge of heredity it can be brought back as a whole. Crossings can be bred out again, changes of race can be corrected by suitable selection."

A number of modern breeds of ponies and small horses are descendants, in part at least, of the tarpan—such types as the wild horses of Dartmoor, the Scandinavian and Iceland ponies, and the Koniks are examples—and they all have one or more physical traits of the original forest horse. Unfortunately, none of these types have retained the bristly mane which is a crucial point of identification of the true wild horse. Breeders consequently were forced to resort to another species of wild horse, the Przewalski Mongolian wild horse, or steppe horse, for the required breeding stock.

Przewalski stallions were bred to Iceland ponies and Konik mares, and the descendants of that cross were inbred among themselves to bring out the tarpan characteristics. In only the second generation, a foal appeared that had the uniform gray coat of the tarpan. Crossings and recrossings among this foal and others were selected to breed out the unwanted traits of the modern breeds and the Przewalski species and emphasize those of the tarpan. Interestingly, even though the breeding program did not emphasize the development of a hard hoof, such a hoof occurred spontaneously after several generations of breeding. Today several herds of the recreated horse live in zoos and animal sanctuaries in America and Europe; they are, as far as can be determined from pictures, skeletons, and zoological analyses, identical to the extinct tarpan.

The aurochs (plural: aurochsen) was a species of cattle that roamed the forests of Europe in earlier times. With the gradual clearing of the forests, the aurochs began to vanish, and the species died out completely in 1627, when the last specimen perished in Poland. They were large, fierce animals, with forward-pointing horns, weighing up to a ton each (and thus fully comparable in weight to the other original cattle species, the European bison). The aurochs played a part in the development of modern domesticated cattle, and its genes were assumed to live on in various cattle breeds. Breeders traveled throughout Europe to select breeding stock from the primitive types of domestic cattle that seemed to show one or more characteristics of the aurochs. Medieval descriptions and drawings, skeletons in zoos and zoological collections, even cave drawings, enabled them to construct an accurate picture of exactly what the aurochs had looked like. A long breeding program was undertaken during which undesirable traits were bred out and desirable ones were emphasized until a new race of aurochs, which bred true to type, was created. Not only did these animals show all the physical characteristics of the original species, they demonstrated temperamental ones as well, being fierce, bad-tempered, and dangerous.

An interesting taxonomic question is whether these new breeds should be considered genuine representatives of the species. Though they are probably indistinguishable from the originals, zoologists are divided on the point. Extinct animals can only be recreated in this way if they form part of the heritage of modern domestic breeds. Unfortunately, most extinct animals have no living domestic descendants, and there is now no possibility of resurrecting them.

For further information, see. P. Street, *Vanishing Animals*, (Dutton, 1961.)

More spectacular recreations are expected to take place in the future when geneticists succeed in extracting viable genetic material from fossil or frozen remains. The most likely extinct beast to be recreated by such methods would be the woolly mammoth. Other candidates would be the moa, a large bird now known only in fossil form, and various types of dinosaurs.

Woolly mammoth specimens have been discovered frozen in Siberian permafrost. Soviet scientists at the Soviet Academy of Sciences in Moscow and at the Institute of Cytology in Leningrad are attempting to find a living mammoth cell that has not been irreparably damaged by the original freezing process. (See *The New York Times*, March 4, 1980.) So far, they have found intact proteins, such as albumin and collagen, in the tissues of the preserved mammoths, but all genetic material such as DNA had been damaged by leaching of phosphorus. If an intact cell were found, it would be grown in a culture medium—itself a difficult task. Genetic material from one of these cells would be inserted in a fertilized elephant egg and implanted into a female elephant. This elephant foster-mother would then give birth to an actual woolly mammoth.

It might eventually become possible to create DNA from fossilized, rather than frozen, remains. If so, then all extinct species, notably dinosaurs, might be recreated.

Strange Animals

Rogue Elephant

A rogue elephant is a vicious elephant, usually, but not always, a male, that separates from the herd and roams alone.

Although, under normal circumstances, the elephant is not dangerous to man—a peaceful elephant usually flees from the smell or sound of man—deviant behavior of elephants turned "rogue" is well documented. A British authority, A. A. Kinloch, wrote: "When in herds they are generally quite harmless, and a child might put a hundred to flight; but a solitary bull is often a savage and dangerous beast, attacking and killing everyone he can. Occasionally, one of these 'rogues' will haunt a certain road and completely stop the traffic as long as he remains. There was one . . . which was supposed to have killed many people, and even destroyed houses." Carl Akeley, the father of modern taxidermy, who believed the elephant the most dangerous of all animals, was seized and terribly mutilated by a bull elephant.

Generally, a rogue elephant catches its victim in his trunk and variously dismembers him, smashing the victim against the ground or against an upright object, or tossing him high in the air. Some, reportedly, take great pains to mutilate their enemies, returning again and again to the victim after death.

The Asiatic elephant, although less temperamental than the African elephant, more commonly turns rogue. It is estimated that in India rogue elephants account for the deaths of more than 50 persons a year. The aggressive behavior of rogues has often caused elephants to be branded as maneaters.

Elephants, however, are strict vegetarians. The misnomer probably arose from the habit of some enraged rogues to play with the limbs of dismembered victims and hold them in their mouths.

There is no proven correlation between solitude or isolation and a rogue elephant's aggressive behavior. It is possible that solitude make rogues uneasy and defensive. However, herds of elephants have also been known to raise havoc, ruin crops, and destroy structures.

It has also been suggested that rogues are old bulls, past their sexual prime, but not all rogues are necessarily bulls nor are they always old.

More likely is the possibility that some infirmity makes the animal bellicose and may also be the reason the animal separates from the herd in the first place. Male elephants fight among themselves, often causing extensive wounds which fester and cause great pain. In many instances, elephants shot and identified as rogues have had such wounds.

In the same vein, the desire for revenge may explain why some elephants turn rogue. According to one writer: "Many bulls go through life with heavy particles of lead imbedded in their skulls . . . one can wonder just how many majestic headaches an old bull will endure before taking a decided dislike to all mankind."

G. P. Sanderson reports a dramatic encounter with an Indian rogue, who took possession of a stretch of road near Mysore, chased many travelers, and savagely killed several natives. Slightly wounded in an unsuccessful manhunt, the rogue disappeared for five months and then reappeared not improved in temperament. Another bloody manhunt finally felled the animal, who stood proudly—head held high, eyes gleaming wickedly—ready to advance until the fatal blow. Then the cause of the animal's savageness was discovered. Two thirds of his tail had been severed in some previous fight or accident, and at the end of the remaining portion was a huge sore which must have caused the animal great pain.

For more information, see: R. Carrington, *Elephants* (Basic Books, 1959) and R. A. Caras, *Dangerous to Man* (Chilton, 1964).

Killer Whales

Killer whales are predator whales which attack small aquatic mammals and other whales, and are reputed to have attacked humans.

The killer whale *(Orcinus orca)* is a large swift creature with over 50 teeth, with males reaching 30 feet in length and females about half that size. It is the most powerful and fleetest member of the family *delphinidae* which also includes most dolphins. It has a striking black and white coloration and prominent dorsal fins, which in old bulls can be over six feet high. The species is distributed in every ocean throughout the world. It has no natural enemies.

Among the killer whale's recorded prey have been seals, sea-birds and walrus. Group hunting maneuvers are often used, depending on the type of prey being hunted. In an incident described in *Grzimek's Animal Encyclopedia*, (Van Norstrand, 1972) a group of 15 to 20 killer whales attacked some 100 dolphins off Baja California, in Mexico by swimming around them in narrowing circles. When the dolphins were tightly crowded, the killer whales rushed into the group one by one. While each whale devoured a few dolphins, the others kept circling.

On rare occasions, killer whales will attack whales belonging to one of the large whale species, usually baleen whales. From three to forty killers may attack at once, some striking at the animal's lower jaw, others biting the victim's pectoral fins. The killers usually feed on the softer body parts, such as the tongue, lips, and parts of the jaw, leaving the rest.

Killer whales communicate with one another by means of underwater acoustical signals. In addition, the bulls signal to the group by slapping the water with their flukes or pectoral fins, or even by leaping out of the water and landing against the surface, broadside, a maneuver known as "breaching." The splash can be heard for five miles.

In a widely reported 1905 incident, a photographer and two dogs on the Scott expedition to Antarctica were stranded on an ice floe surrounded by killer whales. The whales succeeded in breaking up the floe from beneath by butting it with their heads, but the prey made a safe escape.

According to two authorities on killer whales, D. R. Martinez and B. Klanghammer, the killer has been maligned through misleading and sensationalized stories. These scientists note that recent studies have shown that the killers generally do not feed on large prey.

Japanese catch records covering over 500 killer whales caught over a 10-year period show that about two-thirds of the stomach contents consisted of fish and cephalopods (squid and octopuses), with most of the remainder consisting of small dolphins. A Norwegian investigator with data on more than 1,400 killer whales came to the conclusion that killers do not attack large, healthy whales. Martinez and Klanghammer report an incident in which they were in a small boat surrounded by killer whales for several hours. The animals made no effort to capsize the boat, and seemed merely curious. After a while, one of the whales created a loud splash against the water, whereupon the entire group disappeared from view.

The first authenticated assault by a killer while against a human being occurred in California in 1972, when a surfboarder briefly came under attack. The circumstances indicate that the whale mistook the surfboarder—wearing a black wet suit and lying on a surfboard—for a sea lion, and withdrew as soon as it perceived its error.

For more information, see: R. A. Caras, *Dangerous to Man* (Chilton, 1964).

Albatross

The albatross is the largest living flying creature. Characterized by great flight capacity and endurance, it can stay away from land for months at a time.

The albatross belongs to the so-called tube-nosed swimmers, which also include petrels and shearwaters. For the most part, the bird lives in the Southern Hemisphere, although some species are indigenous to the North Pacific.

The wingspan of the albatross may reach twelve feet or more, and the bird may weigh more than twenty pounds. A life-span of 36 years has been recorded. The bird's diet consists chiefly of squid, fish, and crabs, which it snaps up from the surface of the water. The albatross seems to sweep down at all light-colored objects. This habit is probably responsible for the belief that an albatross will attack a drowning person. According to W. Jameson, author of *The Wandering Albatross,* (Morrow, 1959), the albatross, which has no fear of man, is not aggressive and can be approached and handled without danger.

The albatross has the rather unusual capacity of shooting out stomach oil to a distance of 10 feet with considerable accuracy. There is some debate on the extent to which this activity can be considered as a defense mechanism, or as a device for making the body lighter for flight. According to A. L. Thomson's *New Dictionary of Birds* (McGraw-Hill, 1964), "the shooting of the oil for defense may have evolved as an elaboration of the widespread habit among sea birds of vomiting the stomach contents to lighten the body" for easier escape.

The albatross spends time on land only for breeding. After going through a protracted and complicated courtship involving display, dancing and bill-rubbing, the female lays one large egg.

The long-distance flight ability of the albatross is legendary. In fact, a marked albatross has been recovered 6,000 miles from where it was originally tagged. In one case, described by Jameson, a bird shot off the coast of Chile was found to have a message around its neck, dated eleven days earlier, from a whaling ship sailing in New Zealand waters, some 3,000 miles away.

The albatross moves primarily by gliding. It does not normally beat its wings and, in calm air, when gliding is difficult, the albatross prefers to rest by sitting on the water.

From Samuel Coleridge's *Rime of the Ancient Mariner,* published in 1798, the belief arose that the killing of an albatross would bring bad luck. Prior to Coleridge's poem, sailors had no compunction about killing or capturing the albatross. The hanging of the dead albatross around the neck of the ancient mariner as penance gave rise to the expression "an albatross around one's neck." Other legends had been associated with the bird, such as the notion that tyrannical skippers would be reincarnated in the form of an albatross. Legend also told of a kinship between the birds and certain ships, and of the bird's ability to walk on water and move through the air "by magic."

The legend about walking on the water is undoubtedly explained by the fact that the albatross has very large feet, which it uses for takeoff and landing.

The legend of flying "by magic" might come from the bird's graceful method of gliding, for the albatross glides without effort. It sails in wide sweeps over the waves, with neck withdrawn, legs extended backwards, and webbed feet protruding slightly beyond the tip of the tail-feathers, moving only to act as a rudder. The long wings, their tips slightly bent, are also motionless. The bird's takeoff is similar to that of a seaplane. It stretches its neck out, spreads its wings, and paddles at full speed into the wind. As soon as it is airborne, it assumed its aerodynamic shape. The precise method by which it manages to stay airborne and regain altitude without moving its wings has often been the subject of speculation. Jameson believes that the albatross utilizes the difference in the wind speeds of the different layers of air. Thus, the energy accumulated during a dive is harnessed to bring the albatross back up to a higher altitude.

Galapagos Albatross. (UPI photo)

Tapeworm and Candiru

A tapeworm is a long, flat parasite that often lives in human intestines.

The candiru is a small catfish that lives as a parasite within other fish, and occasionally parasitizes humans and other large animals.

Tapeworms are the chief members of the class Cestoidea of the flatworm phylum. About 1,500 species of tapeworm have been identified, though only a limited number are known to infest man. The body of the adult worm is usually divided into segments or proglottids.

There are two stages in the life of a tapeworm—larval and adult—and each stage is spent in a different individual host. In fact, the larva and adult of any one tapeworm species usually parasitize two different species.

Larvae can parasitize a large variety of animals, infesting any of several organs in large numbers. In contrast, adults parasitize only vertebrates (fish, amphibians, reptiles, birds, or mammals); furthermore, they can survive only in the digestive tract, often of one species exclusively, and usually only one adult can survive in a single host.

Among the common forms of tapeworm that infest humans are the pork, beef, dog, and fish tapeworms. Infestation usually results from eating inadequately-cooked meat.

The larvae of the pork tapeworm usually inhabits pigs, but can sometimes live in man. The adult worm, found only in man, resembles a dirty, white piece of tape, up to 22 feet long. Each adult produces thousands of eggs, which are passed out in human feces and ingested by pigs when they eat food that has been in contact with such feces. When the eggs hatch, the larvae migrate to various tissues of the pig's body which may later be ingested by humans. In the rare cases of a human larval host, the larva can cause such serious problems as damage to the eyes or the nervous system; however, a person infested by the adult of the species suffers only minor ill effects.

The adult of the beef tapeworm also lives only in the human intestine, while the larva may live in cattle, zebus, buffalo, and other cud-chewing animals. Beef tapeworm is common wherever beef is eaten, although cold storage is fatal to the parasite.

Once inside a human host, the beef tapeworm attaches itself to the wall of the intestine by suckers on its head. Infected patients are sometimes subject to abdominal pains.

New proglottids are continually formed and the beef tapeworm can grow to 50 feet in a 20-year life-span. The worm is hermaphroditic, with each proglottid producing first sperm and then eggs. Since the long worm is folded back on itself, sperm from one proglottid fertilize the eggs from another.

A large piece of the worm will sometimes be spontaneously discharged. In addition, from two to 12 fertilized segments, or proglottids, will break off every day. They are not self-sufficient organisms and they die within a short time, releasing their eggs. The proglottids are capable of motion, and may pass out of the infested person into his clothing or bed linen.

The larvae of the dog tapeworm can live in various animals, including man. The adults, found only in dog intestines, are only three to six millimeters in length, but the larvae which may migrate to the brain, lungs, or limbs of the host can grow to the size of a grapefruit within five years. They can be removed by surgery. Victims may pick up the infestation from infected soil or from contact with infested dogs.

Fish tapeworms may remain in a human host for years without any symptoms. Anemia may then develop, though elimination of the worm leads to recovery.

Various effective drugs have been developed to expel tapeworms. Segments of worms or whitish eggs on the feces are signs of infestation.

The varieties of tapeworm whose adult can infest only humans are considered highly host-specific, that is, they have become adapted to life within one particular species only. These parasites have no mouth or digestive canal of their own. They absorb food, already largely digested by the host, through their surfaces. Their metabolism requires low concentrations of oxygen, as found in the digestive tract.

How then could parasite have lived before mankind evolved to its present form? In some cases, it is believed the parasite species must have evolved along with the host species.

In fact, it is sometimes possible to determine if two species of animals have a common ancestor by examining their parasites to see if they are closely related, indicating a common parasite ancestor. This was done in the case of the South American bird, the cariama, whose parasite was found to be related to that of the European bustard. Subsequent research confirmed the genetic relationship of the two birds.

For more information, see *Grimzek's Animal Life Encyclopedia* V. 1 and S.C. Kendeigh, *Animal Ecology* (Prentice-Hall, 1961).

The candiru *(Vandellia cirrhosa)* is a thin, translucent catfish without scales, from 1 inch to 2½ inches long, found in the upper Amazon River.

It lives in the gill chambers of larger catfishes, where it apparently feeds on the skin tissue and blood of the host. It is not known whether it can survive outside a host.

The fish has been known to enter the urethra, anus, or vagina of human and other animal bathers, where it can lodge by extending the spines on its gill covers. Inflammation, bleeding, and sometimes death can result, at least according to folklore among the peoples living along the Amazon.

The candiru is blind and is believed to depend on its sense of smell to guide it to a host. It can be caught by suspending a cattle lung in the water.

The candiru is the only vertebrate (animal with a backbone) known to be an endoparasite—a parasite that lives inside the body of its host.

For more information, see: Thomas C. Cheng, *The Biology of Animal Parasites* (Saunders, 1964).

Manatees, Dugongs and Mermaids

Manatees and dugongs are large aquatic mammals believed by some to have helped give rise to the legends of mermaids.

The manatee and dugong comprise the order Sirenia, or sea cows, along with Steller's sea cow, probably extinct since the 18th century, and several fossil forms. They are the only mammals, other than whales and dolphins, who are completely adapted to life in the water. Some experts surmise that they share a common ancestor with the elephant. Both manatees and dugongs are listed by the U.S. Fish and Wildlife Service as endangered species.

The manatee can be as long as 15 feet and weigh up to a ton. It has a stout, fish-shaped body with a flat, horizontal, rounded flipper at the end; no hind limbs, and two fore limbs in the shape of small flippers near the head. the latter is small and has a square, bristled snout. The upper lips are divided into halves, which can move independently and are used like forceps to hold food.

There are three species of manatee. One inhabits the Atlantic Coast of Florida, the Gulf Coast and the shores of the West Indies. Another lives in the Amazon and Orinoco river drainages, and the third plies the coasts and rivers of tropical West Africa. They are all active mostly at night. Although solitary most of the time, manatees sometimes congregate in large groups.

Because of their voracious appetites (they consume 60 to 100 pounds of vegetation a day), they have been used successfully to clear channels choked with weeds, and are often legally protected for that reason.

Dugongs are similar to manatees, but their tail flippers have two pointed branches, and both their snout and fore flippers are larger than those of manatees. They vary from seven to eleven feet in length. They shun fresh water, preferring shallow, tropical seacoasts. Their habitats range from East Africa to the Solomon Islands.

Dugongs are nocturnal, and they travel in pairs or in groups of as many as six. They often stack sea grass along the shore to eat at some later time. They have been variously described as sluggish and affectionate.

Steller's sea cows, which were first described by Europeans in 1741, were hunted to extinction by 1768. They lived along the shores of Bering and Copper islands in the Commander Islands group of the North Pacific. Individual sea cows were reported to measure up to 25 feet long.

The crew of a Russian whaler reported sighting six Steller's sea cows in the waters off Navarin, on the East Coast of Siberia in July 1962; however, the authenticity of the report has been disputed.

The manatee and the dugong are economically valuable. They are sought by many peoples for their hides, meat and bones, and are also a source of oil. Magic and folk medicine have special uses for certain parts of the dugong. In Madagascar, for example, fat from its head is believed to be a headache remedy, and its tallow is taken as a laxative.

It has long been a matter of speculation whether sea cows gave rise to the myths about mermaids and sirens. Some authors claimed that these animals nurse their young in a human-like posture, keeping their heads erect while holding their infants by a flipper.

We now know, however, that manatees nurse in a horizontal position, with their heads and those of the nursing infants underwater. The mother does not hold her offspring by her flippers. The dugong nursing position is thought to be similar.

There is no question, however, that after mermaid myths did arise, they affected the way mariners perceived sea cows. Columbus wrote, after apparently observing manatees on his first Caribbean voyage: "The three sirens lifted their bodies above the surface of the ocean, and although they were not as beautiful as the painters have made them, their round faces were distinctly human in form."

For additional information, see J. Knox Jones Jr. and R. Roy Johnson, "Sirena" in *Recent Mammals of the World* (Ronald, 1967), and Claude Levi-Strauss, *Tristes Tropiques*, (Adler, 1968).

Synchronous Fireflies

Synchronous fireflies are species of fireflies that form dense swarms in trees where the males flash on and off in unison. These species, which are found from India to the Philippines and New Guinea, have been studied by John and Elisabeth Buck (see "Synchronous Fireflies," *Scientific American,* May 1976).

According to the Bucks, the ability of "a group of organisms to repeat an action simultaneously and at regular intervals seems to be confined to man, to a few kinds of katydids and crickets that chirp in synchrony, and to certain fireflies of Asia and the Pacific." They state that in most cases where animals seem to be acting simultaneously, they are actually rapidly following a leader. For example, although fish in a school often appear to change direction simultaneously, according to the Bucks, this is simply an example of "rapid mass responses to the movements of a leader."

In order to prove that two organisms are acting synchronously, the possibility that one of the organisms is simply quickly following the lead of the other must be excluded. To do this, one must measure the time it takes an organism to start an action after it has been exposed to the stimulus which prompted the action and then compare this time with the time it takes other organisms to start the same action. If the latter time differences are smaller than the former time, the different organisms could not have had the time to follow each other's lead and, consequently, must be acting in an independent, yet snychronized rhythm. If this is the case, each organism must have its own resetable internal clock that enables it to keep a rhythm. When a group of organisms has synchronized their internal clocks, the members of the group are able to act synchronously.

The Bucks designed two experiments using a group of people sitting in a lecture hall to illustrate this phenomenon. In the first experiment, each person was asked to hold a coin. He was to wait until he heard someone else tap with a coin and then to tap with his own coin as quickly as possible. It was found that no one could tap his own coin in less than 150 milliseconds after the leader tapped his coin. In the second experiment, the people in the audience were again asked to close their eyes and hold the coin. This time, they were to start tapping the coin and attempt to get into a regular rhythm with each other. Once they had accomplished this, the experimenter measured the time interval between the earliest tap and latest tap each time the group tapped in unison. Generally, this interval was found to be less than 130 milliseconds. This proved that the members of the audience could not be listening for each other's taps, but were independently keeping a synchronous rhythm.

The Bucks discovered that synchronous fireflies take a minimum of 150 to 200 milliseconds to flash after they are exposed to a stimulus (such as a light). On the other hand, when all the fireflies flash in unison, the last flash occurs only 20 milliseconds after the earliest. This, the Bucks concluded, proved that the fireflies are truly synchronized and not just following each other's lead.

Fireflies of each particular species flash at characteristic intervals. If a firefly is isolated from the other fireflies of its species, it will continue to flash at the interval characteristic of its species.

Male fireflies flash to attract females. In a jungle with heavy foliage, a firefly's flash has less chance of being seen by a female; therefore, it is advantageous for a group of males to get together in one place and flash in unison. This possibly explains why synchronous flashing evolved, but the exact details of the process are not yet known.

Geckos

A Gecko is a small lizard belonging to the family *Gekkonidae,* characterized by the ability to run up walls and across smooth ceilings.

Geckos are typically small, ranging from 1⅕ to 6 inches in length. The family Gekkonidae contains 650 species, distributed around the world, mostly in warm climates. Geckos are harmless but noisy. Their name is said to be an imitation of their call, which ranges from a chirp to a bark. The most widespread North American species, the banded gecko *(Coleonyx variegatus),* is found from Panama to the Southwestern United States.

Many species are highly specialized for climbing on flat surfaces. They can run, in any direction, on vertical sheets of glass and creep over ceilings. A single toe can support the whole weight of the gecko.

The secret of the gecko's climbing ability is adhesion. The gecko's toes have special pads with a velvety appearance. The pads are covered with tiny, curved hairs called setae. The setae cause the adhesion but there is no generally accepted explanation of how they work.

Recent studies by Anthony P. Russell of the tokay (*Gekko* gecko) have demonstrated that this highly specialized species has numerous adaptations which serve to take full advantage of the setae and to protect them from severe damage (see *New Scientists,* September 25, 1975 and October 16, 1975). The bones, muscles and tendons of the lower limbs, and unusual blood sinuses in the toes, together with an unusual gait work both to make maximum use of setae and to give protection. The skeletal peculiarity of the gecko's foot gives the lizard an unusual way of moving—the whole body moves forward while the foot remains in place against the surface. The gecko's body pivots around the foot. When the gecko lifts the foot, he peels it off the surface, removing the tips of the toes first. When he puts the foot down, the backs of the toes touch down before the tips. This is possible because the toe bones are not cylindrical but strongly depressed in the middle enabling the foot to bend backwards. In another special adaptation, the gecko's toes are widely splayed out, more than 180 degrees. This enables the gecko to run head first in a variety of directions—down, up, or laterally.

The foot muscles which control the gecko's unusual foot movement are also specially adapted. Unlike most lizards or birds, the feet and forelimbs are heavily muscled. The foot muscles also cover the bones which control the peeling-back motion of the toes in a feather-shaped pattern. This feather-shaped arrangement makes it possible for more tendons to be attached to the plates holding the setae. Blood sinuses lie between the toe bones and the pads of setae. The toes put pressure on the sinuses when the gecko's feet touch the surface, and the sinuses, in turn, apply hydrostatic pressure on the setae.

In contrast to other lizards, which generally keep four or three feet in contact with the surface they are climbing, the gecko runs up a wall applying only two limbs at a time and only one limb part of the time. The whole cycle of the gecko's movement—all four feet placed down and removed—takes only one-sixth of a second.

The gecko's appetite is enormous. Its diet consists largely of insects, and inhabitants of tropical and sub-tropical cities often keep them as household "exterminators." Geckos are sold specifically for this purpose. In particular, their appetite for cockroaches is so ravenous that one or two geckos will keep a home free from the pests.

Hagfish

The hagfish (*Myxine glutinosa*) is a slimy, ugly eellike creature that literally ties itself in knots as it pursues its prey.

The hagfish preys on other fish by attaching its teeth to the victim's gills. The hagfish then slides its tail into a knot—this is possible because its cartilaginous backbone is highly flexible—and slides the knot forward along its body until it is pressing against the prey. Using the leverage of the knot, the predator gnaws its way through the skin of the host fish, burrowing deeper into its prey until it is completely inside the fish's body. The hagfish then consumes its victim from the inside, leaving only a hollow shell of skin and bone.

Fireflies

Fireflies are incredibly efficient producers of light. In an ordinary electric bulb, only 4 percent of the energy output is in the form of light; the rest, 96 percent, is heat. In the firefly, by comparison, over 90 percent of the energy is given off as light. The firefly's light is "cool," almost devoid of heat. The insects have been used in Brazil and China as a cheap and efficient light source: six large fireflies can provide enough light to read a book.

The firefly produces light through a a chemical process. In a special organ near the tail, light-sensitive chemicals and enzymes combine with oxygen from the air to produce the well-known glow. Special nerves control the flashing mechanism. Laboratory researchers have isolated the four active ingredients in firefly luminescence: luciferin (an inorganic substance known to emit light when oxidized, luciferase (a catalytic enzyme), magnesium ions, and adenosine triphosphate (a naturally-occuring compound that mediates muscle contraction. When these four substances are mixed in a test tube, light is produced. This method of lighting is too expensive to produce on a commercial scale, however.

Electric Fish

The most powerful electric fish is the South American electric eel, which can generate a discharge of 600 volts at 2 amperes. This is enough to kill prey such as fish and frogs and to stun larger predators. The eel's current is enough to light more than a dozen ordinary household light bulbs. The electrical shock, however, is not continually produced but is rather a single split-second burst of energy. It is produced from thousands of linked generator cells, called electroplaques, in the eel's tail. An adult eel possesses 700,000 of these cells, which together occupy 40 percent of its body.

In addition to its shock discharges, the eel produces weak intermittent pulses from other electrical organs. This electricity is used as a sort of underwater sonar, for it creates an electrical field around the fish, changes in which reveal the presence of obstacles or prey.

Other electric fish produce current by the same process as the electric eel. The African electric catfish is nearly as powerful as the eel, while other African fish produce only a few volts of current. Electric fish are not limited to fresh water; the electric torpedo fish of Atlantic and Mediterranean waters generates enough current to stun or kill smaller fish.

Female Ostriches

During the ostrich breeding season in East Africa, two to seven female ostriches lay their eggs in one communal nest, which may contain up to 40 eggs. One dominant female, or "major hen," then incubates the nest. But since the bird can only keep about 20 of the eggs warm, she pushes the other eggs out of the nest. She seems to be able to distinguish her own eggs from the others, for she seldom jettisons her own eggs. Brian C. R. Bertram of King's College in Cambridge, England reported this phenomenon in *Nature*, May 17, 1979. He theorized that the eggs which are pushed out of the nest serve to buffer the rest from predation.

Transvestite Flies

The breeding habits of the scorpionfly (*H. apicalis*) lend themselves to a strange impersonation in which certain males mimic females.

Breeding is *supposed* to take place in this manner: a "normal" male scorpionfly captures an insect and uses it to entice a female, who, if she is impressed with the prey, consents to intercourse and eats the prey during copulation.

The sex act occasionally goes awry when a "transvestite" male mimics a receptive female by fluttering his wings and moving his abdomen in a certain way. When the "normal" male offers the prey as an enticement to breeding, the transvestite snatches it and flies off with it.

These successful thefts provide the mimic with a large food supply and cut down the time spent hunting for prey by nearly 50 percent.

Animal Phenomena

Animal Senses

Animals possess senses more highly developed than man's, and some species even possess senses in addition to the normal five.

Every species of living thing adapts itself to its environment by developing one or more of the five senses that will optimize its ability to find food, avoid predators, communicate with other members of the species, and move about. On a scale of all animal species ranked by acuteness of senses, man would rank roughly in the middle. In the human species, the five senses—sight, hearing, touch, smell, taste—are well developed, though none highly so. This suits man's omnivorous, mobile, communicative, adaptable nature. Other animals are more "lopsided" in their sense profiles, often developing one or two of the senses to levels of tremendous acuteness and letting the others remain relatively unused.

Birds as a group have a very highly developed sense of sight. Some of the high-flying species, especially scavengers like the vulture and the carnivores like the eagle, have eyesight at least eight times as keen as a man's. A buzzard can pick out a beetle on the ground from hundreds of feet in the air. Owls possess eyesight especially adapted for nighttime hunting, with retinas packed with rod cells, the vision receptors that are sensitive to low light levels. Owls also have tremendously acute hearing, and are able to pick out and home in on the rustle of a mouse moving on the ground, a sound inaudible to the human ear. Other birds, such as the sparrow, have less acute hearing that is often skewed toward high-frequency sounds. The sparrow would perceive human conversation only as an ill-defined rumble of low-pitched sounds, and the bass notes on a piano would be completely inaudible.

Various sense adaptations are detectable in mamalian species. Hunting species usually emphasize either sight, hearing, or smell; herbivores use either smell or sight in food-gathering, and smell for detection of predators. Eyesight is often further refined in mammals, depending on the species' principal food sources. Hunters, which must be able to see prey by detecting small movements, have vision dependent on rod cells in the retina; rod cells are color blind but are very sensitive to movement, especially at low light levels. Animals which gather food, such as some monkeys, have an entirely different vision system. Their retinas are supplied mostly with cone cells, which are color-sensitive and able to discriminate among stationary objects; such vision enables the animal to locate fruit on trees, for instance, or nuts where they have fallen on the ground. Still other species have a so-called selective sense of vision; the animal's brain is programmed to recognize only those visual stimuli that are important to its survival. A frog, for example, "sees" only two classes of objects: prey (such as flies and other small insects) and large moving objects which might be predators.

Some hunting species, such as the entire dog family, have phenomenally developed senses of smell. Dogs have over 200 million olfactory cells, as compared to man's 5 million, and experiments have indicated that a dog is literally a million times better at detecting odors than a man. Most dogs have rather poor eyesight, however. Dogs' eyes lack the cone cells that are necessary for color vision, and a dog's visual world appears entirely in shades of gray—like the picture on a black-and-white television set. In addition, most canines are nearsighed, and so their world is blurry as well as colorless. Nor do dogs possess a discriminating sense of taste. They eat only flesh and bolt their food quickly, unlike other animals, such as herbivores, which need to taste their vegetable food in order to ensure that it is edible and not poisonous.

The sense of smell is also highly developed in certain insects, especially those for whom scent plays a part in the mating instinct. Butterflies can detect each other miles away during the breeding season, by smell alone. A female butterfly carries a minute quantity of perfume amounting to no more than 1/10,000 of a milligram. She releases tiny quantities of this scent on the air, and, even in this huge dilution, the male butterfly can detect her at distances of up to seven miles. Other insects use the sense of smell in food-finding.

Certain beetle larvae are sensitive to the smell of carbon dioxide. They feed on special vine roots, and these roots give off carbon dioxide. The larvae are sensitive to no other smells, but they can unerringly locate the vine that provides its food supply.

The sense of hearing is perhaps most spectacularly developed in the bat. Bats have only dim eyesight (though they are not blind), but their hearing has been elaborated into an intricate radar-simulating mechanism of phenomenal sensitivity. When flying in the dark, bats emit high-frequency squeaks; the return echoes enable the bats to maneuver without bumping into objects and even to home in on such fast-moving targets as flying insects. How bats manage such fine turning is still a mystery. All bats seem able to recognize their own echo signals, never confusing them with those of another bat even when flying in groups of thousands. Experiments have been conducted to try to "jam" the bats' radar signals. Loud signals, broadcast on the bats' wavelength and 2,000 times as loud as the bats' own squeaks, failed to confuse the bats, who still were able to recognize their own echoes.

Among the insects, bees can see ultraviolet light, which is invisible to humans. Because ultraviolet light is not stopped or absorbed by clouds, bees can "see" the sun even on overcast days. This ultraviolet sensitivity is a crucial part of the bees' navigation system, enabling the insects to locate flowers at great distances from the hive. Bees also seem to have literally a "sixth sense" entirely outside the 5 ordinary senses; this sense manifests itself as a sensitivity to the earth's magnetic field and is another aid to navigation. Certain other animals species, such as migratory birds, also seem to show signs of this magnetic sense. (See *Animal Navigation*)

Another literal sixth sense is found in rattlesnakes. In an experiment at the University of California, it was established that rattlesnakes could locate mice unerringly even with their eyes taped shut. This was not due to either acute smell or hearing. Rather, it was discovered that two small dimples on each side of the snake's head, between its eyes and nostrils, were heat-sensing organs. Heat-sensitive cells enabled the creatures to detect live prey by the heat they gave off. The snakes were even able to determine the prey's size and shape.

Animal Navigation

Many animal species orient themselves and navigate by means of senses unknown to humans. Various animals have been found to be sensitive to ultraviolet light, barometric pressure, sun and star locations, polarized light, magnetism, airborne odors, and infrasound.

Early studies of bird migration showed that far-ranging species such as the Canada goose and the Arctic tern had "star maps" imprinted in their brains by means of which they aligned themselves during nighttime migration flights. Birds can also detect changes in atmospheric pressure, can distinguish between airborne odors indigenous to different locales, and can detect atmospheric infrasounds undetectable by humans (such infrasound is ultra-low-frequency vibration produced by ocean waves, earthquakes, magnetic storms, and even by the aurora borealis).

Birds as well as insects are sensitive to ultraviolet light (light waves at the upper end of the frequency spectrum, which are invisible to man). Experiments with pigeons have demonstrated that the birds develop a conditioned response to various patterns projected by ultraviolet light, thus proving that they are sensitive to rays of these wavelengths. It is thought that birds use this mechanism to determine the sun's position on cloudy days. Certain insects possess this same ability; and they can detect colors and patterns in the natural world which are invisible to humans. Preliminary research has also found evidence that hummingbirds, toads, lizards, and newts may also be sensitive to ultraviolet light.

Honeybees use a somewhat more sophisticated system based on polarized light. Polarized light is caused by particles of moisture in the atmosphere; it manifests itself as two points of light whose waves vibrate in a particular way. Daytime sunlight is always polarized to some degree, with the direction and intensity of the polarization related to the sun's position. Bees rely on polarized light when the rays of the sun are hidden by clouds, trees, or other obstacles.

When bees discover a nearby source of nectar, they dance a simple, circular pattern (left). When the food supply is distant, the bees perform a more complicated "waggle" dance (right). (© 1979 by The New York Times Company. Reprinted by permission.)

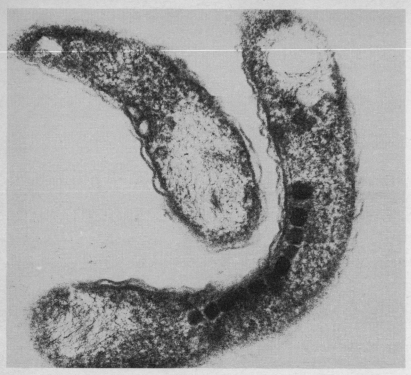

Electron micrograph of thin sectioned magnetic cell. (D.L. Balkwill, D. Maratea)

Researchers have discovered more than 2,000 dance patterns used by bees to give other members of the hive information about distant nectar sources. When a new source is discovered, a bee returning to the hive performs a sort of "waggle" dance that reveals the location of the food in relation to the sun's direction. (See *The New York Times,* November 13, 1979.) The bees always dance along a line that points to the polarized light source farthest from the hive. When two polarized light sources are the same distance from the hive, the dancing bees invariably refer to the polarized source on the right-hand side of the sun. Researchers conclude that the bees' brain and nervous system are programmed with a complex and consistent "wiring mechanism" that keeps them from making mistakes.

Other animals navigate by means of the earth's magnetic field. Evidence of this ability has been found in pigeons, robins, bees, and bacteria. Such "magetotactic" animals actually have particles of magnetite embedded in their brains or elsewhere in their bodies. Magnetite is a naturally occurring magnetic compound made of iron and oxygen (Fe_3O_4). It is also known as lodestone and was used in making early compasses.

Magnetotactic animals make magnetite from iron compounds which they ingest with their food. The actual mechanism for this process has not yet been determined. It is theorized that in the act of cell division, magnetic cells pass on half of the magnetite chain to each daughter cell, thus maintaining the magnetic orientation.

Magnetism-sensitive bacteria have been found in such diverse locations as the Baltic Sea, San Francisco Bay, and swamps in New Zealand and Australia. These bacteria always swim toward the magnetic pole, that is, they swim north in the Northern hemisphere and in the opposite direction in the Southern hemisphere. Researchers theorize that the bacteria use this magnetic orientation to locate the vertical direction. (See *Science News,* April 28, 1979.) In the Northern hemisphere, for instance, north is always down, i.e., the vertical component of the earth's magnetic field is stronger than the

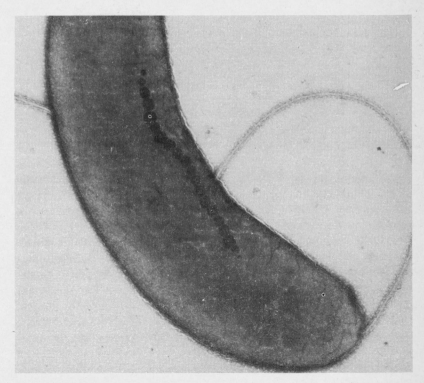

Magnetic bacterium found in a freshwater pond. (R. Blakemore, N. Blakemore)

horizontal component. Thus the bacteria, in swimming north, are also swimming downward toward the sediment or ooze where they prefer to live.

Magnetotactic spirillum bacteria each contain a chain of cubic crystals, usually 22 of them, which contain the magnetite. The size of the magnetite particles is crucial to the proper working of the organism's magnetic sense. If the crystals are too small, heat energy reorients the molecules and blots out their magnetic properties. If the crystals are too large, they point in several magnetic directions, thus canceling the usefulness of the property. Richard Frankel of the Massachusetts Institute of Technology characterized the bacterial magnetite particles as being the ideal size for their purpose: "The bacteria have solved an interesting problem in physics by producing particles of magnetite just the right size for a compass." (*Science News,* April 28, 1979.)

Industrial scientists are exploring the possibility of using bacteria to produce microscopic magnets. Such magnets would be useful in electronic miniaturization and also in drug technology, where they might be used to guide drugs through the bloodstream.

Ape Intelligence

Since 1966, when a chimpanzee named Washoe first began to learn American Sign Language, or AMESLAN, a scientific controversy has raged on the subject of whether apes actually exhibit signs of human intelligence. The debate originally centered around the ability of chimps and gorillas to communicate intelligently but has recently widened to include the question of ape self-awareness.

Washoe, taught by Beatrice and R. Allen Gardner, behavioral psychologists at the University of Nevada at Reno, was the first ape to exhibit language ability. Since 1966, other apes have also been schooled in language. Among the most well known are Nim, a chimp taught by Herbert Terrace of Columbia University and the subject of *Nim* (Knopf, 1979); Lucy, another chimp, trained by Roger Fouts at the National Institute of Primate Studies; Sarah, under the direction of David Premack of the University of Pennsylvania; Lana, who learned the symbolic language "Yerkish" at the Yerkes Regional Primate Center in Atlanta, taught by Duane Rumbaugh; and Koko, a gorilla who learned sign language from Francine Patterson, a psychologist at the Gorilla Foundation in Stanford, California.

Each of these apes has developed significantly large vocabularies, recognizing nouns, like "fruit," "candy," and "banana," and verbs, such as "give," "hug," and "take." At times, these apes combine these words in remarkably appropriate descriptive definitions. Lucy, for instance, did not know the word for citrus fruit and called them instead "smell fruit." Lana, who likewise did not know the correct word for orange, referred to one as "apple which is orange." Watermelons were called "candy drink" or "drink fruit", and cucumbers were known as "banana which is green." Washoe knew the words for "water" and "bird;" the first time she saw a swan, she called it a "water bird."

Apes using sign language have what is known as cross-modal ability. That is, they understand two different languages (spoken words and sign language) and can make correspondences between the two. When the trainer speaks the word for spoon, the ape then makes the sign-language for spoon. In work at the National Institute of Primate Studies, a group of AMESLAN-familiar chimps have actually used the sign language to communicate with each other.

In addition to recognizing the meanings of certain words, apes also seem able to string such words together in meaningful sentences. Sarah, for instance, learned to "write" using cut-out plastic symbols that represented certain words. In order to get an apple from her trainer, she had to write "give Sarah apple", by arranging the plastic symbols for "give," "Sarah," and "apple" in the right order. She also understood the meaning of "if" and "then," which are more complex syntactically than simple nouns and verbs. When given the choice between an apple and a banana, Sarah learned to understand that only if she chose the apple would she also receive a piece of chocolate. She was able to read two symbol-sentences and choose the right one in order to get the desired reward of the chocolate.

Gorillas have traditionally been considered less intelligent than chimpanzees, but Koko, a female gorilla at the Gorilla Foundation in Stanford, California, apparently learned sign language faster than Washoe, the chimp. She and other gorillas also scored higher than chimps on set learning tests, a sensitive method of testing ape intelligence. Koko has exhibited the same creative way of combining known words to describe an object for which she does not know the name.

Critics of ape research assert that supposed ape "intelligence" and language ability is due solely to drill, imitation, or mere conditioned response. From this viewpoint, apes have exhibited no more ability than could be taught to a dog or even a pigeon. Critics maintain that a patient instructor, using simplified step-by-step methods, could teach any other animal to duplicate the apes' supposed feats. Herbert Terrace of Columbia University, an ape researcher and the teacher of Nim, came to the conclusion that Nim's achievements were overrated and were attributable to pure drill.

Terrace maintains that though apes can acquire large vocabularies (because they have an excellent memory capacity), they are not actually able to string words together in truly meaningful, independently created sentences. This syntactic ability is considered a distinction of the human race alone. In reviewing videotapes of Nim's behavior Terrace concluded that almost all of Nim's "conversation" was actually just a response to his teachers' sign language. (See *The New York Times,* October 21, 1979.) Many of Nim's responses merely repeated in whole or in part what his teacher had just said. Nim rarely initiated conversation, and he apparently did not grasp the fact that conversation was a two-way street, for he interrupted constantly in a haphazard manner. Instead of learning to construct longer and longer sentences that might prove his language ability, after a certain point Nim simply added words in long nonsense run-on sentences; such as "Give orange me give eat orange me eat orange give me eat orange give me you."

Duane Rumbaugh of Georgia State University, Lana's trainer, also supports the case that ape ability has been overrated. In *The New York Times,* October 21, 1979, he stated: "Lana showed some sensitivity to the rules of grammar, but we have no evidence that she productively comprehended syntax and the meaning of words. Her performance was inconsistent. We couldn't call it a reliable behavior."

Terrace believes that ape trainers may misinterpret ape "language" in their eagerness to believe that apes are truly displaying human-type intelligence. Referring to Washoe's reference to a swan as a "water bird," Terrace notes that this construction did not necessarily prove that the chimp was creating a new term to describe an animal she had never seen before. She may have merely been saying that she saw "water" and "a bird." He believes that other instances of supposedly creative ape intelligence may be the result of misinterpretation on the part of trainers. "The trouble is," he says, "that the meaning is in the eye of the beholder. Without a well-analyzed film record and a complete listing of all the animal's utterances, any claim of an ape's using language is questionable."

Koko's trainer, Francine Patterson, has postulated that such questionable results as Nim exhibited are due to the fact that the training period was too short and too many persons were involved, leading to confusion and lack of progress on the ape's part. Patterson believes that an ape needs the reassurance and guidance of one particular trainer and a long training period, perferably more than five years. Koko exhibited unstructured behavior during the first years of her training, but she now has a good grasp of advanced language concepts such as puns and rhyme.

Besides language ability, researchers have discovered evidence that apes also possess self-awareness, i.e., the ability to recognize themselves in a mirror. This has long been considered an exclusive characteristic of the human race.

Experiments have shown that chimps and gorillas learn to identify themselves in a mirror in much the same way that a human infant does. A baby does not recognize its reflection until it is about two years old; before that time, it typically responds to the mirror image as if it were another baby. After that age, babies show signs of self-awareness. In a similar manner, chimpanzees learn to recongize their images in a mirror. At first, they make various social gestures before the mirror, as if the image were another ape. After several days, however, the ape learns to use the mirror to examine itself; it grooms parts of the body it has not been able to see before, examines the inside of its mouth, etc. This proves that the chimp realizes that it is looking at its own reflection.

Dr. Gordon Gallup, professor of psychology at the State University of New York in Albany, reported experiments in which chimps were anesthetized and one eyebrow painted over, with a bright red, odorless, nonirritating dye. When the chimps awoke, they examined themselves in the mirror, touched the reds spots and smelled their fingers. This is very similar to the reaction that would be expected from a human being, according to Dr. Gallop, "if, upon awakening one morning, he saw himself in a mirror with red spots on his face." Chimps who have not been trained to use a mirror do not make this response. They do not realize they are seeing themselves in the mirror and do not touch or smell the red spots on their foreheads. Obviously, the response to the mirror has to be learned.

Primates other than man and the apes seem unable to ever learn the mirror response. While they may learn to take advantage of the mirror's reflective properties in various simple ways, they do not graduate to an awareness of self. Painted with the same red dye as chimpanzees, rhesus monkeys or macaques make no response when they view themselves in the mirror. Self-awareness does not seem to be learned, no matter how many months or years the monkey is exposed to the mirror.

The neurological basis for self-awareness has so far not been discovered, although it is obviously connected to the level of brain development achieved by the particular species. Self-awareness may appear in a species when the brain's cortex achieves a specific number of complex interconnected neurons.

Koko, 4½-year-old female gorilla, and Francine Patterson, her teacher and companion. (UPI photo.)

Or it may develop more gradually as a matter of degree, in which various species, depending on their evolutionary development, have greater or lesser degrees of self-awareness.

It is suspected that other highly-developed species besides apes may also be self-aware. Whales, porpoises, and perhaps elephants, which all have relatively large brains, would be the obvious candidates. Testing would be difficult, but Dr. Gallup has outlined one possible test. A porpoise could be shown an underwater television image of itself, and some object could be introduced behind it. If the porpoise turned to look at this object, this would be presumed proof that the animal also realized that it was looking at its own image.

Gallup has postulated that man's awareness of death may be shared by apes. An ape, especially after seeing the death of a companion, may receive an idea of its own end.

The question of ape self-awareness is treated in detail in *The Ape's Reflexion*, Adrian J. Desmond (Dial, 1979).

Spider Courtship

During or after the act of mating, the male spider is often devoured by the female. Male spiders have evolved a number of interesting ways to avoid this fate.

Slow motion pictures of spider courtships have been made by Michael H. Robinson and Barbara Robinson, two researchers at the Tropical Research Institute of the Smithsonian Institute in Panama. Their nine years of research indicate that most spider courtships fall into three specific categories. (See *The New York Times*, June 12, 1979, p. C-1.)

The first category, designated Group C behavior, is the safest for the male. It has been observed in eight spider genera including 27 species. During courtship, the male does not advance onto the female's web at all. The safety of the procedure lies in the male's insistence that mating take place away from the female's own domain. The male spins a "mating thread" from his perch on a branch to the outer ring of the female's web. By rubbing the thread with his legs, he transmits courtship vibrations to the female in her web. His repertory of signals includes drumming motions and elaborate high-amplitide twanging vibrations. Wooed by this courtship ritual, the female leaves her web and advances along the mating thread. If she is sufficiently placid, mating takes place at the male's end of the thread. If the female appears aggressive or threatening, however, the male cuts the thread before the female reaches him, thus saving himself.

Group B behavior entails more risk for the male. It has been observed experimentally in 11 species. The male enters the female's web, proceeding cautiously while transmitting his mating vibrations along the rays of the web. He eats a hole in the center of the web and spins his mating thread across it. He then indulges in a variety of leg-rubbing, pounding, and jerking maneuvers to lure the receptive female onto the thread. If the female makes threatening gestures, the male simply jumps off the mating thread.

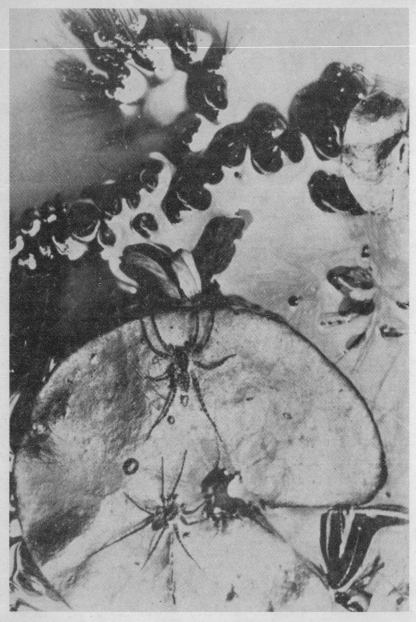

Male spider making courtship gestures to the female. (New York Public Library Picture Collection)

Group A courtships are dangerous and often deadly for the male. They have been observed in four genera including 12 species and are believed to be the most primitive form of spider mating on an evolutionary scale. In these species, the male is very small and the female relatively gigantic. The male takes no precautionary measures except occasionally to eat portions of the female's web in order to limit the female's mobility. His mating vibrations are not always enough to pacify an aggressive or hungry female, and he is often devoured before, during, or after mating. In some species, the male is so small compared to the female that he may survive simply because he is not worth eating.

A few rare species use an entirely different courtship ritual: the male spins a web of silk around the female, tying her down so that she will not be able to move during the actual mating. This maneuver may have developed very early in the history of spiders and later led to the use of the mating thread. The male first walks around the female, rubbing her legs with his; this presumably prepares the female for mating. Then the male crawls back and forth across her body, wrapping her in layers of silk.

It is not known why female spiders have a tendency to eat the male after courtship. This behavior is also observed in other insect species such as the praying mantis. The most logical explanation, though unproven, is that the female simply regards the male as she would regard any other insect, that is, as a prospective meal.

STRANGE NATURAL PROCESSES

Olfaction

Olfaction, or the process of smelling, is the principal means by which animals receive chemical clues about their environment. It has long been known that many species communicate by means of scent, and evidence is mounting that there may also be chemical communication between humans. Such communication may be entirely subliminal, and the participants may be unaware that it is taking place.

Olfaction between animals is common. In black tail deer, alarm or fright causes an odorous substance to be released from a gland on the outside of the hind leg. This chemical, sniffed on the air by other deer, prepares them for possible flight, causing them to lift their heads repeatedly in the alert posture. Chemical signals play an even more common role in reproductive behavior. In many species of insects, for instance, an odorous compound emitted by a single female can attract males over great distances.

In monkeys such as the marmoset and the tamarin, olfaction plays a prominent role in both social and sexual organization. With secretions from glands on their chests and genital region, dominant members of a tribe signal their status by marking their territory. It appears even that dominant females of these monkey species may be able through some undiscovered chemical means to suppress the fertility of females lower on the social totem pole.

Though "subdominant" females mate normally with males, they do not become pregnant. Only the dominant females achieve normal pregnancy.

The possibility that chemical communication might take place between humans has traditionally been ignored by science. The possibility was not taken seriously until 1968, when the Monell Chemical Senses Center was established in Philadelphia; this was the first institution devoted to basic research on the two chemical senses, taste and smell. The human sense of smell has often been dismissed as a merely vestigial organ. It is true that the olfactory sense is processed in an evolutionarily primitive part of the brain—this may account for the intensity of olfactory memories—but it is not true that the sense of smell is rudimentary or undeveloped. The human nose, though of course not as sensitive as that of a dog, is nevertheless far more sensitive than any analytical laboratory instrument and is capable of detecting faint odors and discriminating between closely-allied scents.

Evidence for human chemical communication is mounting. Researchers at Oxford University in England and at the Brain Behavior Research Institute at Sonoma Hospital in Eldridge, California have shown that there is an olfactory link between mothers and babies. Six-day-old infants can discriminate between their mothers and other women by scent alone. A six-week-old baby, while asleep, will move its head and make sucking motions toward a piece of cloth moistened with its mother's milk but will not respond to a similar cloth moistened with another woman's milk or with cow's milk.

Certain reproductive processes also seem to be affected by chemical communication between individuals. One of the most interesting manifestations is the fact that women living in close proximity to each other, such as roommates in college dormitories, often seem to develop synchronized menstrual cycles. Since it has been shown that neither diet nor environmental factors account for this fact, presumably some sort of chemical signal is passed between the women. A study by Michael Russell at San Francisco State University proposed a possible mechanism for this communication. Russell extracted liquid substances from the perspiration of one woman and then applied these substances to 16 female volunteers. Three times a week for four months he applied a smear of the liquid, masked with alcohol, to the upper lips of the volunteers. After four months, the cycles of the 16 women had noticeably synchronized. At the beginning of the experiment, their cycles had started an average of 9.3 days apart. After the experiment, the time difference had narrowed to 3.4 days.

Although the specific substance responsible for chemical synchrony was not isolated, other experiments indicate that it may be closely related to

109

a protein hormone known as LRH (luteinizing hormone-releasing hormone). LRH acts via the pituitary gland to trigger ovulation in women. Close relatives of LRH have been developed that have the opposite effect, inhibiting ovulation. Such "LRH analogs" are highly effective birth control devices. In a study at the University Hospital in Uppsala, Sweden (reported in *Lancet*, August 4, 1979), applications of LRH analog by nasal spray stopped ovulation in all the women who participated in the study.

There is also evidence for links between olfaction and emotion. A study at the Hatfield Polytechnic in Hertfordshire, England showed that "male" and "female" olfactory chemicals could affect human feelings and judgment. (See *Science News*, April 28, 1979.) Student volunteers wore paper surgical masks before voting for candidates for the student body secretary. Unknown to them, the masks had been impregnated with tiny amounts of liquid derived from male or female perspiration. The scent was entirely undetectable to the volunteers. The results were interesting. The male students seemed unaffected by either the "male" or the "female" scent. But the female students showed sharp differences: volunteers inhaling the female chemicals tended to vote for student-government candidates with quiet, retiring personalities, while those wearing the male masks tended to vote for candidates exhibiting aggressive, outgoing personalities. As this process was completely subliminal, it implies that human beings may be prone to many more chemical olfactory stimuli than is now realized.

Immunities

Immunity is the ability to withstand the effects of a poison or other biological agent, such as an antibody. There are many natural varieties of immunity, two of the most complex of which are fetal immunity and progressive immunity.

An unborn fetus is immune to the attack of its mother's antibody system. The fetus is technically a foreign object within the mother's system and would normally be quickly attacked by the mother's immunity system. A complicated hormonal sequence prevents this from happening; failure of any one of the steps in the process may be the cause of certain forms of infertility or miscarriage. Researchers at the Weizmann Institute of Science in Rehovot, Israel describe what is basically a two-phase system to protect the infant embryo. (See *Science News,* February 17, 1979.) A special uterine layer, the decidua, contains factors that inhibit maternal antibody production. These antibody-suppressors have not yet been identified but appear to be especially important during the first stages of pregnancy. During later stages of pregnancy, a placental hormone, progesterone, prevents the build-up of white blood cells which usually attack and destroy foreign tissue.

Progressive immunity is an entirely different phenomenon whereby various animal or insect species gradually acquire immunity to specific poisons. It occurs most often in insect pests, which build up resistance to chemical pesticides such as DDT. It has also been noted in certain rodents, especially the house rat (*Rattus rattus*) and the even more common Norway rat (*Rattus norvegicus*), which have developed immunity to several rodenticides.

Progressive immunity has been known since 1911 but has only become important in the years since about 1950, when pesticides began to be used in large quantities. According to the United Nations Food and Agricultural Organization, 364 insect species have developed immunities to pesticides being used against them. (In 1965, there were only 182 resistant strains, and in 1968 there were 228.) This includes both crop-destroying and disease-carrying insects. Many mosquito species have become immune to DDT, dieldrin, organophosphate, and carbamate, all of which were previously-effective pesticides; as a consequence, some tropical countries are showing 30 to 40 times increase in the number of cases of malaria.

In certain cases, double-, triple-, and quadruple-resistant insect strains have developed, indicating that the pest is immune to several varieties of pesticide at once. Such problems aggravate control of the pests. In addition to mosquitoes, the most successful insects at developing progressive immunities are houseflies, black flies, and fleas.

Progressive immunity is developed as a result of natural selection among individuals possessing genes that confer immunity. The actual mechanism of immunity usually depends either on enzymes that detoxify the poison or properties that slow down penetration of the pesticides. Besides these biochemical and enzymatic adaptions, a few insects have also developed special behavioral adaptations. One variety of common housefly for instance, has "learned" not to alight on surfaces which have been sprayed with a particular insecticide. A major factor in the development of progressive immunity is the speed with which most insects (or rodents such as rats) reproduce. The reproductive cycle of the housefly lasts two weeks. Many generations are born in a year, and significant new genetic adaptations may appear in a matter of only a few years.

Progressive immunities could theoretically occur in longer-lived species, even in man, but such immunities would take dozens of generations, and hundreds of years, to manifest themselves.

Hormonal control methods have been tried as substitutes for chemical pesticides in certain instances, but according to the 1979 annual report of the U N Environmental Program such methods are not a foolproof answer. Already some insect species have become immune to the hormone controls. Two examples are beetles, which have acquired resistance to growth inhibitors, and houseflies, which are developing immunity to the supposedly fatal bacteria *Bacillus thuringiensis*.

Further details on progressive immunity may be found in *The New York Times*, June 5, 1979, p. C-1.

Obesity

Obesity, or fatness, is usually thought of as being caused by simple overeating, but new scientific evidence links this condition with several intriguing and little-known bodily mechanisms.

All food consumed by the body is either excreted as waste, burned as fuel to maintain the body temperature, or deposited as fat in body tissues. Persons who consume more than they need to keep themselves warm will gain weight in direct proportion to the amount of excess food they consume, according to most theories of obesity. Most obesity treatment consists of either overcoming the emotional problems that allegedly lead to overeating in the first place or controlling the brain's appetite control mechanisms through the use of drugs.

Recent research indicates, however, that obesity may not be as simple as all that. Two developments in particular support this conclusion. One is the discovery that bodily chemicals play a role in triggering the urge to eat. The other is a reevaluation of the role of "brown fat," brown fat cells that may dramatically affect the individual's potential to gain weight.

David L. Margules of Temple University propounded the theory that beta-endorphin, a naturally-produced peptide that has effects similar to those of opium, may be responsible for inducing a wide range of changes in the body. In particular, beta-endorphin may be particularly involved in preparing the body for starvation conditions and, in animals, preparing for hibernation. Release of the peptide into the bloodstream would create a "pre-famine" hunger that would lead to immediate heavy overeating. It would also initiate an integrated series of adaptive reactions in the body that would result in more efficient storage of excess calories in fat cells. The body would thus be prepared to face a period of either starvation or hibernation. Among the known actions of beta-endorphin which could lead to this hunger response are a lowering of the respiration rate and the body temperature, slowing of the heart beat, conservation of water, and increased extraction of nutrients in the kidneys by the concentration of urine.

Such a "starvation" or "hibernation" response is of no practical value to modern man, who is not usually faced with either situation. However, if the beta-endorphin system malfunctioned, it might lead to urgent overeating even when starvation was not threatened. Margules's experiments with hamsters (reported in *Science News,* November 24, 1979) indicates that beta-endorphin is indeed involved in hibernation. If an antagonist to beta-endorphin is injected into a hibernating hamster, the animal wakes up quickly, experiencing shivering and an increased heart and respiration rate. It is hypothesized that in human beings the body's natural system of checks and balances usually keeps levels of beta-endorphin at safe levels. Overeating would be triggered only in those individuals who suffered a natural imbalance in bodily hormones.

Obesity has also been linked to the presence or absense in the body of brown fat cells, which are present in small but varying quantities in all people. Dr. Michael Stock of Queen Elizabeth College in London, England, formulated a theory that brown cells may function as miniature heat engines that burn off excess calories. Individuals with particularly active brown cells would be protected against obesity, because the cells would burn excess calories before they would be deposited as ordinary fat. Whenever the individual overate, the brown cells would simply "run hotter," converting the excess food into heat energy. People with inactive brown cells would lack this valuable mechanism and would be particularly prone to put on weight if they overate.

Experiments with rats seem to bear out this theory of obesity. Dr. Stock's tests with "brown cell" rats showed that such animals could eat 80 percent more than a group of ordinary rats while only putting on 27 percent more weight. The other 53 percent of excess food energy seemed to disappear without a trace. The only explanation was that it had been metabolized in the body and given off as heat. Brown fat cells are the presumed source of this metabolization.

Researchers theorize that brown cells evolved originally not as a means to combat overeating but as an auxiliary heat source to augment body heat in times of extreme cold. Experiments with rats raised in cold environments showed that brown fat cells might account for as much as three-quarters of the animals' entire heat production. In a temperate environment, the brown cells would not be needed for heat production but could be used instead to burn off excess caloric intake. Genetically obese rats either have fewer brown fat cells than normal rats or they lack the bodily chemicals known as nucleotides that control the operation of the brown fat cells.

It is not known whether this research on rats is directly applicable to humans. Stock himself has stated that there is no other evidence that brown fat is actually active in adulthood, although it has long been known to be active in children. Dr. Philip James of the University of Cambridge in England found in experiments with obese woman that there was indirect evidence that overweight women were burning off far fewer calories as heat than were lean women. (See *The New York Times,* March 18, 1980.) The discovery of a mechanism to control and regulate brown fat cells would provide a relatively easy and foolproof method of weight-control.

Regeneration

Regeneration is the process by which an animal grows back a lost limb or organ. It is common in lower animals such as starfish and lizards, but it appears that it can be artificially stimulated in species as complex as man.

Starfish are the champion regenerators of the animal world. If one of its five points or legs is cut off, a starfish will grow another one in its place. Not only that, but the severed limb will actually regrow four additional legs to create a whole new five-limbed individual. Some species of lizards and salamanders have the ability to regrow a severed tail but do not have the spectacular adaptability of the starfish.

In mammals, the process of regeneration is limited. Traditionally, it applies only to three main organs: liver, skin, and bones. Broken bones will knit; skin will mend; and as much as two-thirds of the liver will grow back from a remaining third. It also appears that the spleen is also capable of at least partial regeneration. The spleen is a poorly understood organ that seems to play some role in combating infections, especially in children. Doctors have long observed that children whose spleens were removed seemed somehow to retain the disease-immunity that the spleen conferred. Howard Pearson of the Yale University School of Medicine discovered that bits of spleen tissue remaining in the body grow into tiny mini-organs that function in exactly the same manner as an intact spleen. As a result of this discovery, surgeons performing spleen removals are careful to leave a portion of the organ in the body to provide the elements of regenerating tissue.

Traditional medicine has long considered the regeneration of limbs an impossibility, but it appears that there are notable exceptions to this rule. The most prominent is the ability of young children to regrow severed fingertips. There are three requirements for this to occur: the child must be under 12 years of age; the cut must be above the first crease of the first joint of the finger; and the wound must not be operated on or surgically affected in any way, for this will destroy its ability to grow back. If the wound is simply bandaged and left alone, the finger starts to regenerate within three weeks, and is wholly restored in 11 or 12 weeks.

Electrical therapy holds out the possibility of regenerating entire limbs. Robert Becker, a researcher at the Upstate Medical Center in Syracuse, New York, discovered that when a salamander regenerates a limb, an actual electrical potential is generated in the limb. It appears that the electrical current causes the cells of the stump to become undifferentiated, much like the cells of a primitive embyro; from these undifferentiated cells grow bone, muscle, and nerve tissue. Becker conducted experiments which consisted of applying electric current to animals which normally do not regenerate themselves. Under the stimulus of the current, the forelegs of amputated rats began to grow back. Such growth was not complete, but it indicated that the power of regeneration was not completely absent in mammals.

Electrical currents applied to human bone fractures which have refused to heal have in some cases stimulated the bones to grow together again. It is presumed that all animals have an innate ability to regenerate lost parts, though this ability may not be easily stimulated. Nevertheless, Becker feels that within one or two decades medical science will have discovered the means to regenerate all of the organs of the body, including the heart and even portions of the brain.

Strange Plants

Bristlecone Pine

A bristlecone pine (*Pinus aristata*) designated WPN-114 had, according to the *Guinness Book of World Records* (Bantam, 1979), the longest life span ever recorded for a tree. The tree grew 10,750 feet above sea level on the northeast face of Wheeler Peak (13,083 feet in elevation) in eastern California. It was found, after studies in 1963 and 1964, that the tree was approximately 4,900 years old. The tree was then cut down with a chain saw.

Currently, the oldest known living tree is another bristlecone pine, named Methuselah, which grows at an elevation of 10,000 feet on the California side of the White Mountains. Its confirmed age is 4,600 years. According to a March 1974 report, this pine has produced forty-eight seedlings.

Dendrochronologists—specialists who study the sequence and difference between rings of growth in trees and aged wood in order to date past events, intervals of time, and changes in the environment—estimate the potential life span of an average bristlecone pine to be almost 5,500 years and that of a "big tree" at 6,000 years. By crossdating living and dead bristlecone pine trunks, ring count dating can extend as far back as 6,200 B.C.

Up to twenty years ago, the mammoth giant sequoias were thought to be the oldest living trees. Then, after some twenty years of research led by Dr. A.E. Douglas at the University of Arizona, including microscopic study of growth rings, it was found that the bristlecone pines may be the oldest

116

living things on earth. In 1958, seventeen bristlecone pines, all growing in close proximity in the White Mountains, had been dated at 4,000 years old or more. Nine of the trees were found in an area that has been named Methuselah Walk. (See Edmund Schulman, "Bristlecone Pine, Oldest Known Living Thing," *The National Geographic Magazine*, March 1958).

The trees, now no more than dwarfed living ruins, show their age. Their trunks, which are little more than eroded stumps, are ten to thirty feet high. However, each tree has a life line, only a few inches wide, of bark-covered growing tissue which leads from the partly bare roots to a thin crown of branches. Each tree is capable of producing cones occasionally.

Planta del Mudo

Planta del mudo strikes people dumb.

In his book, *The Strangest Things in the World* (Public Affairs Press, 1968), Thomas R. Henry describes a plant being cultivated in the botanical garden of the University of Caracas that may be a blessing to henpecked husbands and harrassed mothers because it can render a person speechless. He states that the plant looks like sugarcane and cites "reliable reports" that a person who chews the plant's stem will be stricken dumb for forty-eight hours.

The plant in question may be one of thirty species of Dieffenbachia of the Arum family (Araceae) found in the tropical regions of the Americas. Several species are grown in gardens in the southern part of the United States and are also commonly used as house plants. The *Dieffenbachia sequin* (the dumbcane proper) and the *Dieffenbachia picta* are the most frequently cultivated species.

Dieffenbachia, a perennial herb, has a green stem which grows three to six feet tall. The leaves are large and oblong and often have decorative markings.

All species of the Dieffenbachia are poisonous. Eating the stem will cause a severe burning sensation in the mouth and throat; the mouth and tongue may swell, possibly causing death by choking. Nausea, vomiting, and diarrhea may also occur.

The causes behind the symptoms are complex. The mechanical effect of the plant's many sharp, little crystals of calcium oxalate, called raphides, partially cause the burning sensation. This effect is intensified by certain chemicals present in the plant. J. W. Hardin and J. M. Arena, in *Human Poisoning from Natural and Cultivated Plants*, say that the chemical effect is more important than the raphides in producing the burning sensation, but they are not certain which chemicals are involved. The causes of the nausea, vomiting, and diarrhea are also unknown.

Dieffenbachia does not directly strike a person dumb. It is the resultant pain and swelling of the tongue which interferes with the ability of some victims to speak. Thus, the impression that one can produce muteness in a person for a predictable period of time without other effects by administering Dieffenbachia, or an extract of it, is false. In the West Indies, forced chewing of *Dieffenbachia sequin* (or sequina) stems was used to torture slaves.

Some other members of the Arum family are also poisonous, such as the roots of the jack-in-the-pulpit, as well as the stems and leaves of the philodendron if eaten in large amounts.

Many poisonous species of the Arum family are rich sources of starch and are specially treated in many areas of the world to make them nonpoisonous food sources. The best known is the taro of Southeast Asia and the Pacific. North America's jack-in-the-pulpit and Great Britain's cuckoopoint— the source of Portland arrowroot—are some examples.

For more information, see J. Hardin and J. M. Arena, *Human Poisoning From Natural and Cultivated Plants*, 2nd ed. (Duke, 1974); J. M. Kingsbury, *Deadly Harvest* (Holt, Rinehart, and Winston, 1965).

The Kapok

The kapok (*Ceiba pentandra*) or silkworm tree has an unusually-shaped trunk that gives it something of the appearance of a square tree.

The kapok, a member of the family Bombacaceae, is native to Central America. The mature kapok is large, up to 150 to 100 feet in height and forty feet in circumference. The trunk has buttresses and it is these that give the tree a squarish look. The buttresses start twelve to fifteen feet up the trunk and can extend out more than fifteen feet from the base of the tree. They function differently from buttresses in architecture, which use compressive force to hold up a building. The kapok buttresses use tensile force not unlike the cables that support suspension bridges. The buttresses of the kapok tree are of a uniform thickness, six to 12 inches all along their length.

Buttresses are common among trees that grow in tropical rain forests.

Such trees generally have shallow roots with little or no taproot. Research has been done on several species to determine whether trees that normally have buttresses developed them in response to strain. The studies showed this not to be the case, however, because buttresses develop in trees sheltered from the wind and in trees too young to have heavy crowns. Nevertheless, trees develop buttresses in such a way as to resist the strongest pulls on the tree—a tree that leans has its largest buttresses on the side opposite to which it leans.

It is generally believed that buttressed trees evolved from trees with strong taproots as an adaptation to life in the rain forest. A taproot, the deep central root found in most trees, serves two functions: to provide support and to insure a water supply by reaching to a soil level deep enough to be permanently damp.

In the often swamp-like environment of a rain-forest, the water-supply function of the taproot is no longer essential, and its supporting function is taken over by buttresses. Since the roots are no longer needed to support the tree, they no longer need to be massive. This is an advantage, because the shorter the roots the greater surface area in proportion to their volume. Consequently, the roots, for their size, are more efficient in absorbing water and nutrients.

For more information, see E. A. Menninger, *Fantastic Trees*, Viking, 1967.

Heat-Producing Plants

Some plants generate heat. The champion heat-producer is probably the skunk cabbage of eastern North America.

Instead of waiting for spring, the skunk cabbage creates its own balmy environment. It begins to grow in late winter, often before the snow has melted. The spadix, or flower cluster, draws on the plant's stored energy to create heat, which is generated by a rapid rate of respiration within the flower cluster. The spadix is surrounded by an insulating sheath which keeps out cold air. The spadix itself is maintained at 72 degrees, which may be up to 50 or 60 degrees warmer than the surrounding air. The heat thus generated is strong enough to melt snow.

Other plants of the same family, the Araceae, also possess heat-generating properties, although not in such great measure as the skunk cabbage.

PREHISTORY

The 800-Day Year

During the Precambrian period, 1.5 billion years ago, the earth may have spun twice as fast as it does today. A day then might have lasted only nine hours, and a year would have consisted of 800 or 900 days.

Paleontologists have long suspected that day length was probably shorter during earlier epochs than it is today, but they did not know how much shorter. (The length of the year is presumed to have remained substantially the same throughout earth's history. The planet has slowed only minimally in its orbital path due to slight effects of sun's gravity.)

Recently, scientists have begun using special high-magnification techniques to examine fossils of bacteria and algae from the Precambrian period. These fossils are arranged in strata called stromatolites, and researchers can identify daily growth layers. Stromatolite analyses of the Biwabik formation in Minnesota and the Bulawayan formation in Zimbabwe Rhodesia have led B. G. Hunt, a weather scientist of the Australian Numerical Meteorology Research Center in Melbourne, to conclude that the earth's day length at that time may have been as low as nine hours. (See *The New York Times*, October 9, 1979.)

This would help explain a mystery that has puzzled science since fossils were first discovered: why did one-celled organisms that appeared on the earth more than three billion years ago not begin to evolve into higher forms of life until 600 million years ago? At the 600-million-year stage, a sudden explosion of diversification and development took place, leading to the appearance of many forms of higher organisms.

The phenomenon of short day length goes a long way toward explaining this problem. During a period of nine-hour or ten-hour days, earth's environment would have been relatively hostile to life. A computer simulation of atmospheric conditions of a fast-spinning earth found that only a relatively small band around the equator would have supported life. Surface winds would have been weaker than they are now, resulting in low precipitation and meager river flow. Reduced wind stress on the ocean surface would have inhibited the upwelling of nutrient-rich waters from the ocean depths. The shallower sections of the ocean, where primitive one-celled organisms developed, would have been unable to support large populations of life forms.

The gradual slowing of the earth's spin is due primarily to lunar tidal drag. The moon's gravity exerts a pull on the water of the earth, causing the oceans to "bulge," thus slowing the earth's rotations. During the Precambrian period, the moon was probably closer to the earth than it is today, which would have increased the atmospheric stress on the earth and further inhibited the development of complex life.

By the end of the Precambrian era 600 million years ago, the earth's day length had increased to an estimated twenty hours. The slowing of the planet's spin has been estimated at approximately 2.5 thousandths of a second per century during recent times, but it may have been more accelerated during the Precambrian era due to the moon's proximity and the greater lunar tidal drag that resulted.

With the longer day lengths came stronger surface weather systems. Heat flowed into the midlatitudes. The force of ocean currents increased. These changes would have radically improved the environment for the evolution of many-celled organisms.

As the number of life forms increased, the amount of ozone in the atmosphere would also have increased. Ozone, a biologically-derived gas composed of three oxygen molecules, comprises a layer of the earth's upper atmosphere that absorbs deadly wavelengths of ultraviolet radiation. Only after sufficient ozone had accumulated as a protective mantle around the earth could life emerge from the seas and begin to inhabit dry land.

For more information, see *The New York Times*, October 9, 1979, p. C-1.

The Extinction of the Dinosaurs

The entire dinosaur population of the earth, from giant Tyrannosaurus to little Archaeopteryx, died out suddenly 63 million years ago. The causes of *any* extinction are poorly understood; an extinction of this magnitude—by far the greatest the earth has ever experienced—represents a first-class scientific mystery.

The earth 63 million years ago, during the late Cretaceous period, was warm and balmy. Broad-leaved vegetation grew north of the Arctic Circle. Mountains were being pushed up by the action of the earth's crust (see *Continental Drift*, p. 143), and such modern ecological features as forests, deserts, and grassy plains were all common. The shallow land along the seacoasts was somewhat more extensive than it is today, and great expanses of swamps and everglade-like marshes ringed the continents. Recognizable reptiles such as crocodiles, lizards, and turtles were present in abundance, but the mammals were poorly represented, the most advanced form of the class at that time being a small tree-climbing shrew-like creature.

The dominance of the dinosaurs was complete. They had evolved over millions of years into a huge array of species that filled almost every ecological niche on the planet. There were both herbivores and carnivores, land-dwellers, swamp-dwellers, and sea-dwellers, giant forms and relatively dwarf forms. The 50-ton Brontosaurus and the recently unearthed "Supersaurus" were the largest. The 8-ton, 20-foot-plus Tyrannosaurus was the biggest meat-eater. Such forms as the "sea-monster" Pleisosaurs inhabited the shallow seas that bordered the continents. Pterosaurs were genuine flying dinosaurs, as well equipped aeronautically as modern birds (their flight pattern was a combination of flapping and gliding), and their breathing systems were also as efficient as those of present-day birds. Archaeopteryx, the smallest dinosaur (crow-sized) had developed feathers. And several land-dwelling species living in the snow-covered regions of what is now Antarctica even had furry coats and manes.

The popular view of dinosaurs as slow, hulking, dim-witted creatures is only partially true. It fits Brontosaurus well enough, for instance, or Triceratops, which was 25 feet long, weighed 1¾ tons and had a brain the size of a walnut. But other species did not fit this primitive mold. The big bird-like Pterosaurs had developed relatively large brains and were certainly no stupider than present-day reptiles. And at least one species was perhaps even more intelligent: Saurornithoides (whose name means "bird-like reptile", as it somewhat resembled a large featherless ostrich), had a large brain, wide-set eyes that gave it stereoscopic vision, and very flexible hands with opposable thumbs that made it capable of rather delicate manual manipulation. Adrian J. Desmond, in *The Hot-Blooded Dinosaurs* (Futura, 1977) has stated that Saurornithoides was separated from other dinosaur species "by a gulf comparable to that dividing men from cows." Such a creature, had it survived, might have evolved into quite advanced forms of life.

Since the first discovery of dinosaur remains in the 18th century, it has usually been assumed that dinosaurs, like modern reptiles, were cold-blooded. Robert T. Bakker of Yale University, in "The Superiority of the Dinosaurs," (*Discovery*, vol. 3, 1968), summarized this traditional view: "Generally, paleontologists have assumed that in the everyday details of life, dinosaurs were merely overgrown alligators or lizards. Crocodilians and lizards spend much of their time in inactivity, sunning themselves on a convenient rock or log, and, compared to modern mammals, most modern reptiles are slow and sluggish. Hence the usual reconstruction of a dinosaur such as Brontosaurus as a mountain of scaly flesh which moved around only slowly and infrequently."

There is, however, no overwhelming evidence to prove that all dinosaurs were cold-blooded. Modern researchers have come to the conclusion that some of them were probably warm-blooded. This conclusion derives from the fact that many dinosaurs were seemingly too active to have been cold-blooded. Cold-blooded creatures spend most of their time inactive. A lizard, for instance, spends 90 percent of its life motionless, only occasionally making a quick lunge at an insect or a fast run to a hiding place. After such exertion, the creature has to "recharge" by lying in the sun. If it moves out of the sun, it becomes sluggish and slow.

It has been theorized that the body temperatures needed to keep some of the larger dinosaurs on the move, or even upright, could not have been provided solely by the sun. The big Tyrannosaurus, for instance, would have found it difficult merely to stand on its feet, much less to pursue and overpower its prey. Its skeletal configuration indicates, furthermore, that it was built principally for walking upright, not for flopping on the ground in the sun.

Hence, the argument that many dinosaur species had warm blood and were much more advanced than formerly believed. Warm-blooded creatures are the only ones capable of rapid, sustained, strenuous activity. In the case of the more active land-dwelling dinosaurs, and especially the flying dinosaurs, it is difficult to see how they could have survived at all had they been cold-blooded. The principal objection to the warm-blooded thesis is that a constant body temperature required relatively large quantities of food for its maintenance. A warm-blooded animal burns 80 to 90 percent of its food merely to maintain its body temperature; the rest fuels the muscles that keep the animal active. It has been estimated that a man-sized lizard if it were warm-blooded would consume 40 times as much food as a cold-blooded one. The amounts of food needed to maintain an even body temperature in such a large species as Tyrannosaurus would have been astronomical.

The end of the dinosaur era was remarkable both for its suddenness and its violence. How long the great extinction took is open to question, but even a few million years would have been an astonishingly quick process by evolutionary standards, a mere eyeblink compared to the eons in which the dinosaurs had already existed. And there is evidence that the extinction may have occurred much more rapidly than this, perhaps in only several hundred thousand years. The dinosaurs were not the only species decimated in the catastrophe. No large families of living things, animals or plants, were spared. Nearly half the species of flowering plants disappeared from the earth, as well as numerous marine organisms from one-celled animals right up through various forms of squids, turtles, lizards, and other aquatic reptiles. In addition, many of the small land-dwelling mammals, both egg-laying and pouched types, were extinguished. The only forms of evolved life that remained were fishes and invertebrates, small mammals, primitive birds, and some reptiles. The largest remaining land creature was the crocodile.

The causes of this massive catastrophe are endlessly debated by scientists, zoologists and botanists. Only twice before in the earth's history has anything remotely comparable occurred. 500 million years ago, when life was still primitive and land creatures had not yet evolved, two-thirds of the various types of marine shell creatures were destroyed. Again, 230 million years ago, half of all the species known from the fossil record disappeared forever. (It was after this cataclysm that the 160-million-year reign of the dinosaurs began.)

Many theories have been propounded to explain the great extinction of the dinosaurs. All, even the most suggestive of them, are open to question. Perhaps the actual event involved several explanations simultaneously.

The most common theory in the public mind, though an erroneous one, is that dinosaurs were snuffed out by an ice age. However, ice ages did not occur until much later than the Cretaceous period, and even if they had, the whole earth would not have been affected. At least some of the many dinosaur species would presumably have survived in the still-tropical bands near the equator. And some of the furred and feathered dinosaurs should have been able to survive the cold even at great distances from the tropics.

Serious scientific theories of the dinosaurs' demise include:

Competition from mammals. This theory holds that mammals competed with dinosaurs for ecological space and eventually defeated them. But this is unlikely, and the truth seems actually to have been the reverse. Mammals had been dominated by the dinosaurs for 135 million years, and the largest mammals during the Cretaceous period were not even as large as the smallest dinosaurs. The mammals did not really begin to emerge from obscurity until after the dinosaurs died out.

Overspecialization. The fact that dinosaurs had been on the earth so long led to the idea that they "over-evolved" and died out from sheer awkwardness. But many dinosaurs were highly adaptable and not at all overspecialized. And this theory still does not explain the suddenness of the extinction.

Egg-stealing mammals. Mammals undoubtedly ate dinosaur eggs, but it is also surely true that various species of dinosaurs preyed on each other's eggs as well. Even with this predation, the dinosaurs had survived well enough for millions of years, so it is difficult to see why they should suddenly have died out at one point in the Cretaceous period. Many animals today eat crocodile eggs, but the crocodiles still survive.

Poisonous plants. When flowering plants first appeared 130 million years ago, some of them developed potent alkaloids in their sap. It is thought that dinosaurs, having poorly-developed taste buds, may not have been able to detect the alkaloids and have been poisoned by them. However, such plants had been around for more than 50 million years when the dinosaurs died out, and the dinosaurs had been thriving on them up to that time.

Epidemic. It has been suggested that an unknown disease or diseases killed the dinosaurs. But would each and every species have been destroyed, along with many species of mammals, plankton, and other sea life, as well as plants?

Geomagnetic reversal. The earth's magnetic poles have been reversed many times during the planet's history. Theoretically, such a reversal could have adversely affected the dinosaurs. This may be partially true, but the magnetic poles had been switched many times during the Cretaceous period as well as the previous Jurassic and Triassic periods without causing massive extinctions.

A change in the oxygen concentration of the air. It has been argued that flowering plants increased the amount of oxygen in the atmosphere, a change with which dinosaurs were unable to cope. This is doubtful, as it does not explain the suddenness of the extinction, nor does it account for the fact that many species of flowering plants died out along with the dinosaurs.

Collision with a meteorite. A large enough collision might have resulted in several simultaneous reactions, including a reversal in the earth's magnetic poles, changes in the sea level along with disastrous tidal waves, and perhaps climatic changes as well. Such a concatenation of events might have spelled the end of many species, but it is hard to see that it would have doomed them all.

The rise of the earth's mountain ranges. This is known geologically as the laramide revolution which resulted in changes in the earth's environment and climate. Such a change did indeed occur, but it seems more likely that it had a beneficial, rather than a harmful, effect on the dinosaurs. By creating new ecosystems, the laramide revolution stimulated the development of new dinosaur species (as well as new species of plants).

These theories have been propounded in various sources, including: Norman D. Newell, "Crises in the history of life," *Scientific American*, February, 1963; Dale Russell, "The disappearance of the dinosaurs," *Canadian Geographical Journal*, vol. 83, 1971; "Supernovae and the extinction of the dinosaurs," *Nature*, vol. 229, 1971; and *The Mysterious World,* Francis Hitching (Holt, Rinehart and Winston, 1978).

Perhaps the most widely accepted theory, though far from being universally subscribed to by all scientists, is the supernova theory. A supernova is a colossal stellar explosion in which a star (larger than the sun) nearing the end of its life cycle collapses inward upon itself and then explodes in a huge ball of nuclear matter. This supernova emits various atomic elements and huge quantities of radiation. Such explosions have been observed at least eight times during recorded history, though none has occurred near enough to our planet to have had significant effects. Statistically, however, it is probable that the earth has experienced at least one supernova within a distance of 100 light years about once every 50 million years. A cosmic explosion at this distance would result in disruptions to the earth's upper atmosphere, a tremendous cosmic ray shower, and an eventual prolonged drop in the earth's surface temperature.

Such a sequence of catastrophic events might well have been sufficient to wipe out all large animals, i.e., dinosaurs, on the face of the earth, as well as many of the smaller mammals that could not either hide from the radiation, or tolerate the temperature changes. Many of the larger plant species would also have died out, as well as many marine animals which could not adjust to the resulting cooler water temperatures. Adrian Desmond in the above-mentioned *The Hot-Blooded Dinosaurs* refers to the supernova theory as follows: "The geologists' lingering aversion to cataclysms notwithstanding, it is becoming difficult to disagree with the idea that the dinosaurs departed with the most spectacular bang since Creation."

The Dinosaurs' Living Relatives

Dinosaurs have been dead for millions of years, but their relatives live on in an unexpected form—birds.

Two scientists, Robert T. Bakker of Harvard University and Peter Galton of the University of Bridgeport, cite numerous similarities between the fossil remains of birds and those of certain types of dinosaurs. Archaeopteryx, a small feathered dinosaur, is often considered the first true bird. And Saurornithoides, a larger dinosaur, had many features in common with our present-day ostrich. Strip an ostrich of its feathers, give it a scaly skin and a long tail, and it becomes almost a dead ringer for Saurornithoides.

Berezovka Mammoth

In 1900, a deep-frozen carcass of a woolly mammoth was discovered in the permafrost of the Siberian Arctic, near the banks of the Berezovka River in the USSR. Since then, many more of the preserved beasts have been found. The manner of their death and preservation is a continuing puzzle to archeologists.

Mammoths roamed the Siberian steppes up to perhaps 8000 B.C., along with sabre-toothed cats, steppe bison, slothes, tapirs, wolves, and armadilloes. The mammoths were slightly smaller than today's elephants. They stood up to 10 feet high and had a pair of broad curving tusks. Their coarse outer hair was up to 18 inches in length and covered a reddish-yellow under-fleece. Tough skin over a 4-inch layer of fat protected them from the cold.

The animals were highly prized by prehistoric man and they figured in many primitive cave paintings. Their meat was eaten or used to bait traps; skin and bones went into the making of tepee-like shelters; horns were used as utensils.

The unearthed carcasses of these mammoths have been in varying states of preservation—some extraordinarily lifelike, others little more than fossilized bones. Many of the skeletons have not been entire, indicating that the carcasses had been disturbed and ruptured while in the ground. Occasionally, great quantities of bones have been found together, as though many individuals died together in one spot. The best-preserved single specimen was that of a 90-kilogram baby found near the Kolyma River by Siberian gold prospectors in 1977. After 40,000 years, it was still in a remarkable state of

The preserved corpse of a baby wooly mammoth, unearthed from the permafrost of the Magadan territory. (TASS from SOVFOTO)

preservation. For instance, it still possessed two appendages or "fingers" on the end of its trunk—the first time this feature had been observed outside of cave-paintings of the period. The baby mammoth was exhibited in the USSR and was nicknamed Dima.

Several unusual things were noted about the preserved mammoths. Some of the beasts were preserved in upright, standing positions, not recumbent or prone. This suggested a sudden death. At least one specimen was found with undigested food in its stomach and buttercups on its tongue. Most were found, not in ice but in the frozen muck known as permafrost. Some were so well-preserved that pieces of their flesh were allegedly fed to sledge dogs.

The orthodox explanation for the mammoth's demise is that they died accidentally through falling into ravines, being trapped in bogs, landslides or mudflows, or by drowning in rivers. They then froze solidly and were preserved in the premanently frozen tundra until today.

However, this explanation leaves many questions unanswered. How, for instance, could the beasts have been frozen in standing positions? Indeed, how did they freeze at all if the temperature was warm enough for buttercups? But the biggest question—the one that creates the real mystery—relates to the actual state of the carcasses' flesh. How could a mammoth have been deep-frozen so quickly that the meat remained well-preserved 40,000 years later? Why hadn't the flesh rotted and the contents of the stomach putrefied?

If a mammoth had fallen into a crevasse in the permafrost, it would have frozen very slowly. The temperature of the permafrost is only a little below freezing. An animal as large and as well-insulated with fat and hair as the mammoth would have taken literally months to freeze solidly. Most of the carcass would have putrefied long before it froze. And even the flesh near the skin, which would have frozen first, would have been dehydrated by the slow freezing process. The actual cells were not dehydrated, however, indicating that they had been frozen quickly, like a side of beef in a modern freezing plant.

To satisfactorily freeze even a side of beef requires temperatures many degrees below freezing—usually minus 40 degrees for 30 minutes. It has been estimated that to deep-freeze a whole mammoth, insulated by thick hair, would have required temperatures of minus 150 degrees—readings which have never been recorded within living history on earth.

It appears then that something extraordinary must have happened to freeze the mammoths. One minute they were grazing on grasses and buttercups, the next they were subjected to temperatures so extreme that they were frozen where they stood. No known variation of climate can explain this.

Much as orthodox science dislikes the idea of 'catastrophism,' it appears that some catastrophic atmospheric cataclysm must have occurred.

The dominant theory suggests an earthquake and volcanic eruption more violent than any recorded throughout history. Such an eruption may have been triggered by massive slippages in the earth's crust or even a sudden change in the earth's axis. Climatic disruptions on a scale never witnessed since would have occurred. Volcanic dust and gas would have been hurled into the upper atmosphere, blotting out the sun. Violent snowstorms, winds, and tidal waves would have raged. If volcanic gases were hurled high enough into the upper atmosphere, they would have been chilled to extreme low temperatures. Funneling back to earth in violent gusts, they would have caused abrupt drops in temperature of up to 200 degrees.

Such cold would have killed all animals instantly, freezing the lungs in a few seconds and literally turning the blood to ice. In only a few hours, an entire adult mammoth would have become a solid block of ice.

Most of the frozen carcasses would of course thaw and rot when temperatures finally moderated again. A few would not—they would fall into holes or be buried by winds, entombed in the permafrost—and these would be the specimens that have been unearthed in modern times.

The question of the demise of the mammoths is considered in: N. D. Newell, "Crises in the history of life," *Scientific American*, February 1963; and W. R. Farrand, "Frozen mammoths and modern geology," *Science*, 1961, 133:729.

Ice Ages

Current theories of glaciation hold that ice ages occurred as a result of changes in the earth's orbital pattern. As these orbital changes follow a predictable cycle and are still occuring today, the earth is likely to enter a new ice age at some time in the future.

According to this theory of glaciation, the key factors in the onset of an ice age are changes in the earth's orbital path and the tilt of its axis. Such changes affect the amount of solar radiation reaching northern latitudes; when the amount of yearly sunlight is insufficient to melt the winter snows, an ice age begins.

This theory was first proposed in the 1920s by the Serbian geophysicist Milutin Milankovitch, based upon earlier work by the French mathematician

Joseph Alphonse Adhemer and the Scotsman James Croll. Milankovitch found four cycles relating to the earth's orbit: (1) a 23,000-year cycle in which the orbital ellipse changes so that the earth's closest approach to the sun varies (today the earth and sun are closest in January; in 10,000 years they will be closest in July); (2) a 41,000-year cycle in which the earth tilts on its axis, so that seasonal differences are either intensified or diminished (when they are diminished, summers are not warm enough to melt polar ice); (3) a cycle of 93,000 years in the eccentricity of the earth's orbital path around the sun, in which the orbit changes from elliptical to more nearly circular; and (4) a similar orbital cycle occurring every 413,000 years.

Studies of sedimentary core samples from the earth have provided evidence of climatic changes matching each of these cycles. The 413,000-year cycle was not scientifically corroborated until 1979, when Madeleine Briskin and James Harrell of the University of Cincinnati discovered evidence of three complete cycles over the past 2 million years.

Because these cycles do not have the same periodicity, one cycle may be at its peak while another may be at its low point. In such cases, the tendency would be for the two cycles to cancel each other out. In cases where one or more cycles reached peaks simultaneously, the resulting climate changes would be expected to be correspondingly drastic.

Although the Milankovitch mechanisms probably provide the driving force for ice-age glaciation, other factors may also play a part; ice ages vary, and the extent of glaciation is never the same from one ice age to another. Current research indicates that conditions in the Antarctic may have a subtle but important effect on worldwide glaciation. It is known that the Antarctic Ocean cools appreciably before the onset of an ice age. During the last ice age (which began approximately 95,000 years ago), the Antarctic cooled about 3,000 years before ice sheets in the northern hemisphere began to grow.

Climate specialists at the Australian National University in Canberra have proposed that slippage of the Antarctic ice may cause this cooling of the Antarctic Ocean. (See The New York Times, March 9, 1980.) Large slippages are believed to have occurred regularly throughout history, most notably 95,000 years ago, when world sea levels apparently suddenly rose about 60 feet, and 120,000 years ago when sea levels rose more than 26 feet. Slippage of large portions of the East or West Antarctic ice sheets into the sea is the only hypothesis that can satisfactorily explain these sudden and catastrophic sea level surges. (If all of the East Antarctic ice were to slip into the ocean today—admittedly an unlikely occurrence—world sea levels would rise 200 feet.)

After slipping into the sea, such ice sheets would tend to become thinner but wider, covering large areas of the ocean and causing the ocean itself to freeze. The brilliant white surface of this gigantic ice-field would reflect enough sunlight back into space to cool the earth's climate appreciably. Glaciation of the northern hemisphere, starting near the North Pole, would then begin.

The severity of any particular ice age probably depended in large part on exactly which causes precipitated it. In many cases, the ice age probably amounted to little more than a periodic cooling of northern hemisphere climates. Full-scale glaciation would have only occurred when all conditions conspired to cut down on the amount of solar radiation that reached the earth. D. Q. Bowen of the University College of Wales proposed: "Perhaps major periods of continental glaciation only took place when a combination of Antarctic [ice] surge and favorable Milankovitch conditions arose."

A complete analysis of current theory relating to ice ages may be found in *Ice Ages: Solving the Mystery*, by John Imbrie and Katherine Imbrie (Enslow, 1979).

The Long Count

The Long Count was a sophisticated system used by the Maya for specifying dates.

The Maya, an American Indian people who, between the third and eighth centuries, had a complex civilization covering southern Mexico, all of Guatemala, and northern Belize (formerly British Honduras), developed a remarkable calendar that is strikingly different from the Gregorian calendar we know today. Although much of Mayan civilization has been forgotten or was destroyed by European conquerors, some Maya who live in remote villages still continue to use many features of the traditional system for keeping track of time.

According to the Mayan calendar, the day runs from noon to noon. The civil year, which is divided into eighteen named months of twenty days each, has 365 days. Since this arrangement totals only 360 days, five days of evil omen are not part of any month. The twenty days of the month are counted from zero to nineteen. Each of the days of the month has a name. Because five of the day names must be used for the extra days that follow the eighteen months of the year, a Mayan day does not always have the same position in a month. For example, if Akbal is the first day of one month in one year, it falls on the sixth day of the month the next year, the eleventh day of the next, and the sixteenth day of the next. In the fifth year, Akbal again falls on the first day of the month.

The year is also divided into twenty-eight consecutive periods of thirteen days. Since this division totals only 364 days, there is one extra day in this year. Each day is assigned a number corresponding to its position in the period in which it falls. Again, a given day will fall at a different time in each thirteen-day period each consecutive year until the thirteen numbers are used up and the whole procedure begins again. Consequently, a day name will have the same day number in the thirteen-day period once every 260 days. The Maya considered the 260-day period the sacred year *(tzolkin)* and marked its beginning with a festival.

In writing a date, the Maya usually first gave the number of the day within its thirteen-day period and the name of the day. Next the Maya wrote the number of the day of the month (i.e., as we would write 12 July). The date does not mention the year because the same date re-occurs periodically

The Mayan calendar. (The University Museum, University of Pennsylvania)

only once every 52 years, a cycle called a "Calendar Round." The earliest Mayan inscription of a date is from Guatemala, dated at A.D. 292.

However, if it was not clear from the context in which 52-year period the date fell, the Maya used the Long Count to specify the period. Time stretched indefinitely into the past and future for the Maya, but they believed that the present universe was created on August 13, 3113 B.C. The Long Count placed a date in relation to this initial date. The number system used is vigesimal, i.e., based on twenty rather than ten as in the decimal system we use. Scholars believe the beginning of the use of the Long Count was between 350 B.C. to A.D. 140. The oldest known inscription of Long Count corresponds to A.D. 320.

The Mayan manuscripts that were not destroyed by the Spanish contain remarkably accurate calculations. The solar year is not exactly 365 days long, but actually 365.2422 days long. The Maya came very close to this figure when they calculated the solar year to be 365.2420 days long. While we make up for the fact that the 365-day year is too short by adding an extra day to leap years, the Maya did not. Instead, because without leap years the dates did not correspond to the seasons, from year to year they changed the date of those festivals and annual activities that depend on the season. They also calculated the movements of Venus so they could predict its position on a given day with great accuracy. Their calculation of the time it takes the moon to revolve around the earth once was also very accurate.

There is evidence that the Maya got their system of timekeeping from earlier civilizations. For example, an inscription has been found in the Mexican state of Vera Cruz which is dated at 31 B.C. The numbers in the inscription show a system of positional notation like that later used by the Maya. Positional notation is a system in which a symbol's value depends on its relative position within a number.

Today, in western civilization, two systems of time-keeping are used—an approximate one for daily life and an exact one used by astronomers. The Maya had one precise system used by everyone. Although the system seems more abstract—in that dates do not correspond to seasons because of the absence of leap years and the number of the year is not explicitly mentioned in a date—in some ways the Mayan calendar was closer to concrete life. Every time period corresponded to certain combinations of deities who determined what would happen within that period. The deities were diverse and associated with metereological conditions, human technologies, sections of the world, moral laws, animals, and every other aspect of human existence. They were known as the bearers of the burden of time, i.e., the characteristics of a particular period that determine what will happen during that period.

The Maya, who conceived everything in analogy with time, ordered their lives according to the patterns by which the calendar was ordered. Even today, the more traditional Mayan villages refer to the calendar to determine who will perform a certain religious or political function at a certain time. They also use the calendar to try to predict the success or failure of all kinds of activities which—to us—would not seem to be related to time.

For more information, see: Eric T. Thompson, *The Rise and Fall of Maya Civilization,* 2nd enl. ed. (University of California Press, 1954); and Miguel, Leon-Portilla, *Time and Reality in the Thought of the Maya* (Beacon, 1973); and Frank Waters, *Mexico Mystique: Coming Sixth World of Consciousness* (Swallow Press, 1975).

Runes

Runes are the written remains of ancient North German tribes, or the alphabet used in these writings.

Over 4,000 inscriptions and several manuscripts in the runic alphabet have been found in all parts of northern Europe, but primarily in Scandinavia and the British Isles. The earliest inscriptions date from around A.D. 200. Varieties of runic scripts were still in use in the twelfth century and runic inscriptions were occasionally used for magic or religious purposes for another 500 years, mostly in Scandinavia.

Historians believe that the runic alphabet, originally having twenty-four letters and reading from right to left, was developed well before the surviving inscriptions were made. The most commonly accepted explanation for the origin of runic script is that it was derived by ancient Goths from the North Etruscan alphabet during the second century B.C. The Etruscans, living in Italy, north of Rome, had in turn derived their alphabet from the Greeks. In support of the Etruscan origin of the runes, two inscriptions have been uncovered in Austria dating from the second and first centuries B.C., written in a Germanic language and using the Etruscan script.

Most surviving runes are inscriptions on objects like jewelry, armor, weapons, and memorial stones, and many seem to have a magical purpose. In fact, the word *rune* is related to the old Teutonic words for secrets and mystery. Some historians have claimed that runic was used for ordinary documents and poems as well, but the few extant runic manuscripts date from a relatively late period.

The Latin script gradually replaced the runic everywhere, due to the influence and example of the Church of Rome, which associated the runes with pagan religions.

Ever since it was established that North America had been visited by Norsemen long before the voyages of Columbus, attempts have been made to find runes that they might have left behind. Several such finds have been announced over the years, but all have proved to be forgeries.

The most notorious example was the Kensington stone rune, which was supposedly unearthed by a Swedish immigrant farmer near the town of Kensington in Douglas County, Minnesota, in 1898. It tells of an expedition of Scandinavians who traveled west from the Atlantic Coast in 1382. But the text contained grammatical froms that were unknown in the 14th century, and the language of the inscription was 19th century Swedish. The letters showed few signs of weathering, and were carved with a one-inch-bit chisel, commonly used in the United States at the time of the stone's appearance. Medieval runes were only rarely carved with chisels.

Nevertheless, some scholars, mostly of Scandinavian extraction, have continued to argue for the authenticity of the Kensington runes and for the other purported North American inscriptions.

For more information, see: Ralph Elliot, *Runes* (Manchester University Press, 1959) and Brigitta L. Wallace, "Some Points of Controversy" in *The Quest for America,* Geoffry Ashe, ed. (Praeger, 1971).

THE EARTH

The Tunguska Fireball

The largest explosion ever recorded on earth occurred in 1908 over a remote region of Siberia. Scientists have still not been able to agree on what caused it.

The explosion took place on June 30, 1908 at 7:17 a.m. in the Tunguska River basin in central Siberia. A dazzling fireball brighter than the sun descended through the daytime sky and was followed shortly by a tremendous explosion. Eyewitnesses 37 miles away at the Vanovera trading station felt a blast of heat at the time of the explosion (it was strong enough to singe clothing and cause flash burns on exposed flesh), followed by a concussive shock wave that threw them to the ground, followed in turn by a loud detonating roar that shook whole houses. Other eyewitnesses at a distance of only 25 miles from the blast were literally thrown into the air. At a distance of 400 miles, horses were knocked off their feet, and the sound of the explosion was heard at distances of over 600 miles. Ground tremors strong enough to break windowpanes and shake buildings to their foundations were felt at even greater distances.

The forests surrounding the blast site were devastated. The area within an 11-mile radius of the explosion was incinerated. Trees were knocked down at distances of up to 25 miles, their crowns pointing radially outward from the direction of the blast. Photographs taken 21 years after the event still clearly show the extent of the destruction.

The explosion left a huge amount of dust in the sky. Incandescent debris was thrown up to heights of 12 miles above the surface of the earth. It has been estimated that the explosion added several million tons of dust to the atmosphere. Effects were noted as far away as California, where the atmosphere was found to have become less transparent than usual, two weeks after the explosion. Microbarograph measurements established the fact that the airborne shock wave circled the earth twice. Seismographic readings around the world recorded an earthquake.

Scientists using modern analytical techniques estimate that the fireball was about four or five miles above the ground when it exploded. Professor Ari Ben-Menahem of the Weizmann Institute in Israel estimated the explosive energy to have been the equivalent of 12.5 megatons of TNT, or the equivalent of a very powerful nuclear blast.

Scientists are still not sure what caused the Tunguska blast, and several explanations have been put forward.

The original investigator of the explosion, the Soviet scientist E. L. Krilov, at first adopted the hypothesis that the explosion was caused by the impact of an iron meteorite much like the one that carved the famous mile-wide Meteor Crater in Arizona. However, the absence at the Tunguska blast site of any sort of large crater ruled out this hypothesis. In his 1921 investigation, Krilov found nothing more than residual meteoric dust and a few small depressions in the earth that could not definitely be characterized as craters.

In the early 1930s, Dr. Fred L. Whipple of the Smithsonian Astrophysical Observatory in Cambridge, Massachusetts proposed that the Tunguska blast was caused by a small comet striking the earth. He estimated the diameter of the comet at 44 yards and its speed at 37 miles per second. The tail of the comet, consisting of gas and dust particles, would have accounted for the thick column of "smoke" that the 1908 observers had described as following the fireball—and would also explain the atmospheric dust present in the air after the explosion. Whipple proposed that the head of the comet, or nucleus, caused the actual blast when the friction of the earth's atmosphere caused it to explode. His "dirty snowball" theory holds that a comet's head is a loose conglomeration of dust and rock held together by ice and frozen gases. Whipple's comet theory still is accepted by many scientists, but there are two significant objections to it. First, no comet had actually been seen approaching the earth in June, 1908. Adherents of the Whipple theory state, however, that if the comet had approached Earth from the direction of the sun, the sun's glare would have blinded observers to it. The second objection to the comet theory states that a relatively "loose" object such as a comet head would be incinerated soon after it entered earth's atmosphere, high in the ionisphere; it would not be sufficiently solid or massive to survive atmospheric friction long enough to penetrate to the 5-mile level where the Tunguska blast occurred.

In 1959, scientists at the British Atomic Energy Authority proposed a nuclear explanation for the blast. They theorized that a meteorite containing a mass of fissionable material reached critical density upon entering Earth's atmospheric field and gave rise to an explosive chain reaction similar to an atomic bomb. The scientists supported their theory by noting that chain reactions have been known to occur naturally (though none has ever actually been observed to lead to an explosion). In 1967, Aleksei V. Zolotov of the Ioffe Physico-Technical Institute of the Soviet Academy of Sciences supported the nuclear theory in an article in the scientific journal *Soviet Physics-Doklady*, by stating that his observations of the blast site in Siberia were consistent with the effects of a thermonuclear explosion. Professor Ben-Menahem of the Weizmann Institute reiterated the theory in 1975, saying that he believed the explosion was caused by "an extraterrestrial nuclear missile." Though the nuclear theory is impossible to disprove, most scientific observers are skeptical of it, finding it hard to believe that any meteorite could contain enough fissionable material—presumably deuterium or tritium—to fuel a nuclear blast.

In 1965, Nobel laureate Dr. Willard Libby and two colleagues proposed the anti-matter theory. They suggested that the blast occurred when an "anti-rock"—a meteorite formed of antimatter—reached the earth and was annihilated. (See also "Experiments to measure the antimatter content of the Tunguska meteorite," *Nature*, vol. 248, 1975, p. 396.) Every atomic particle has an identical but opposite twin, differing from it only in characteristics such as electrical charge; this is antimatter. When two such opposite particles meet, they destroy each other in a burst of gamma rays. Opponents of the antimatter theory point to the fact that if an "anti-rock" approached the earth, it would be annihilated as soon as it encountered matter in the form of Earth's atmosphere. It would theoretically not be able to penetrate to the 5-mile level of the Tunguska explosion.

In 1973, A. A. Jackson and M. P. Ryan, Jr., both of the Center for Relativity Theory of the University of Texas, puslished an article entitled, "Was the Tungus Event Due To a Black Hole?" (See *Nature*, vol. 245, 1973, p. 88.) A black hole is a theoretical object of small size and such density that its gravitational field does not permit the escape of any material, not even light rays. Such an object entering the atmosphere, the authors reasoned, would cause a shock wave comparable to the Tunguska experience. The black hole would then pass straight through the center of the earth and exit somewhere in the mid-Atlantic. However, no shock waves or disturbances occurred on June 30, 1908 in the Atlantic.

The idea that the Tunguska blast was the explosion of an extraterrestrial spaceship has cropped up regularly, originally in 1946 in a science fiction story by Alexander Kazantsev; in 1976 by John Baxter and Thomas Atkins in *The Fire Came By* (Doubleday); and most recently in a series of 1979 articles circulated by Tass, the Soviet news agency.

The latest scientific explanation of the Tunguska explosion, and perhaps the simplest and clearest, was put forward by Dr. L. Kresak of the Slovak Academy of Sciences in Bratislava, Czechoslovakia (see *The New York Times*, January 30, 1979, p. C-1). Keith Hindley (in *Science News*, June 30, 1979, p. 424) also propounds the same explanation, i.e., that the blast was caused by the explosion of a meteorite. Statistically, this is not unlikely, for most meteorites that enter the earth's atmosphere explode at some distance above the ground, disintegrating and in many instances vaporizing completely after being pressurized and heated to incandescent strength by the friction of the earth's atmosphere. The Tunguska event is thought by the proponents of the theory to have been caused by a meteorite of this type. (Very few large meteorites—usually only very rare iron meteorites—penetrate to ground level as did the great Arizona meteor.) Meteorite fireballs of the Tunguska type—though much smaller and higher in the atmosphere—have been observed repeatedly, most notably the Sumava (Czechoslovakia) fireball of 1974 and the Ozarks fireball of 1969. It is theorized that the Tunguska meteorite was simply a particularly large variety of this class that penetrated deep into Earth's atmospheric field before exploding. The results of such an explosion would have been a dense cloud of iron and silicate spherules, the condensed remains of the meteorite, which still abound at the Tunguska site today.

If the Tunguska explosion was indeed of meteoric origin, could it happen again? A million-ton meteorite of the Tunguska class can be expected only once a century. Such a meteorite would probably be part of the debris of comet Encke, which has littered the solar system with dust, meteors, and meteorites. The earth plows through this material twice a year, producing the Taurid meteor shower of October/November and the B-Taurid shower of June/July. (The fact that the Tunguska event occurred at the height of the B-Taurid period in 1908 is suggestive evidence of its meteoric origin.) Such a meteor could probably not be detected before its entry, so the incandescent fireball would appear quite unexpectedly.

For further details, see Rupert Furneaux, *The Tungus Event* (Panther, 1977).

Continental Drift

The theory of continental drift holds that the surface of the earth is in constant motion. The theory, while generally accepted in the scientific community, has neither been proven nor disproven, but is still undergoing study.

The theory was first proposed in 1912 by Alfred Wegener, a German meteorologist, as an attempt to explain certain anomalies of contemporary geological and anthropological thinking. The theory presented itself to Wegener as a possible answer to a number of questions that had perplexed scientists, such as: Why did the coastlines of South America and Africa seem to "fit" each other so well? Why did geologically identical mountain systems appear on both sides of the North Atlantic? How could tropical ferns have been growing in Greenland when glaciers were covering Africa? Why did the lemur monkey live in two small areas on opposite sides of the Indian Ocean? Why did mountains occur in ranges? In fact, why did mountains occur at all?

Wegener's theory, derided by scientists at the time of its proposal and for 40 years thereafter, advanced the idea that the continents were in constant motion and had once occupied positions far different from those they occupy today. The theory suggested answers for all the questions that had perplexed Wegener. Mountain ranges, for instance, could be explained as the result of the titanic buckling that took place when two continents collided. And the mirror-image coastlines of South America and Africa would make sense if the two continents had in fact been joined together during past epochs. And the lemur monkey's oddly separated habitats would be no mystery if the two sides of the Indian Ocean had once been connected.

The continental drift theory did not become scientific orthodoxy, however, until the advent of paleomagnetic dating techniques, which were first suggested by the British geophysicists F. J. Vine and D. H. Matthews in 1963. Paleomagnetic dating measures the direction of magnetization that is preserved in a rock at the time of its formation. The paleomagnetic "stripes" in an ancient rocky landmass (and especially in the rock layers underlying the ocean floors) show the original alignment of the land in relation to the pole. Naturally, when it was discovered that the paleomagnetic alignment of various parts of the earth did not point north and south, it became evident that the land masses must have shifted their positions in the eons since their formation. Refinement of paleomagnetic techniques enables researchers to construct a "wander path" for the various continental land masses.

The entire surface of the earth, including oceans as well as the land-masses, is carried on about a dozen shifting "plates" that move slowly in various directions. The energy for these titanic movements is derived from the earth's internal heat, which is carried upward by convection from the earth's center like thick soup bubbling in a cauldron. The meeting place of two plates is often particularly unstable, giving rise to volcanoes, fault lines, rift valleys, and undersea trenches. California's San Andreas Fault, for instance, marks the boundary of the Pacific and North American plates. The mid-Atlantic ridge is the joining point for the Eurasian and African plates on the east with the North and South American plates on the west. The Red Sea and the valley of the Dead Sea in Israel are both positioned along the dividing line between the African and Arabian plates.

The principal upwelling of the earth's heat—and consequently the initiation of continental drift—is currently taking place in the great mid-ocean ridges of the Atlantic, Indian, and Antarctic oceans. The displaced land masses are being brought together elsewhere, gradually being forced back down under the earth's crust, by the shrinking of the Pacific Ocean and the Mediterranean Sea.

The current state of the theory of continental drift proposes a history of the earth's continents beginning 500 million years ago. At that date, there were three land masses on the earth's surface—a prototype of Eurasia, a prototype of North America, and a large southern continent dubbed Gondwana, which was composed of South America, Antarctica, Africa, Australia, and India. 500 million years ago, the Armorica plate split off from Gondwana and headed north. Armorica contained what would one day be southern England, Wales, the northern parts of Spain, France, Germany, and Poland, and possibly also New England and Newfoundland. The Armorica plate collided with North America about 450 million years ago, throwing up the Appalachian chain of mountains (which were higher then than the Himalayas are now). The combined new continent of North America-Armorica was in turn rammed by Eurasia (known to geologists as the Baltic Shield and the Russian Platform) 50 to 100 million years later. This collision formed the Caledonian mountains of England and Wales, a chain which originally extended through the Netherlands and Germany into Poland. North America and Eurasia were now welded into one single northern continent, dubbed Laurasia.

The southern continent of Gondwana drifted northward about 300 million years ago and collided with the northern land mass. This caused the formation of new mountain ranges all along the line of impact. The Alps, the Pyrenees, the Alleghenies, and the Canadian Maritimes all derive from this period. The entire land mass of the globe was now welded into one supercontinent known as Pangea. At that time, the East Coast of the United States abutted Morocco, while Europe was attached to the northern face of Canada. South America hugged the southern part of Africa, while the Indian subcontinent was wedged in between East Africa and Antarctica. Australia was an extension of Antarctica.

It was the gradual breakup of Pangea, beginning about 200 million years ago, that gave rise to the earth's crustal arrangement as we know it today. By the end of the Triassic period 180 million years ago, the northern continent of Laurasia had begun to split apart from Gondwana, creating the infant Caribbean and Mediterranean seas. And Gondwana itself had begun to break up. Specifically, a wide Y-shaped oceanic rift split it into three parts, setting free India and Antarctica/Australia.

65 million years later, at the end of the Jurassic period, the continents had drifted even further. The beginnings of the North Atlantic pushed north from the Caribbean, starting to split Laurasia into its two components of North America and Eurasia. India, freed from Gondwana, drifted north, creating the Indian Ocean between it and Antarctica/Australia. The birth of the South Atlantic began in a long narrow rift between Africa and South America.

At the end of the Cretaceous period 65 million years ago, the South Atlantic had widened into a major ocean. The North Atlantic was still extending itself northward. Europe began to split off from North America, carrying with it the ancient Armorica plate that bore southern England and the northern coasts of France and Spain. Antarctica and Australia were still joined, but a new rift carved Madagascar off from the East coast of Africa. India was still on the move, heading northward toward Asia.

The Cenozoic period of the last 65 million years saw our present continental arrangement take place. The North Atlantic widened considerably, completing the fissioning of Laurasia. Australia broke off from Antarctica. And India finally bumped into Asia, welding itself to the larger continent and pushing up the Himalayan chain in the process.

What will happen to the face of the globe during the next 50 million years? Extrapolation of current crustal action indicates that there will be several major changes in the earth's surface. The Atlantic and Indian oceans will continue to expand at the expense of the Pacific. Australia will drift northward toward the East Indies. East Africa will be ripped away from the mother continent as the East African subplate rotates. Africa itself will move northward, collapsing the Mediterranean Sea. North America will continue its northwest drift, sundering the Isthmus of Panama. And Baja California along with a sliver of coastal California will tear away from the North American continent and drift out to sea as the Pacific plate grinds away at the San Andreas fault. Ten million years from now, Los Angeles will be on a long narrow island abreast of San Francisco. In 60 million years, Los Angeles will slide into the Aleutian trench off Alaska.

Further information may be found in *Science News*, June 9, 1979, p. 373; *Scientific American*, October, 1970, p. 30; S. K. Runcorn, *Continental Drift* (1962); and T. F. Gaskell, The *Earth's Mantle* (1967).

Hot Spots

"Hot spots" are specific areas of the earth's crust where heat from the planet's interior rises close to the surface. They are thought to be responsible for a number of unexplained geologic features scattered over the face of the globe.

W. Jason Morgan, a geophysicist at Princeton University, is credited along with J. Tuzo Wilson with originating the hot spot theory.

The most easily observed instance of hot spot activity is the Hawaiian Islands. Each of the islands that make up the chain are thought to have been originally created as the Pacific Plate moved slowly over a fixed hot spot in the earth's crust. The heat from the hot spot caused volcanic activity which eventually pushed the Hawaiian Islands above the surface of the sea. Such volcanic activity still continues at the southeastern end of the island chain where Mauna Loa and Kilauea are both active. Their positioning suggests that the islands as a whole are sliding to the northwest. By this reasoning, a new island should eventually appear off the southeastern tip of the island of Hawaii.

Such an island has actually been observed growing upward from the Pacific floor. Known as Loihi, it lies 25 miles off Hawaii and is at present still 3,200 feet below the surface of the ocean. Researchers have dredged fresh basalt from Loihi's summit, which indicates that recent volcanic activity has occurred. And Loihi is the epicenter for heavy swarms of low-energy earthquakes that are characteristic of underwater volcanoes.

Studies in the Easter Island chain have indicated that a hot spot may be responsible for several of them. One, San Felix, is an active volcano and is presumed to be located directly over the hot spot. San Ambrosio is 30 kilometers to the east, and its lava is dated at approximately 2.9 million years. The Nazca Plate is known to move at a rate of about 10 centimeters per year, which would have placed San Ambrosio directly over the presumed hot spot at the proper time 2.9 million years ago.

Reunion Island in the Indian Ocean—often dubbed "Hawaii South"— is formed by two volcanic mountains, one of which is fully mature, the other of which is just coming to maturity. Given that the Indian Ocean Plate is moving in a northwesterly direction, a hot spot under Reunion would explain the origin of the two mountains.

The most extensive scenario of hot spot activity concerns the so-called Bermuda rise, a large upthrust area in the Atlantic which carries the Bermuda Islands. Princeton University geophysicists Morgan and Thomas Crough theorize that the Bermuda hot spot has been responsible for a large number of geologic features over more than 100 million years. (See *Science News*, July 28, 1979, p. 69.) Sixty million years ago, for instance, the present coast of North Carolina would have been over the hot spot. North Carolina sits upon a large unexplained underground feature known as the Cape Fear arch. Wilson and Crough propose that the Bermuda hot spot gave birth to the Cape Fear arch.

In a similar way, the general area of Appalachian uplift noticeable today from West Virginia to Alabama is also thought to be attributable to the action of the Bermuda hot spot 70 million years ago. At the 90 million year point, Arkansas would have been over the hot spot. The diamond deposits found today in Arkansas may have been laid down at that point. Deposits of the mineral kimberlite are known to occur over hot spots, and the kimberlite deposits of Kansas, laid down 112 to 114 million years ago, may also be due to the Bermuda hot spot.

The presence of kimberlite may provide a handy means of tracking hot spot activity in other parts of the world. By mapping the locations of known kimberlite deposits, geophysicists would have a ready-made track of the route of the continental land mass over the hot spot. The actual location of the hot spot would be pinpointed at the end of the kimberlite chain.

New England Earthquakes

New England and the contiguous states of New York and New Jersey form the second most active earthquake region in the continental United States (after California), but seismologists cannot explain why the quakes occur.

The New England area, loosely defined as stretching from the St. Lawrence River in Canada to northern New Jersey, receives an average of four to six earthquakes a month. The quakes usually do not measure over 4.5 on the Richter scale. (The Richter scale was devised in 1935 to measure the intensity of earthquake motion recorded on seismographs. A quake at the 3.5 level can cause moderate damage, depending on the population density of the area where it occurs, while one that registers 6.0 can cause severe damage.) The most powerful recent tremors in New England occurred in April, 1979 (registering 4.0) and in June, 1973 (registering 4.3), but the most serious quake ever to hit the region was probably the Cape Ann (Mass.) earthquake of 1755, which destroyed a large part of Portsmouth, New Hampshire.

New England quakes are not as strong as California quakes (which regularly measure up to 5.0 or 6.0 on the Richter scale), but they are felt over wider areas than the California tremors, sometimes to distances as much as 900 miles from the New England epicenter.

Boston College's Weston Observatory in Weston, Massachusetts is the headquarters of the Northeast Seismic Network, which monitors New England tremblor activity. Government concern over the safety of nuclear power plants and hydroelectric dams led to the buildup of the network's monitoring stations to the present total of nearly 50. The network has pinpointed seven major centers of earthquake activity in the New England area: Cape Ann in Massachusetts, central New Hampshire, southern Connecticut, northern New Jersey (including the New York City metropolitan region), Montreal and Quebec City in Canada, and a third Canadian location on the St. Lawrence River.

Geologists cannot satisfactorily explain why New England has earthquakes at all. Most earthquake-prone regions of the world, such as California, are near a fault line where two land masses or "plates" rub against each other. New England, however, has no active fault lines and is located near the center of a plate. One theory, called the "glacial rebound theory," attributes the

148

area's seismic activity to the fact that New England was covered by a mile-thick blanket of ice during the last Pleistocene ice age, which ended about 12,000 years ago. The theorists surmise that the New England land mass is still "bouncing back," slowly and unevenly, like a compressed sponge.

Richard Holt of Weston Geophysical Research, Inc. proposed a more recent theory that the earth's crust in the New England region contains buried "plutons" or hard rock shafts that pierce the geologic plate like reinforcing rods in concrete. These plutons would act as stress centers, focusing siesmic activity whenever the plate shifted. In support of this theory, Holt stated that at least two plutons had been found in the Cape Ann Area.

Dr. Edward Chiburis of the Northeastern Seismic Network has stated that New England's chances of having an earthquake in the 5.0-to-6.0 range during the next half-century is roughly 50 percent.

For further documentation, see *The New York Times*, April 19, 1979, p. A-16.

The Palmdale Bulge

The Palmdale Bulge is a strange unexplained swelling in the earth's surface north and east of Los Angeles. It is not known if the actions of the bulge are related to earthquake activity of the nearby San Andreas fault.

The Palmdale Bulge was discovered in 1976. Records going back to 1959 indicate that the affected area of California may have risen and subsided several times between 1959 and the present. At certain points, particularly near Palm Springs, the landscape may have risen as much as 18 inches. Since 1974, the bulge seems to have deflated somewhat and to have moved to the north, where it is now centered in the Mojave Desert about 40 miles north of Los Angeles.

Swellings of terrain similar to the Palmdale Bulge have occurred before severe earthquakes in Japan (1961), the Philippines (1971), and China (1975). The Palmdale bulge is therefore suspected to be an earthquake precursor, though it appears to have swelled during the early years of this century without a major quake occurring.

In 1979, it appeared that the Palmdale area, rather than rising vertically, was expanding in a horizontal direction. Scientists at the U.S. Geological Survey in Menlo Park and at the NASA Jet Propulsion Laboratory in Pasadena used sophisticated radio astronomy and laser technology to ascertain that the

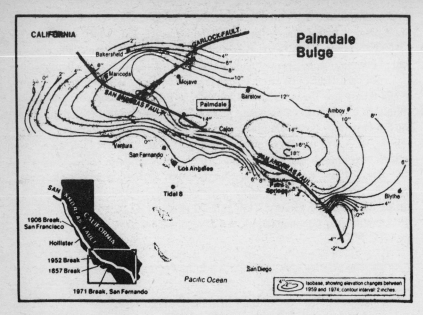

The area around the Palmdale Bulge in California is laced with fault lines. (© 1979 by The New York Times Company. Reprinted by permission.)

landscape had expanded about 22 centimeters in a northeast-southwest direction. (See *Science News*, December 15, 1979.) Pasadena, for instance, was now further away from the city of Goldstone than it had been previously. One researcher commented: "It looks like Pasadena moved west."

It is not known what caused this rapid stretching—or what its effects may be. On the one hand, it may forewarn of an earthquake. On the other, it may merely be an odd geological anomaly peculiar to this region.

Some geophysicists think that the Palmdale Bulge does not exist at all but is simply the result of measuring error. In support of their case, they point to the admitted difficulties of making accurate measurements by laser, which are open to distortions caused by the effects of water vapor in the air. The so-called "Palmdale stretch" they attribute to a systematic error in the calibration of leveling rods used for the survey.

Most scientific observers, however, believe the Palmdale Bulge is real, despite the inevitable errors that creep into measurement surveys. In this case, the bulge undoubtedly has some significance for the earthquake-prone region, though geophysicists unfortunately do not know exactly what that significance is.

Detailed information on the Palmdale Bulge is contained in *The New York Times*, March 27, 1979, p. C-1.

The New Madrid Fault

The New Madrid Fault in the mid-Mississippi Valley is not as well known as the San Andreas fault in California, yet it was responsible for the most severe earthquake in United States history. The great Missouri quake of 1811 leveled every building for miles around, swallowed the village of New Madrid, and tossed the Mississippi River from its bed.

Little is known about the fault. It is believed to be actually a 175-mile system of faults running from Illinois to Arkansas, deeply buried beneath 2,000 to 3,000 feet of Mississippi River sediment. This sediment layer magnifies the shock waves of a quake, thus creating the possibility of greater surface effects than are possible with such shallow faults as California's San Andreas fracture.

Several large population centers lie within the New Madrid Fault zone—St. Louis; Memphis and Nashville, Tennessee; Evansville, Indiana—as well as nine nuclear power plants. It has been estimated that a major quake in the area would cause ten times as much damage as a similar quake in California.

THE PHYSICAL WORLD

Lightning

Lightning is a visible transfer of atmospheric electricity between a cloud and the earth, or between two clouds.

Lightning usually occurs during thunderstorms, but it is also associated with volcanoes, sandstorms, and snowstorms. In thunderstorms, the electrical energy needed for lightning is generated in cumulonimbus clouds, which are shaped like towers with their bases one-half to one-and-one-half miles above the ground and their tops from seven to ten miles above the ground.

The top of the cloud has a high proportion of positively charged particles, while the base has a high proportion of negatively charged particles. The causes of this separation are not precisely known but are related to the rapid movements of air masses and moisture and the collision of icedrops and raindrops.

The negative charge at the base of the cloud causes the ground beneath the cloud, especially at its highest points, to become positively charged. A huge electrical potential builds up, since the air between the cloud and the ground normally acts as an insulator. When the potential reaches a critical level, a lightning stroke occurs and conveys the cloud's negative charge to the earth.

Time-lapse photographs of lightning reveal that each stroke involves several stages:

(1) the leader, a group of negative charges, moves toward the ground in a stepped, or zig-zag path, stopping before each turn. The air in its path becomes ionized, making it an excellent conductor of electricity.

(2) as the leader approaches the earth, opposite charges accumulate in the area of descent, and a brief discharge rises up to meet the leader. This discharge can be heard as a click.

(3) a return stroke moves back *up* the leader's path, at great speed and at currents of up to 200,000 amperes. This is the visible lightning stroke. It heats up the air in its path, causing it to expand suddenly; the expansion is heard as thunder.

(4) a "dark" leader, a group of negative charges, moves back down the stepped column of ionized air without stopping and is followed by a second return stroke. As many as forty-two strokes have been counted in rapid succession.

Lightning strokes between clouds are more frequent than cloud-to-ground strokes, but less is known about their dynamics.

The adage that one should avoid isolated trees during a thunderstorm is quite valid. While the treetop attracts lightning, the trunk and roots are usually poor conductors, and the flash is apt to jump to a nearby, prominent object, such as a human, which would be a better conductor. Also, a tree may explode when the charge turns the sap in the trunk to steam.

A lightning shock may stop a victim's heartbeat and breathing while doing little damage otherwise. Victims often suffer burns as well. External heart massage and artificial respiration can revive the victim in such cases.

The simple lightning rod invented by Benjamin Franklin remains the basis for all systems that protect buildings from lightning. In this system, the charges accumulating in the ground are safely dissipated in the air by means of metal conductors leading to sharp points on the roof. Thus, lightning strokes are usually avoided, but if they occur, the conductors lead the charge to the ground, avoiding the building itself.

It is possible to be killed by lightning even if you are not actually hit by the stroke itself. In a phenomenon known as return shock, a lightning bolt can cause related electrical discharges over a wide area. A human being standing on open ground during a thunderstorm will build up a positive charge along with all other nearby objects. When lightning strikes, the surrounding ground suddenly becomes negatively charged. This causes a strong electric shock in the human body, in some cases severe enough to endanger life.

For more information, see: Sir Basil Schonland, *The Flight of Thunderbolts* (Oxford University Press, 1964); Martin A. Uman, *Lightning* (McGraw-Hill, 1969).

Ball Lightning

Ball lightning is a mysterious form of electrical disturbance in which small balls of fire move through the air. Because there is no accepted scientific explanation for ball lightning, it is often dismissed as merely the result of hallucination, optical aftereffects, or spots before the eyes. However, there is a large body of reliably documented incidents of ball lightning, and the phenomenon seems to be a true one.

Ball lightning is usually described as a luminous floating sphere which moves through the air at varying speeds and lasts from several seconds to several minutes. Usually the sphere is about the size of a grapefruit, but it can range from one centimeter up to more than a meter.

The general properties of ball lightning were described by J. D. Barry in the *Journal of Atmospheric and Terrestrial Physics*, 29:1095, 1967, as follows: "Ball lightning is most commonly observed as a ball-shaped object with a burning appearance, and radial dimensions less than 40 centimeters Although it appears similar to a burning globule, its surface is generally dimly illuminated with a lack of protruding flames. It is generally first observed in a slow descending motion, apparently from a thundercloud, but does not fall directly to the ground. It commonly assumes random motions a few decameters above the ground, or a slow horizontal flight. It appears to behave independently of external forces, as it is frequently observed to be unaffected by conductors. It does, however, seem to have an occasional affinity for enclosures. It can deviate from a straight path to enter a room through a doorway or a partially opened window. The ball lightning is sometimes accompanied by the presence of a sharp repugnant odor, such as that associated with an electrical discharge. The ball lightning has a short lifetime, usually only a few seconds. It can decay silently or explosively, although the latter decay mode is most frequent."

Ball lightning seems definitely to be connected with thunderstorm activity and is often reported by airplane pilots. A survey of 4,000 NASA personnel indicated that ball lightning might occur much more frequently than had been thought. The phenomenon would presumably account for many

Ball lightning. (M.R. Lyons/NEW SCIENTIST)

unidentified "UFO" reports; more often, however, appearances of ball lightning simply go unreported.

Cases of ball lightning—or what appears to be ball lightning—have been reported throughout history. One of the earliest cases that was actually documented occurred in St. Petersburg, Russia, in 1753. G. W. Richman, an early experimenter with lightning, and I. Sokolov were present in a laboratory during a thunderstorm. Part of the laboratory apparatus consisted of an ungrounded lightning rod. At the height of the storm, a fist-sized glowing ball appeared at the end of the rod and floated through the air. It detonated as it approached Richman. Sokolov lost consciousness; Richman was killed. His body had a red spot on the forehead, and two holes were in his shoes. (This case was reviewed by J. R. Powell and D. Finkelstein in an article in *American Scientist,* May/June 1970, 58:262.)

Many cases were reported during the 19th century. In Paris on July 5, 1852, during a violent thunderstorm, a tailor in a fourth floor apartment saw a "fireball" the size of a human head emerge from the fireplace "as if driven by a gust of wind." The fireball dislocated the screen that covered the fireplace. No heat emanated from the ball, though it was luminous. Floating just above the floor, it moved across the room "like a cat." Returning to the chimney, it rose suddenly and detonated, destroying part of the chimney. (See *On Earth and In the Sky,* by W. Ley, Ace Books, 1957.)

On July 23, 1878, an incident was reported aboard a yacht near Southampton, England. (See *Nature*, December 1895, 53:152.) During a heavy thunderstorm, a bright light appeared near the upper part of the mast of the yacht. It was described as a fireball of a delicate rose-pink color, about 4 or 5 inches in diameter. It descended slowly through the air, finally hitting the deck with a loud detonation. A crewman standing 25 feet away was knocked down but not hurt. A strong odor of ozone was apparent for some time after the explosion.

One of the best documented modern cases of ball lightning occurred inside the passenger cabin of an airplane on a late night flight from New York to Washington on March 19, 1963. One of the passengers was Professor R. C. Jennison of the Electronics Laboratories at the University of Kent in England, who described the occurrence. Several seconds following a loud thunderclap, a luminous spherical object emerged from the pilot's cabin and floated down the aisle of the passenger compartment. It glowed with a blue-white color and had a "thick," solid appearance. It was about 8 inches in diameter and floated about 30 inches off the floor. It drifted down the length of the aisle before disappearing.

What exactly is ball lightning? Many scientists discount it as folklore or hallucination, maintaining that ball lightning is merely an optical after-image left on the retina of the eye after a bright flash of light such as that caused by a lightning bolt. However, this explanation does not seem adequate for ball lightning observed indoors, where the witness has not been blinded by a lightning flash. It also discounts the evidence of presumably reliable observers like Jennison.

Various explanations have been put forward to explain ball lightning. D. Finkelstein and J. Rubinstein have proposed that ball lightning represents a direct-current glow discharge. The electroluminescence that occurs in lightning channels could, according to the theory, create detached spheres of glowing air. (See *Physical Review*, 135:A390, 1964.) M. D. Altschuler proposed in *Nature* (November 7, 1970, 228:545) that the energies contained in ball lightning could only be explained on the basis of some form of nuclear phenomenon. Such a nuclear source might be created when protons are accelerated down a lightning channel, thus forming radioisotopes in the air. The decay of these radioisotopes would then presumably liberate the energy displayed by the ball lightning.

E. T. F. Ashby and C. Whitehead proposed an antimatter theory of ball lightning. (See *Nature*, March 19, 1971, 230:180.) They postulate that antimatter can be comparatively stable in the presence of ordinary matter. Gradual annihilation of the antimatter would liberate the energy given off by the ball lightning. The flux of antimatter from outer space is presumed to be concentrated by thunderstorms into densities that give rise to ball lightning.

The most recent proposal is that of G. C. Dijkhuis of Zeldenrust College in the Netherlands, presented in *Nature*, (March 13, 1980, 284:150). Dijkhuis proposes that ball lightning consists of superconducting ionized gas created by ordinary lightning bolts. Gas is ionized by proximity to a lightning bolt. Vortices, known as plasmas, are then formed in the gas. These plasmas would behave as superconductors, tending to spin in the same direction as the particles of which they consist. Dijkhuis maintains that this is the only explanation for ball lightning which accounts for the fact that ball lightning is seen inside the cabins of sealed airplanes; ball lightning from other hypothesized sources would be effectively screened out of this environment.

Further information on ball lightning is found in S. Singer, *The Nature of Ball Lightning* (Plenum, 1971); and R. H. Golde, ed., *Lightning*, vol. 1 (Academic, 1977).

Gravity Waves

Einstein's general theory of relativity maintains that gravity waves exist. But gravity is such a weak force that scientists have not yet succeeded in making instruments sensitive enough to detect its presence. It is intuitively obvious that gravity exists—the lesson of Newton's apple is irrefutable—but its actual physical presence has yet to be proven.

Other forces in nature are represented by easily-detected waves. A wave is defined as a cyclic or pulsating disturbance that propagates itself through space; the wave is the means by which any particular force manifests itself. Besides gravity, the other force that dominates the earth's general existence is electromagnetism. Its waves are common everyday phenomena: light, X-rays, ultraviolet rays, and electricity are among its various forms. Gravity waves would presumably be directly analogous to electromagnetic waves: they would carry gravity just as light carries electromagnetism.

Gravity is the universal "glue" that pervades everything, from the smallest subatomic particle to the most massive star. Every object in the universe exerts a gravitational attraction on every other object. The magnitude of this attraction is quite small, however. Only in objects as large as the earth or the sun does gravity become a force to be reckoned with. On the level of individual atoms or subatomic particles, the effects of gravity are negligible. The electrostatic force between two electrons, for instance, is literally trillions and trillions of times stronger than the gravitational force.

Einstein's general theory of relativity—which first predicted the existence of gravity waves—was published in 1916, but not until the 1950s did scientists actually set about trying to discover the waves. The waves were expected to be so unimaginably weak that extremely sensitive instruments had to be constructed. Most experiments to date have involved the use of long aluminum bars in a procedure originated by Joseph Weber, a physicist at the University of Maryland. Weber's method is to make the bar as motionless as possible, so that any motion then detected in it is presumably due to the passage of gravity waves. This involves isolating the bar in an elaborately cushioned vacuum chamber and chilling it almost to absolute zero (4 degrees Kelvin).

Gravitational waves should theoretically cause slight vibrations in the bar. In a three-meter aluminum bar, the strongest gravity wave that could be expected in our galaxy would only cause a net motion equal to the diameter of one atomic nucleus, or about 1.5×10^{-16} centimeter. Results of experiments using Weber bars have so far been inconclusive. The purported gravity waves have left such equivocal traces that one analyst can claim that a certain set of data prove gravity's existence while another analyst can equally plausibly argue that the data disprove it.

Newer experiments are being designed with bars of sapphire or silicon in place of aluminum, since those two substances are known to be particularly sensitive to vibrations.

William F. Fairbank, a physicist at Stanford University and a gravity experimenter, believes that gravitational experiments have failed because they were too insensitive: only a really large star explosion, he says, would have produced gravity waves strong enough to be detected by such primitive means. (See *Science News*, December 8, 1979, p. 392.)

Other new experiments are being designed using a device called SQUID—Superconducting Quantum Interference Device—which should be able to detect gravitation from star explosions anywhere in the Milky Way. In the future, advanced technology may make possible the use of evacuated tubes 12 to 15 miles in length. These tubes, used in conjunction with satellites, might succeed in providing a large enough target for elusive gravity waves.

The most successful recent experiment was performed between 1974 and 1978 by astronomers from the University of Massachusetts. The experimenters used a giant radio telescope to track the movements of a double star in the constellation Aquila. The two stars spin around each other about once every eight hours at a velocity of 660,000 miles per hour. According to Einstein's theory, gravity waves radiated into space by the two stars would slowly drain energy away from them, with the result that their orbits would move ever closer, causing a shortening in their orbital period. The slow-down would be very small, only 1/10,000 of a second per year.

Four years of observation of the orbiting pair showed that indeed they were slowing down—and by exactly the 4/10,000 of a second that Einstein's equation predicted. The experimenters claimed that these results showed that gravity waves did exist, although they had not detected the actual waves themselves.

Information on gravity is contained in P. G. Bergmann, *The Riddle of Gravitation* (New York, 1968); and J. Weber, General Relativity and Gravitational Waves (New York, 1961).

Holography

Holographic photography is a method of recording three-dimensional images on two-dimensional photographic plates. When illuminated, a holographic photograph gives the illusion of a solid object or scene magically suspended in space.

Sometimes called the photographic equivalent of hi-fi, holography was first proposed as a theoretical possibility by Dennis Gabor in 1947. At the time, there was no practical method of making holographic photographs because all known light sources were inadequate. With the invention and development of the laser in the 1950s and 1960s, however, a source of highly-aligned light beams became available, and holography was a practical possibility. Gabor received a Nobel prize in physics in 1971 for his part in developing the theory of holography.

Holograms are produced without a camera, a lens, or a negative. The holographic plate is simply a thin, semi-transparent film that records the images projected by the laser beam. To record a scene or object, light from

Hologram. (Dr. Karl Pribram/Stanford University)

Hologram. (Dr. Karl Pribram/Stanford University)

a laser is first split into two beams by a prism. One beam—called the reference beam—is deflected directly to the holographic plate. The other beam is bounced off the object to be photographed, then redirected to the holographic plate. The two beams reconverge at the plate, combining to imprint a holographic image.

It is the interference pattern of the two beams that creates the holographic photograph. The easiest way to visualize this process is to compare it to what happens when two pebbles are dropped into a pond. Both pebbles set up concentric circles of waves that radiate out from them. Wherever the two sets of waves collide with each other, an interference pattern is created. If the crests of two waves meet, they create a new wave that is twice as high; if a crest and a trough meet, they cancel one another out, leaving smooth water; if two troughs meet, they make a trough twice as deep. In the same way, the two beams of light from the laser set up an interference pattern of the holographic plate.

The holographic plate, in ordinary light, appears to have a grainy grayish surface upon which no images or pictures are visible; nothing can be made out except a vague series of concentric circles. However, when a laser beam of the correct frequency is shined through the plate from behind, the holographic image springs to life. It is visible as an incredibly realistic representation of the photographed object or scene. If the viewer looks at it from different angles, the perspective of the image changes as he moves, with the result that he can see "around" and "behind" objects in the scene.

Three-dimensional moving holographic pictures—holographic movies—are a recent development in the field. They are produced by shining laser beams through ordinary 35-mm. movie film to produce a holographic film. The simplest way to project the film is to display it inside a wide glass cylinder, illuminated with an ordinary incandescent light bulb. When the viewer moves around the cylinder, the pictures appear to move. As the viewer stops, however, so does the action. Holographic movies may also be projected before an audience in the usual manner, but this method is still quite primitive. The angle of vision is so small that only a few persons can view the moving picture at a time.

One of the most interesting features of holograms is that each fragment of the holographic plate contains the entire image. If part of the hologram is cut away, the whole image still remains. In fact, if a laser light beam is passed through only a tiny point of the hologram, the entire scene will still be projected, although this view of the scene will be from a slightly different perspective than the view created if the laser beam is shined through another point on the hologram.

It is expected that holograms will provide a much more efficient way of storing information than microfilm, since holograms can squeeze so much more information into a single point on the plate. It has been estimated that a hologram the size of an ordinary postcard could store all the information contained in 3,000 telephone books.

More details on holography can be found in M. Wenyon, *Understanding Holography* (Arco, 1978).

THE UNIVERSE

The Big Bang

The universe is believed to have begun with a "Big Bang," a gigantic explosion which created every bit of matter that now exists.

The Big Bang theory, which involves making several exceptions to general relativity theory, maintains that the universe was born from a "singularity" of infinite density and infinitessimal volume. It has been proposed that this entity may have resulted from the collapse of a previous universe which then erupted through a space-time "wormhole" to form the present universe. The initial Big Bang explosion would have occurred at temperatures so extreme that they are meaningful only in terms of relativistic energies of individual subatomic particles.

In *The First Three Minutes*, Steven Weinberg of Harvard University, spells out what presumably happened during and immediately after the Big Bang. Subatomic particles, the building blocks of all matter, began to form a few hundredths of a second after the explosion. At first, the extreme temperature would have prevented the formation of any but the most elementary particles. Electrons and their anti-matter counterparts, positrons, are both nearly weightless and would have been some of the earliest recognizable particles to emerge. The particles that make up the "heavy" nuclei of atoms—protons and neutrons—came later. After 3 minutes and 46 seconds, the fledgling universe had cooled sufficiently for a proton and neutron to hold on to one another; this formed deuterium, or the nucleus of what would eventually be an atom of helium. Not until 600,000 *years* later did temperatures cool to the point at which nuclei could link up with electrons to form true atoms.

The Big Bang would have produced a unified, undifferentiated, rapidly expanding cloud of subatomic particles. Such a perfectly uniform hot gas could theoretically have gone on expanding forever. There is no actual rule of physics that states that particles in this gas cloud should have joined together to form atoms—and yet they did. Why?

Some theoretists simply assume that the necessary density variations (on the order of 2 percent) existed in the gas. A more popular theory holds that gravity pulled the particles together; but gravity is a very weak force that does not operate at the subatomic level, and it is difficult to see how it could have provided the necessary impetus. A third theory is that of Gordon Lasher, an IBM physicist, who proposed a refinement to the Big Bang theory in which shock waves of a particular kind were propagated in the primeval gas, thus knocking particles together to form atoms.

Lasher starts with the fact that at the moment of the Big Bang, only the most elementary particles would have existed. These are known in physics as quarks. They are in reality hardly particles at all but rather "collections of potentialities." One of the specific properties of quarks is that they do not exist in a free state (they have been observed only in the laboratory). If a dense fluid of free quarks had existed at the precise point in time when the universe began, the quarks' inherent instability would have set up shock waves and perturbations as soon as the primeval quark fluid began to expand.

The situation would have been somewhat analogous to opening a bottle of soda water. When the bottle is opened, pressure is released, allowing the dissolved gas in the soda to expand. Bubbles form spontaneously, causing the liquid to fizz. In the same manner, the expanding quark fluid is thought to have created "bubbles" as the quarks spontaneously coalesced. This process would have generated tremendous temperatures and catastrophic shock waves. These shock waves could have provided the initial impetus to knock particles together into atoms—and atoms together into stars and galaxies.

It has also been hypothesized that supernovas may have played a part in the formation of the early universe. Dr. Jeremiah Ostriker of Princeton University proposed that shock waves from huge supernovas propagated outward through the young universe, causing the collapse of gaseous material into stars and galaxies. (See *The New York Times*, February 17, 1980, p. 1.) This concept could help account for the continuing evolution of the universe. As described by Dr. Philip Charles of the University of California at Berkeley, one of the initial supernovas would have caused perhaps 1,000 new stars to form. A million years later, about ten of these stars would have become supernovas themselves, exploding and triggering the formation of new stars.

Large galaxies were theoretically formed by the chain-reaction explosions of perhaps twenty to one hundred huge supernovas. Quasars, distant objects thought to be new galaxies in the formative stages, emit particularly strong X-rays. It is believed that this heavy radiation resulted from the explosion of the supernovas that gave birth to the quasars. The sun and its planets probably started forming about 4.6 billion years ago following a supernova explosion.

Quasars

Of all the objects in the sky, quasars are probably the most enigmatic. They appear to be the brightest and remotest objects in the universe, but while astronomers can describe some of their characteristics, they have as yet no real idea of their true nature.

The discovery of quasars in the early 1960s was wholly unexpected. The first quasars were described by Allan R. Sandage of Hale Observatories and Maarten Schmidt at Mount Palomar, and since then over 200 quasars have been found and named. At first they were assumed to resemble stars and were therefore named "quasi-stellar radio sources," or quasars for short. They have since been found to resemble no known objects in the universe, and they appear to be far brighter than any star. By measuring the amount of "red shift" in the spectrum of light emitted by a distant object, astronomers are able to calculate its velocity and its distance, and, by inference, its intensity. (See *Red Shift*, p. 172.) By these measurements, quasars turn out to be extremely distant objects—in fact, the most distant objects in the universe—up to 10 billion light years from the earth. (A light year is 5.8 trillion miles, the distance light travels in a year.) This would also make quasars some of the oldest objects in the universe, as the light rays we now detect from quasars started their journey toward earth 10 billion years ago.

Quasars seem to be receding from earth at astronomical speeds approaching the speed of light. A quasar identified in 1974 by a team of Arizona astronomers has been "clocked" at 177,000 miles per second, faster than any previously observed quasar. Because quasars are so far away, they must be almost inconceivably brilliant in order to be detected on earth at all. They appear not only to be brighter than individual stars but brighter than whole

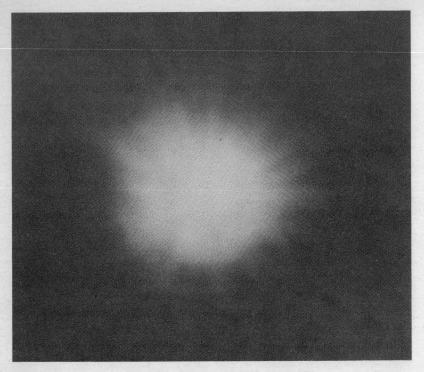

An artist's impression of a quasar. (Hamlyn Group Picture Library)

galaxies. For instance, our own galaxy, the Milky Way, contains 100 billion stars, many of them more powerful than the sun. Yet a single quasar is 200 times as bright as the entire Milky Way.

A pair of "twin" quasars was discovered in 1979 by astronomers at Kitt Peak National Observatory in Arizona. The paired objects appeared to be 150,000 light years apart—not a huge distance by cosmic standards—and to have identical light spectrums and velocities. This was an extraordinary coincidence and it was suggested that perhaps the two quasars were in fact one and the same—and that the light emitted from the quasar had been split in space into two mirror images. Such a split could theoretically occur, according to Einstein's general theory of relativity, if the light from the quasar encountered a massive object on its way to the earth. Such an object would act as a "gravitational lens," bending the quasar's light rays and splitting them apart like a wedge. To produce the effect noted at Kitts Peak, such an object would have to be incredibly massive, a galaxy or black hole at least 10 trillion times as massive as the sun. Further observation of the twin quasars by astronomers at the National Radio Astronomy Observatory near Socorro, New Mexico, however, indicates that the two quasars are not exact mirror images of each other. One of them appears to have two jets of material shooting out from it. It would seem, then, that the two quasars are in fact closely-paired twins which were probably formed and evolved at about the same time and in the same environment.

So far, astronomers have not been able to explain exactly what quasars really are, and in particular how an object can be so bright and so fast-moving. One theory propounds that quasars are formed by large numbers of stars exploding in rapid succession. Exploding stars, or novas, are well known to scientists—about once per century such an explosion takes place in the Milky Way—and it is conceivable that a chain reaction of supernovas could occur in various parts of the universe, one supernova touching off others like a falling row of dominoes. Such a constellation of supernovas would presumably approach the brightness of a quasar.

It has also been suggested that quasars might represent, in some as yet unexplained way, the interaction of matter and anti-matter. (See *Antimatter*, p. 174.) When these two substances collide, they annihilate each other in a tremendous burst of energy. If quasars were in fact cosmic furnaces for the destruction of matter and anti-matter, it would account for their incredible brilliance.

Perhaps the most disturbing possibility, however, is that quasars in reality are not distant objects at all and are much closer to the earth, and much less bright, than currently thought. As it is, quasars' velocity, brightness, and distance are only inferences based upon the degree of their observed red shifts. If it should turn out that the scientific dogma of red shift is inaccurate or incomplete, quasars might have to be radically reevaluated. Such a scientific upset would cause reverberations in every area of astronomy as well. This possibility, based upon observed anomalies in red shift, has been espoused by, among others, Dr. Harold Arp of the California Institute of Technology (see *The New York Times*, October 16, 1979, p. C-1), who has argued that quasars may actually be very young objects to which the normal laws of red shift do not apply.

Black Holes

A black hole is a collapsed star of such extreme density that its gravitational pull prevents the escape of any material, even light rays, from it. Even if it is white hot, it cannot be seen and appears to be literally a hole in space. Not all physicists and astronomers believe that black holes even exist, and no one can describe exactly what takes place inside them, for the normal laws of physics break down when applied to such dense objects.

Because black holes emit neither light nor radio waves, physicists can only infer their characteristics, and indeed their very existence, from their effects on neighboring stars. The reality of black holes was first proposed to explain the strange behavior of Epsilon Aurigae, a giant star 60,000 times as bright as the sun, which fades to half its usual brilliance every 27 years. It was presumed that Epsilon Aurigae must be one of a pair of stars that revolved around each other and that the other star must "get in the way" of Epsilon Aurigae's light rays. However, this partner was itself invisible, emitting no light rays of its own. The only explanation seemed to be that it was a super-massive object that gave no direct physical evidence of itself. It was labeled a black hole.

Support for the existence of black holes comes from other observed astronomical anomalies as well. Instellar gas being sucked into a black hole by the black hole's intense gravitational field would theoretically be expected to become superheated and give off X-rays before vanishing. Such X-rays have in fact been detected precisely as postulated.

Astrophysicists believe that black holes are created by the collapse of old and dying stars. When the supply of nuclear fuel within a star begins to be exhausted, the star implodes, i.e., collapses inward. Relatively small stars of approximately the size of the sun become small cool objects known as "white dwarfs." Somewhat larger stars, over half again as large as the sun, implode with such violence that a huge explosion of gas, known as a supernova, results; a tiny part of the star's mass, known as a neutron star, remains as a super-dense core at the center. In even larger stars, 50 times or more the size of the sun, the supernova explosion is correspondingly greater and the remaining mass in the center is thought in some cases to be so small and tightly packed as to become a black hole. A collapsing star 10 times bigger than the sun would theoretically leave behind a black hole only 40 miles in diameter.

This theory of black hole formation is lent support by observations of Cassiopeia A, a celestial object that has long been one of astronomy's strangest mysteries. Cassiopeia A is located 9,000 light years from earth and is the strongest radio source in the heavens after the sun. It is a gigantic shell of gas that is the remains of a supernova explosion which, from its measured rate of expansion, can be pinpointed as having taken place late in the seventeenth century. Even though this supernova would have been of an intensity surpassing every other star in the sky, it was not noticed by any astronomers of the time, an almost inconceivable oversight. Russian astrophysicist Iosef S. Shklovsky has suggested that the exploding star that created Cassiopeia A collapsed, not into a neutron star, but into a black hole. (See *Nature*, June 21, 1979.) A supernova with a black hole at its center would not have been visible on earth, since only those supernovas with a neutron star center emit visible light. Further support for this hypothesis comes from the fact that no iron-group elements are to be found in the spectrum of Cassiopeia A; this implies that all heavy elements such as iron must have remained behind, presumably in the black hole, when the supernova exploded.

Because they are so dense and have such strong forces of gravity, black holes suck up any matter that enters their gravitational fields. This effect has been observed in HDE 226868, a star in the constellation of Cygnus, which is believed to be paired with a black hole. HDE 226868 is losing clouds of gas from its perimeter, and the gas is presumably being absorbed by the neighboring black hole.

Black holes hold no possibility of being explored, for a space probe would be demolished by the black hole's gravity before it could approach or enter the object itself. Nor could any radio transmission escape from the black hole. A black hole is surrounded by what is known as an "event horizon." This is the point at which the object's gravity decreases to the extent of allowing the escape of light rays. Inside the event horizon, no light rays can emerge. Beyond the event horizon, they move at greater and greater speeds—like a rocket at lift-off—as the black hole's gravitational field is left behind. Precisely at the event horizon, light rays can neither escape nor be pulled back, an intriguing situation that means that light stands still. Events that take place on the event horizon would thus be visible forever. For instance, a space probe, at the moment in entered the event horizon, would be frozen in time as a light image, even though the probe itself continued to hurtle into the hole. Since the image would remain forever, time would in effect be standing still.

Because matter is superheated as it enters a black hole, thus giving off great quantities of energy, some theorists have proposed that in the far distant future, black holes might be used by man as energy sources. The black hole would function in effect as a cosmic garbage can or incinerator, sucking in any unwanted rubbish that was aimed in its direction and giving off valuable energy in return.

What eventually happens to black holes? Presumably, like all stars, they have a finite life span. Stephen Hawkins, a British scientist, has suggested that they slowly "evaporate." At this stage in the history of the universe, however, only very small black holes would have reached the point of cosmic senescence and disappeared; most presumably have a long remaining life still ahead.

Red Shift

The red shift is an astronomical phenomenon in which light rays reaching the earth from deep space sometimes seem to have been "stretched out" in relation to normal light rays. Astronomers and physicists are in disagreement as to both the causes and the meanings of this mysterious behavior.

When light from a glowing stellar object such as a star or galaxy reaches the earth, the rays can be broken up in an astrological observatory, using prism techniques, into the familiar rainbow spectrum. Lines can be observed at particular points in the spectrum, interspersed between the vivid colors. These lines are caused by specific elements in the distant light source which emit light of one particular wavelength. Under certain conditions, these lines are shifted toward the red end of the spectrum. The wavelengths of the rays emitted by the elements in the light source are therefore longer than they would ordinarily be. There is also an analagous but opposite blue shift, in which the incoming light rays are shortened and thus shifted toward the blue end of the spectrum.

Edwin Hubble, an American astronomer generally regarded as the father of modern cosmology, proposed the current explanation of red shift in the 1920s. He postulated that the red shift effect is due to distance, i.e., the further a star or galaxy is from the earth, the greater its red shift. A corollary assumption was that the further away a star or galaxy was, the faster it must be receding from the earth. It is a generally held assumption now that the red shift alone is enough both to determine the distance and velocity of a distant cosmic light source.

A number of anomalies have cropped up, however, which throw doubt upon the accuracy of the present interpretation of the red shift. One such problem concerns our own sun. Light coming from the edge of the sun seems to display a significantly greater red shift than light emanating from its center. This cannot be explained under the current red shift thesis, which implies that all light rays emanating from the sun should show substantially the same amount of red shift. Another anomaly concerns the faint radio background, still detectible in the universe, of the original "big bang" which is widely believed to have given birth to the universe. Edward S. Cheng and researchers at the Massachusetts Institute of Technology and Princeton University have discovered that this cosmic radio background appears to be stronger in one direction than in another, which seems to violate the hypothesis that it should be equally strong no matter from which direction it is picked up on earth.

Several possible explanations for these anomalies have been proposed. Though astronomers still agree that light from rapidly receding stellar objects is shifted toward the red end of the spectrum, it now seems that red shift may be caused by other agencies besides distance and velocity.

Theorists at the Israeli Institute of Technology in Haifa have demonstrated that in some cases red shifts might be caused simply by gravity. By this thesis, the mass of a stellar light source would be capable of affecting the wave lengths of the light it emitted.

Observations by numerous astronomers have shown that certain galaxies which are apparently closely linked in space show entirely different red shifts. According to standard theory, they should show nearly identical red shifts. It has been argued that such galaxies are not really linked at all but merely look that way due to accidental juxtaposition on photographic plates, but the phenomenon occurs in so many instances that the probability of such galactic associations being merely illusory is rather small.

Other astronomers argue that quasars may cause unexplained anomalies in red shift patterns. Quasars are mysterious poorly-understood radio sources in deep space. (See *Quasars*, p. 167.) The spectra of quasars often show such massive red shifts that they seem to be receding from us at the speed of light. This would seem to indicate that they must be near the outer edge of the universe, billions of light years from earth. However, it is then difficult to explain how they can appear so bright to us. At that distance, they would have to be far more intense than entire galaxies, an uneasy assumption at best. Observations by a number of astronomers have indicated that some quasars may actually be relatively nearby, which would help explain their observed brightness but would make their large red shifts even more mysterious. One possible explanation is that such quasars may be composed of newly formed "young" matter which has an inherently high red shift.

Further information on red shift may be found in *The New York Times*, October 16, 1979, p. C-1.

Antimatter

The laboratory discovery of antimatter began in the 1930s. Since then, it has been shown that for every particle of matter created, a corresponding particle of antimatter is also created. The two particles are identical except that they carry opposite charges.

Thus, the negatively charged electron has as its antiparticle the positively charged positron. The antiproton is the negatively charged counterpart of the normal proton. Antineutrons are the antimatter twins of neutrons. Antiparticles have been found for virtually all subatomic particles.

The section of the universe that contains the earth and the solar system is made up almost entirely of matter, but it has been theorized that other sections of the universe may be composed predominantly of antimatter—antisuns, antistars, antiplanets, etc.

When particles of matter and antimatter collide, they annihilate each other, releasing several new particles and a burst of energy. When a positron and an electron meet, for instance, the resulting annihilation produces two gamma rays of precisely 511 kilo-electron-volts each.

The laws of physics state that the universe should contain equal amounts of matter and antimatter. Any act of creation—including the creation of the universe—should be balanced between the two. If there was zero before the creation, there must be a net total of zero after, also. That is, the amount of matter must exactly cancel the amount of antimatter.

The problem for cosmologists is that this balance between matter and antimatter is not actually observed in the universe. Very little antimatter has actually been detected, except in the laboratory. And yet, exactly equal amounts of matter and antimatter should theoretically have been created at the moment of the birth of the universe. One theory attempts to explain the lack of observed antimatter by postulating that antimatter is somehow inherently unstable and has decayed to the vanishing point since the beginning of the universe. Another theory holds that antimatter galaxies and stars exist in distant parts of the universe and that they have not yet been detected on earth.

There are problems with both of these theories, however. The idea that antimatter is unstable has been partially refuted by the findings of an experiment conducted in 1979 by researchers at New Mexico State University and the Johnson Space Center in Houston. (See *The New York Times*, October 17, 1979.) Using sophisticated measuring equipment sent into the upper atmosphere by helium balloon, they found traces of antiparticles in space. In particular, antiprotons were discovered that were apparently far from unstable. The age of antiprotons in cosmic rays can be determined by measuring the radioactive decay of certain of their atoms. The antiprotons detected in the experiment appeared to be on the order of ten million years old. This would appear then to weaken the hypothesis that antimatter undergoes rapid decay.

The theory that bulk antimatter—antigalaxies, antistars, etc.—may exist elsewhere in the universe has not yet received conclusive experimental verification, either. Various experiments have been carried out in attempts to locate such concentrations of antimatter but have been, at best, only partially successful. In a 1978 experiment at Bell Laboratories and Sandia Laboratories in New Mexico, researchers discovered evidence of heavy concentrations of antimatter, specifically positrons, at the center of the Milky Way. The researchers felt, however, that these positrons were probably not evidence of bulk antimatter. More likely, they simply resulted from high-energy bombardments such as take place in laboratories under experimental conditions. Positrons would have resulted, then, from the radioactive decay from supernova explosions or from the collision of cosmic rays with interstellar matter. The presence of antistars is held to be the least likely explanation for the abundance of antimatter. (See *Science News*, May 6, 1978, p. 292.)

These difficulties of antimatter theory result basically because of the scientific tenet that the laws of physics never change. Physical laws are supposed to be universal, applying at all times and in all places. R. L. Golden of New Mexico State University has noted that scientific conundrums such as that relating to antimatter would evaporate if the laws of physics changed under different conditions. (See *Science News*, October 27, 1979.) In that case, the parity of matter and antimatter might no longer apply, say, under the conditions of extreme gravity found in a black hole or those of extreme temperature experienced at the birth of the universe.

175

Closed Universe

The "Big Bang" that created the universe sent stars and galaxies hurtling into space in all directions. The universe is still expanding as a result of this initial explosion. Will the universe eventually stop expanding? The "closed universe" theory says that it will. The "open universe" hypothesis says that it will go on expanding forever.

The closed-universe theory proposes that the universe is a cyclic phenomenon, eternally expanding and contracting. The birth of the present universe may have taken place when a previous universe collapsed inward upon itself and then exploded outwards again. The universe is still expanding at tremendous rates. In 60 million years, however, this outward rush is expected to stop. The universe will then fall in upon itself, collapse to a single point, and then explode again, starting the whole process again.

The eventual fate of the universe depends on how much mass actually comprises the universe. If the universe and all its parts—galaxies, stars, interstellar gas and dust—add up to a certain critical level of mass, then the gravitational force of this mass will eventually stop the outward flight of the universe. Gravity will then pull the universe back in upon itself, like a collapsing balloon.

Principal support for the closed-universe theory originally came from experimental observations that the intergalactic spaces of the universe were filled with a cosmic "radio flux" that seemed to have been generated by the original Big Bang. This radio flux was assumed to represent clouds of cosmic gas which had never coalesced into stars or galaxies. These huge amounts of intergalactic gas were assumed to provide the added mass that would bring the universe to the critical level required before gravity would cause it to implode; the actual mass of stars and galaxies alone is *not* sufficient to overcome the outward drift of the universe, but the added mass of the gas would just tip the scales.

Several astronomical observations have cast doubt upon these assumptions, making it more likely that the "open" or expanding-universe theory is the true one.

Observations by the X-ray satellite *Einstein* have indicated that there may actually be very little intergalactic gas in the universe. The X-ray "radio flux" that was previously believed to come from pervasive gas clouds has actually been shown to originate instead from stars, galaxies, or quasars. If little or no intergalactic gas exists, the universe will not achieve a critical mass and will go on expanding forever.

Evidence gathered by astronomers at the Harvard/Smithsonian Center for Astrophysics in Massachusetts, the Steward Observatory and the Kitt Peak National Observatory, both in Arizona, suggests furthermore that the universe is actually expanding twice as fast as had previously been believed. (See *The New York Times*, November 14, 1979.) The universe may also be younger than suspected, only nine billion years old rather than the fifteen to eighteen billion years previously estimated.

If the open-universe theory turns out to be correct, the universe will go on expanding forever, becoming colder and deader with passing eons. Recent research into the basic laws of physics, such as the Second Law of Thermodynamics, tends to support this hypothesis. Dr. Ilya Prigogine, Nobel Prize chemist in 1977, stated: "At the moment, we know from experiments that the Second Law of Thermodynamics applies to the universe at short range, but gravitational effects are not well understood. We know little about the formation of black holes, and so on. To speak about the universe as a whole, to call it a closed system doomed by the Second Law, that is an extrapolation that goes beyond the present limits of knowledge. But I think that the universe is not closed, and that we cannot assume it is doomed by the Second Law." (See *The New York Times*, May 29, 1979, p. C-1.)

Cannibal Galaxies

Some galaxies are cannibals, swallowing up smaller galaxies that approach too closely to the major galaxy's gravitational field. Galaxies, even small ones, consist of hundreds of millions of stars in addition to primordial gas clouds.

The first scientific evidence of galactic cannibalism was reported by astronomers at the Cerro Tololo Interamerican Observatory in Chile. Studies of a galaxy known as NGC 1316 showed evidence that it had consumed a smaller galaxy with a mass roughly equivalent to 100 times that of our sun. Analysis of radio signals from NGC 1316 indicated that the smaller galaxy continued to rotate inside it; the parent galaxy does not rotate at all. The radio profile of NGC 1316 indicates that it has a deformed bulge, much like a snake that has swallowed a rat.

Because many other large galaxies also exhibit such bulges and deformities, it is assumed that galactic cannibalism is quite common.

UNIDENTIFIED FLYING OBJECTS

Extraterrestrial Life

The idea that life may exist on other planets in the universe is an accepted scientific hypothesis. Dr. Carl Sagan, an astronomer at Harvard University, and Dr. Frank Drake of the National Radio Astronomy Observatory, have estimated that intelligent life may have evolved on at least 1 million planets in our own galaxy alone. Highly advanced technological civilizations are also thought to exist in most of the other tens of billions of galaxies scattered throughout the universe. Though we have had no convincing and incontrovertible proof of the existence of extraterrestrial life, it is assumed by many scientists that such life must surely exist: there are simply so many stars in the universe that *some* of them must have solar systems capable of supporting life.

It is generally assumed that life will spontaneously arise on any suitable planet provided that the surface temperature is moderate enough for there to be liquid water on the planet's surface. Higher forms of life will evolve if the planet remains continuously equable for long periods of time. Organisms capable of conducting photosynthesis will arise in 800 million years. Intelligent life comparable to our own requires a time span of from 3 to 4 billion years.

A suitable planet for the evolution of life, in addition to having a stable temperature, would also have to possess all or most of the elements that go into the make-up of living things—elements such as carbon, oxygen, hydrogen, nitrogen, iron, etc. When these elements are present in a primitive salt-water solution such as existed on the young Earth, spontaneous chemical reactions—especially those triggered by electrical shocks like lightning—give rise to simple amino acids, sugars, and nitrogenous bases that are the building blocks of life.

While these arguments in support of the existence of extraterrestrial life are undeniable, they have been challenged by a more recent view that postulates that evolved life, if it exists at all on other planets in our galaxy (the Milky Way), may not be nearly as common as has been widely assumed. Several reasons are cited. In the first place, there may be fewer planetary systems in the Milky Way than was at first thought. Most stars belong to binary pairs—they are twins, in effect—and this condition prevents the formation of planetary matter. Dr. J. Patrick Harrington of the University of Maryland has stated (see *The New York Times*, November 4, 1979, p. 12) that "the formation of a planetary system is a rare event." No planets outside of our own solar system have so far been detected. Barnard's star, which is relatively close to the sun, exhibits anomalous behavior that was once believed to be attributable to the presence of planets, but new observations have shown this view to be incorrect. (See *The New York Times*, November 4, 1979.)

Furthermore, a planet hospitable to life must contain the requisite large number of basic chemical elements. (The Earth itself contains nearly one hundred in naturally-occurring forms.) Most planets are probably of much simpler composition, however, consisting mostly of light elements like hydrogen and helium. These planets would closely resemble Jupiter and Saturn and would be unable to support life as we know it.

A life-supporting planet must also be positioned at a precise distance from its sun, so that it is neither too hot nor too cold. The continuously habitable zone (CHZ) around a star is quite small. Michael H. Hart reported (see *Science News*, January 29, 1977, p. 68) that if the earth were 5 percent closer to the sun, the planet would be too hot to support life: a "runaway greenhouse effect" would have occurred 4 billion years ago. And if the earth were 1 percent further from the sun, it would have undergone permanent glaciation 2 billion years ago. Further, if the earth's orbital path were more elliptical than it is, the planet would suffer from disastrous yearly extremes of temperature that would also prevent the occurrence of evolved life.

A computer simulation of the CHZ's around various other types of stars in the Milky Way established that continuously habitable zones were rare. (See *Science News*, February 24, 1979, p. 121.) Stars which are smaller and less luminous than the sun have correspondingly smaller CHZs. Stars whose mass is less than 83 percent of the sun's have *no* continuously habitable zone at all. Stars larger than the sun have slightly wider CHZs, but are beset by other problems. A star only 10 percent larger than the sun would emit so much ultraviolet radiation after 4 billion years that life would probably be unable to exist on dry land. And a star 20 percent larger than the sun would probably have been too hot to support life after a mere 400 million years.

All attempts to detect life from other worlds have as yet been unfruitful. Since 1960, radio telescopes have been monitoring the skies, but no intelligible signals have been identified. Astronomers on earth have also been sending out radio signals, but no replies have yet been received, nor can they be expected for many years. It would take 300 or more years for such an earth-originating signal to reach even a "close" star. If the signal elicited a response from an intelligent civilization, it would take another 300 years for the signal to return to earth.

Even if the earth were to prove unique in the galaxy as the only planet to harbor life as we know it, that would not rule out the possibility of other forms of life existing elsewhere in the universe. Dr. Gerald Feinberg of Columbia University and Dr. Robert Shapiro of New York University have stated (in *The New York Times*, November 11, 1979, p. 12) that life need not necessarily be based on water and carbon, as it is on earth. A silicon-based life chemistry might be a possibility at very high temperatures, and it is even possible to conceive of a kind of radiation-based life form that would depend on the organization of energy rather than matter.

The UFO Phenomenon

A Gallup poll released in 1978 indicated that 9 percent of those polled had seen a UFO. This figure corresponds to a national total of 13 million American adults who claim to have witnessed an unidentified flying object.

The modern UFO phenomenon began in 1947. The term "flying saucer" was coined in that year when Idaho businessman Kenneth Arnold saw nine discs flying in formation and said that the motion of each disc resembled a "saucer skipping over water." UFO reports became more common in subsequent years, with particularly intense waves of sightings, or "UFO flaps," occurring in 1952, 1957, 1965–67, and 1973–74. UFO reports have also been widespread in most other countries of the world, especially the Soviet Union.

Most UFO sightings are eventually explained in terms of relatively common natural objects or occurrences. Thus, most UFOs turn out to have been airplanes, weather balloons, meteors, planets, etc. The U.S. Air Force, in its Project Blue Book investigation of over 13,000 UFO sightings, concluded that roughly 94 percent yielded to convincing natural explanations, a figure with which even critics of the Air Force study have agreed. An explained UFO becomes an IFO, or 'identified flying object.'

Statistically, most UFO sightings occur at night and in rural areas. Few UFO reports emanate from cities, probably for the reason that the bright lights of a city make it difficult to view the night sky with clarity. Astronomers as a group report fewer UFO sightings than other segemnts of the population, presumably because they are skilled at identifying natural or stellar objects that other observers confuse with UFOs. In a 1976 poll of members of the American Astronomical Society (AAS), 2 percent of those polled reported having seen unidentified flying objects.

The UFO phenomenon has generated a great deal of study, discussion, and controversy since 1947. Various agencies of the U.S. government, such as the Air Force, the Department of Defense, and the CIA, have at one time or another devoted serious attention to the subject. A succession of Air Force projects, code named Sign, Grudge, and Blue Book, were terminated in 1969 when the Air Force formally withdrew from the UFO field on the recommendation of a lengthy study conducted by the University of Colorado (known as the Condon Report). Many other public and private UFO study groups are currently in existence, such as the Center for UFO Studies (CUFOS) and the National Investigations Committee on Aerial Phenomenon (NICAP).

A running debate between UFO believers and UFO skeptics shows no sign of abating. Supporters of the theory that UFOs are actually spacecraft from alien worlds base their arguments upon the sheer numbers of UFO sightings that have occurred and continue to occur. Even though most of these sightings are eventually explainable in natural terms, proponents of this theory state that there are still so many unexplained reports that at least some of them must represent visitations from elsewhere in the galaxy. Critics of the UFO believers point to the lack of incontrovertible, tangible evidence of UFO visitations, declaring that this lack is highly suggestive that all UFOs are actually explainable in natural terms.

The pro-UFO faction includes a number of prominent Americans, including former President Jimmy Carter. Carter sighted a UFO on the night of January 6, 1969 while he was still governor of Georgia. That UFO has since been shown rather conclusively to have been the planet Venus, but

Carter is on record as having said: "I'm convinced that UFOs exist because I have seen one."

The term 'UFO' is often considered as being synonymous with 'spacecraft,' an error in semantics that often leads to confusion on the subject. A UFO is exactly what its name stands for, i.e., an unidentified flying object. Merely because it is unidentified or unidentifiable does not necessarily mean that it is a spaceship from another world. In answer to the question, "Do UFOs really exist?", the technically correct reply is, of course, "Yes." Unidentified objects do exist. It should be understood, however, that this is not the same thing as saying that alien spaceships necessarily exist.

Supporters of the extraterrestrial explanation for UFOs have suggested that UFOs may represent other extraterrestrial phenomenon apart from spacecraft, among them "interpenetrating universes" and "psychokinetically generated by-products . . . quasi-physical." UFO debunkers, on the other hand, feel that extraterrestrial or supernatural explanations are unnecessary, and that even farfetched natural explanations are more convincing and more probable statistically than extraterrestrial explanations.

Explanations for UFOs

The statistical records show that almost 95% of all reported UFO sightings are readily explainable in natural terms; this figure is agreed to by both UFO supporters and UFO debunkers. Mistaken sightings occur simply because ground observers are not thoroughly familiar with all the objects, manmade or natural, that sometimes appear in the sky. Thus, any strange object that is not immediately identifiable is likely to be reported as a UFO. Since the first 'flying saucer' sightings in 1947, objects as disparate as balloons or birds, meteors or mirages, have been mistaken for supposed extraterrestrial spacecraft.

The following is a list of the most common sources of UFO misidentifications:

1. **Meteors**. Fireball meteors are reported as UFOs more often than any other objects. Any UFO reported as glowing with brilliant light and moving at a high speed is likely to prove to have been a meteor. Such fireballs often follow trajectories that appear from the ground to be nearly horizontal, thus leading unsophisticated viewers to suspect that the object must be an

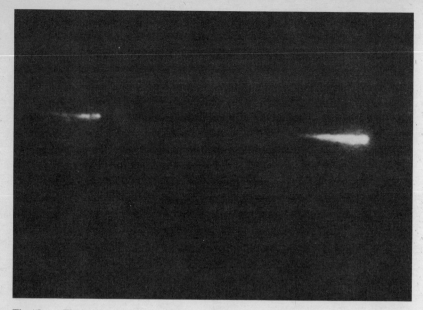

The "Iowa Fireball" over Peoria, Illinois on the afternoon of June 5, 1969. (Al Harkrader/ *Peoria Journal Star* photo)

airborne craft moving under its own propulsion. Meteor UFO sightings are most common during annual meteor showers in October/November and July.

2. **Stars and planets**. Many astronomical bodies have been reported as UFOs. For instance, there are cases on record of pilots taking dangerous evasive maneuvers to avoid hitting an object that turned out to be the moon. The most common astronomical UFO is Venus, which often appears in the sky as a brilliant morning star and has become known as the "Queen of the UFOs." It may seem difficult to believe that planets could give rise to such gross misconceptions, but UFO investigators regularly receive reports in which planets are mistaken for UFOs that are alleged to have emitted beams of light, glowed with different colors, moved or spun, or changed shape. Any UFO which is reported as a bright, stationary (or slowly rising) point of light must be suspected of being a planet.

3. **Airplanes**. Aircraft of various kinds, particularly slow-flying planes (which produce little sound) and planes with colored lights or searchlights, are easily mistaken for unidentified flying objects.

4. **Balloons**. Weather balloons and information-gathering balloons are regularly released by meteorologists and scientists and are just as regularly mistaken for unidentified craft.

5. **Clouds**. Various highly unusual cloud formations occur during freak weather conditions and appear as close approximations of classic "flying saucers."

6. **Anomalous Radar Propagation**. This phenomenon is responsible for many so-called "radar UFOs." Under certain weather conditions, usually involving temperature inversions, radar signals cause strange mirage-like blips on radar screens, known as "angels" or "bogies." These phantoms are often indistinguishable from the radar blips caused by genuine aircraft.

7. **Satellites and rockets**. These manmade objects are repeatedly reported as UFOs. Orbiting rocket debris gave rise to many of the so-called "astronaut UFOs."

8. **Plasma**. Plasma, or ball lightning, is a poorly understood natural phenomenon. Often occurring near power lines, free-floating plasmas glow with various colors and move at varying speeds. It is not known how many UFO reports they may account for, but several classic sightings have been tentatively attributed to them. (See *Ball Lightning*, p. 155.)

9. **Visual anomalies**. Tricks of vision, such as mirages and reflections, are responsible for a percentage of UFO reports. Many heavenly bodies, even the sun and moon, when appearing under mirage conditions, cannot be immediately identified and are reported as UFOs.

10. **Birds**. Either single birds or flocks have led to a number of UFO reports. Owls and sea-gulls seem to have been the main culprits.

In illustration, the Air Force Project Blue Book tallied identified UFOs, or IFOs, from 1953 through 1965 placing them into the following categories:

Meteors	1,396
Aircraft	1,367
Stars & planets	940
Balloons	691
Satellites	563
Missiles & rockets	93
Searchlights	89
Chaff, birds	75
Flares, fireworks	63
Reflections	61
Clouds	48
Mirages, inversions	43

Special attention must be given to two other UFO categories: hoaxes and hallucinations. Many UFO reports, especially those involving photographs of alleged UFOs, turn out to be hoaxes. Hallucinations, though not involving intent to deceive, may be equally misleading. Hallucinations of various kinds occur more frequently than is realized, especially to impressionable people, and often an initial stimulus is elaborated in the viewer's mind into a complex tale of a UFO sighting. "Highway hypnosis" is a relatively common but little-known affliction that can affect long-distance drivers, especially at night. It leads to hallucinations of various objects standing on the highway or at the side of the road. Another optical anomaly known as the autokinetic effect, while not an actual hallucination, also accounts for many mistaken UFO reports. Autokinesis is a sort of optical illusion in which stationary objects, such as stars or planets, appear to move, especially if the observer stares at the object fixedly.

Lastly, there is the problem of the unreliability of human testimony. UFO investigators, even dedicated UFO believers, remark over and over on the inability of most observers to accurately describe what they see. If a group of people jointly spot a UFO, their later testimony in most cases is astonishingly disparate. Air Force investigations during the period of Project Blue Book showed that, in general, engineers and scientists were the most reliable witnesses; only 50 percent of their reported UFO sightings could be ruled out conclusively as misperceptions. Other groups scored less well. Surprisingly, airline pilots and radar technicians did quite poorly; 80 to 90 percent of their UFO reports were based on clear misperceptions of what they saw.

Selected Listing of Pre-1900 UFO Reports

1270. Bristol, England. Aerial craft observed over city. The craft caught an "anchor" in a church steeple, and an occupant of the ship who scampered down a ladder to free the anchor was "burned and asphyxiated" by the earth's atmosphere.

1561. Nuremberg, Germany. Circular disks observed by many people in the neighborhood of the rising sun. The disks "appeared to fall to the ground as if it was all on fire and everything was consumed amid a great haze."

August 7, 1566. Switzerland. A large number of "black balls" were observed moving at high speed toward the sun. They made a half turn and seemed to collide with each other. Many turned "red and fiery" before the lights disappeared.

March 6, 1716. England. The astronomer Edmund Halley observed an object that illuminated the night sky with such brightness that he could read a printed text by its light.

1794. London, England. An observer saw a light in the dark part of the moon. It appeared within the circumference of the moon's circle, "light like a star, as large as a star, in the dark part of the moon."

October, 1816. A large glowing crescent-shaped object seen by many observers over Edinburgh, Scotland.

May 11, 1845. Naples, Italy. Astronomer at a Naples observatory reported seeing a number of luminous discs that left trails in the sky.

March 19, 1847. London, England. A spherical object was observed rising straight up through the clouds.

October 26, 1853. Ragusa, Sicily. A brilliant disc was observed moving through the sky in a westward direction during the early morning hours.

August 11, 1855. Sussex, England. Several luminous round objects were visible for an hour as they crossed the sky. The objects had "spokes like a wheel."

April 6, 1856. Colmar, Germany. A dark object, rounded at one end and pointed at the other and making a low-pitched sound, was seen in the sky.

October 10, 1864. Paris, France. A French astronomer named Leverrier observed a glowing tubular object over Paris.

July, 1868. Capiago, Chile. An aerial object emitting both light and noise was observed. The sound had a metallic clashing quality.

March 22, 1870. A ship in the Atlantic Ocean observed a light gray disc in the sky. The object seemed to have a long tail and it flew against the wind.

August 1, 1871. Marseilles, France. A large red disc hovered over the city for ten minutes.

April 24, 1874. Prague, Czechoslovakia. A "blinding white" object was seen to cross slowly over the face of the moon. It continued to remain visible afterwards.

September 7, 1877. Indiana. Dark objects crossed the sky with lights flashing at four-second intervals.

May 15, 1879. Persian Gulf. The British warship *Vultur* observed two giant luminous wheels as they spun slowly and descended toward sea level. They remained visible for over a half hour.

November 17, 1882. Greenwich, England. Greenwich Observatory reported a large green disc with a mottled appearance. The object was also apparently observed in continental Europe.

July 3, 1884. New York State. Observers over many parts of the state reported seeing a bright round craft with dark markings.

May 25, 1893. Sea of Japan. A formation of disc-shaped objects emitting smoke trails was reported by two British warships.

April 14, 1897. Kansas City. Observers described a torpedo-shaped aerial object. A searchlight shone downward from the craft.

The Record of U.S. Government Involvement

Since 1947, various agencies of the U.S. government have been closely concerned with UFO monitoring and investigation, though they have not always admitted it to the public. UFO experts outside of government have been highly critical of this state of affairs. It appears through recently released government documents that various federal agencies are still involved in the UFO field, if only in a monitoring capacity, despite government denials.

Government involvement in the UFO field began in 1946, when Scandinavians reported sighting cigar-shaped objects in the sky. It was suspected that the Russians were developing a secret weapon with the help of captured German scientists. The CIA (then known as the CIG) started monitoring the situation at that time. When the first "flying saucers" appeared in U.S. skies a year later, the Air Force got into the act, enlisting the help of the FBI in trying to find out what the UFOs really were. J. Edgar Hoover, head of the FBI, assisted the Air Force on the condition that he have "full access to discs recovered."

A security lid was clamped on the subject of UFOs in July, 1947. The Air Force publicly stated that UFOs were either misidentification of natural objects or products of the imagination. Privately, Air Force officials appeared to be as baffled by UFOs as anyone else. Reactions among government officials ranged from naive credulity to paranoid suspicion to outright hostility. In September, 1947, the Army Chiefs of Staff told the Air Force that "the phenomenon reported is of something real and not visionary or fictitious." The Air Force then set up Project Sign to look into the UFO phenomenon.

Project Sign found no evidence that UFOs were Soviet secret weapons, which had been the Air Force's greatest fear. The project's final report, classified top secret, concluded that UFOs were of interplanetary origin. Air Force General Hoyt S. Vandenburg rejected this conclusion for lack of proof, and the report remained classified for the next 12 years.

Another project, code named Grudge, followed. It, too, found no evidence of Soviet secret developments and thus no direct threat to U.S. national security. A press release following the termination of Project Grudge gave the impression that the Air Force was no longer interested in UFOs; but the Air Force continued to collect UFO reports through its regular intelligence channels.

In 1952, a record number of UFO reports led to the establishment of Project Blue Book and the reentry of the CIA into the UFO field. A UFO "flap" in Washington, D.C. in June 1952 precipitated CIA action. From the start, the agency's involvement was kept secret from the public. A 1952 CIA memo stated that "no indication of CIA interest or concern [should] reach the press or public, in view of their probable alarmist tendencies. . ."

The CIA secretly investigated several private UFO organizations at this time, as well as scrutinizing dozens of individuals suspected of "subversive UFO activities." This may have been the genesis of the myth of "the men in black," mysterious UFO investigators who allegedly appear shortly after UFO sightings to question or intimidate witnesses. The CIA recommended that UFO groups be watched "because of their potentially great influence on mass thinking . . . The apparent irresponsibility and the possible use of such groups for subversive purposes should be kept in mind." Surveillance of UFO organizations and enthusiasts continued through the 1950s and 1960s.

Increasing criticism of the Air Force handling of Project Blue Book compelled the Air Force to commission an independent UFO study from the University of Colorado. This study, issued in 1968 as the "Scientific Study of Unidentified Flying Objects," is the now-famous Condon Report. It occasioned a great deal of comment and led to the Air Force's official withdrawal from the UFO field.

The Condon Report received a great deal of criticism for presumably sweeping the UFO phenomenon under the rug. The report concluded that "further extensive study of UFOs probably cannot be justified in the expectation that science will be advanced thereby. . . . We do not think that at this time the federal government ought to set up a major new agency, as some have suggested, for the scientific study of UFOs."

Critics noted that the University of Colorado investigators were unable to find satisfactory explanations for one-third of the UFO cases they investigated. The critics felt that for this reason, the Condon study should have recommended further study of UFOs on a scientific basis. The report was quite candid about the unexplained UFO cases, making no effort to explain them away, as Project Blue Book had done occasionally. Blue Book had, for instance, dismissed the famous Lakenheath UFO as a case of "anomalous radar propagation," whereas the Condon Report admitted frankly that "the probability of anomalous propagation of radar signals . . . seems to be small;" the Condon Report even went so far as to state that "the preponderance of evidence indicates the possibility of a genuine UFO in this case." Condon's critics charged that it was inconsistent to make such statements while simultaneously recommending that the Air Force abandon the UFO field.

As to the problem of what the federal government should do with UFO reports received from the general public, the report concluded: "We are inclined to think that nothing should be done with them." On that recommendation, the Air Force withdrew formally from the UFO field in 1969.

It appears, however, that not only the Air Force but other government agencies have, despite denials, retained an interest in UFOs. For instance, a number of suspicious sightings occurred over nuclear missile and bomber bases in 1975, most notably at Malmstrom Air Force Base in Montana. A Defense Department memo marked confidential stated that efforts by Air Force and SAC helicopters and F-106s had failed to identify the UFOs. The memo concludes: "I have expressed my concern to the Air Force Information Office that we come up soonest with a proposed answer to queries from the press to prevent overraction by the public to reports by the media that may be blown out of proportion."

The Air Force itself today admits only a "transitory" interest in UFOs. Its advice to the public is: "If you see a UFO and you feel the situation warrants it, call your local police." The CIA's current interest in UFOs professedly lies only in "its responsibility to forewarn principally of the possibility that a foreign power might develop a new weapon that might exhibit phenomena that some might characterize as a UFO." A 1976 CIA memo indicates that the CIA is still involved in the UFO field, at least to the extent of monitoring UFOs on an unofficial basis. Another CIA memo states that the agency "has been receiving UFO-related material from many of our Science and Technology sources. . . . These scientists include some who have been associated with the Agency for years and whose credentials remove them from the 'nut' variety."

Is the government still harboring secret unreleased documents relating to UFOs? Representatives of Ground Saucer Watch (GSW), which successfully sued the CIA for the release of UFO documents, maintain that the CIA was very sparing in the records it released. "What has been released to us seems to have been rather carefully selected," said one of GSW's lawyers. GSW suspects that the agency is withholding several hundred documents in addition to 57 which have admittedly been withheld for security reasons.

Government records have, in some cases, become so disorganized that rumors of continuing secrecy still crop up. It is constantly rumored among UFO buffs that the government has other explosive UFO secrets, such as voice-prints from extraterrestrial beings or the remains of a crashed flying saucer. The Project Blue Book files have become so badly scrambled by years of research without proper refiling that many desired documents are now hopelessly buried somewhere in the hundreds of file boxes.

Officially, government agencies have withdrawn from the UFO field. The current government position on UFO's can be summed up by the words of a federal aviation official: "If you get a piece of the thing, fine. But don't bother me with anything else."

Five Case Studies in UFO Identification

Aurora, Illinois, April 29, 1978

The police department of Aurora, Illinois (a suburb of Chicago) received ten reports of a UFO sighting on the night of April 29, 1978. The reported observations were between 10:30 p.m. and midnight.

Witnesses reported seeing a round saucer in the night sky, with lights rotating around its perimeter. The reports varied as to the size of the object, one witness estimating it at 25 feet, another as the width of a football field. It was further suggested that there might have been more than one saucer— a large "mother" ship and one or more smaller craft.

The most detailed report was filed by a couple identified as Mr. and Mrs. S, who reported a close encounter with the object. The saucer appeared over their car, and as they drove home to summon their neighbors, the saucer followed them, flying at treetop level and angling upward periodically to avoid the trees. The craft was round, they said, with a dome on top. As they reached their home, the saucer hovered motionlessly above them for some time, then shot away toward the East in "the blink of an eye." At no time could they detect any sound from the saucer.

Their neighbors' television set blanked out at the same time. Mr. and Mrs. S could not sleep for several nights after the experience, and the neighbor reported that he "gets chills" just remembering the incident.

The sightings were reported to Center for UFO Studies (CUFOS), and an investigator was sent to look into the reports. The description of rotating lights on the saucer was an immediate clue to its real identity, as UFO investigators have over the years received hundreds of similar descriptions. The unidentified objects in these cases have been advertising planes, light-bodied aircraft with a frame carrying rows of electric lights that blink on and off in sequence to spell out an advertising message. The investigator contacted a Chicago advertising company that confirmed that it had sent up an illuminated plane on the night of April 29. Time and location checked perfectly with the reported UFO sightings.

When such a craft is seen from below or from an acute angle, the advertising message is not readable; an observer sees only rows of lights flashing from one side to another. This accounts for eyewitness reports of a "rotating saucer." Such a plane makes very little noise due to the fact that it flies very slowly; the sound of its engine can easily be masked by the noise of a car's engine, for instance. If the plane is flying directly toward or away from an observer, rather than across his field of vision, it often appears to be "stationary." The absence of perspective or of reference points in the dark night sky increases the illusion.

The local TV station confirmed to the investigator that it had had technical difficulties at the studio on the night of the sightings, causing some interference and interruptions on local TV sets. This accounts for the blanked-out television set.

This case illustrates how easy it is for observers to be misled when viewing strange objects in the night sky. UFO witnesses habitually describe not only what is perceptually available to them but also what their imaginations lead them to suspect may be there. CUFOS investigator Allan Hendry refers to "the pervasive emotional climate that appears to be surrounding the entire UFO subject, one that succeeds in distorting even the most common-place sightings into exaggerated miracles."

Louisiana, October, 1967

Policemen in several communities reported observing, chasing, and being chased by a UFO in the early morning hours on four successive days. The most impressive sighting was on October 20, 1967. Police officers noticed the UFO in the sky at 4:36 a.m. It appeared as a bright red football-shaped light as big as the moon. The police car followed the object, which receded before it. When the officers turned around and headed back to the town, the UFO caught up with them and followed them. The car was moving at 70 mph, and the UFO appeared to be approximately 500 feet behind it and at an altitude of 500 or 600 feet.

A forest service pilot took off shortly after 5 a.m. two days later in a Cessna in an effort to sight the UFO. He was in contact by radio with both the airport radar operator and ground observers. The radar operator reported to the pilot that he had the target on the scope. The pilot sighted the object, reporting that it was about 1,000 feet above him. He gave chase, and the UFO receded ahead of him. He climbed to 3,500 feet but the object always remained above him. At first sighting, the object had appeared to be one-half to two-thirds the size of the moon, but as it receded, it shrunk to the size of the head of a pencil. The pilot gave up the chase at 6 a.m., and the object was still visible in the eastern sky, a brilliant white light, when he landed.

At first, this case gave the appearance of a first-rate UFO sighting, but it fell apart under investigation. The radar operator reported that he had no way to be sure that the object on his scope had been the UFO. He had only one steady target on the scope, which he assumed to be the Cessna, although he could not even be certain of that. An intermittent target had also appeared on the scope for short intervals, but he pointed out that it was quite vague and could well have been a "ghost return."

The police officers stated to investigators that the UFO on each of its four daily appearances changed from red to orange to white as it climbed in the sky. On each occasion, it seemed to take a final position in the eastern sky, hanging motionless at a high altitude, at 7 or 8 a.m., "looking like a star."

This suggested that the UFO might have been a heavenly body. Venus at that time was a very bright morning star, rising at about 2:50 a.m. It was bright enough to remain visible until the late morning hours. Weather records indicated that a heavy mist or ground haze was present on the mornings of the sightings. This would have caused a magnified appearance of the planet and given it the observed red glow. As the planet rose in the sky, it would have become progressively whiter and smaller. The apparent diminishing size would have made it appear that it was moving away from an observer. The

Cessna pilot, when he heard this explanation, agreed that it might have been possible that he was pursuing Venus.

The position that the object finally took in the sky, as described by witnesses, correlated exactly with Venus' position. And when police observers were shown Venus in the morning sky, they agreed that it appeared identical to the UFO.

It thus appears certain that the UFO was Venus. The reports of the policemen that the UFO appeared at a distance of 500 feet and chased them illustrate the extent to which eyewitnesses can misinterpret what they are seeing.

North Central USA, Spring, 1967

This case was reported in the University of Colorado's Condon Report published in 1969. The location is identified as 'North Central' and the witnesses are not identified by name.

The seven witnesses—three couples and a single man—were hunting raccoons on an isolated ranch in the middle of the night. Two of the couples were visitors from a midwestern city. The third couple, as well as the fourth man, were local ranchers. The three wives waited in a pickup truck while the four men foraged at distances of up to a half-mile from the truck. The men carried flashlights which they illuminated only for brief intervals as needed.

At about 11:30 p.m., all seven witnesses saw a glowing object gliding toward them in the sky. Several of them noticed small red, white, or green lights on the object. One of them estimated its size as 50 feet in diameter and reported that its brightness alternated between dim and very bright. When the object was immediately overhead, a brilliant cone-shaped beam of light suddenly flared downward over the observers, blinding them momentarily. Three of the witnesses reported that the light beam hovered motionless over them; two felt that it followed a moving path. As suddenly as it had appeared, the light was extinguished and the object disappeared.

One of the witnesses reported the sighting to a local Air Force base and sent a report to National Investigations Committee on Aerial Phenomena (NICAP). Investigators visited the site in June, 1977 and interviewed the seven witnesses.

The witnesses' reports differed rather widely, illustrating the fact that people perceive events in widely varying ways. Five felt that the unidentified aerial object had approached from the northwest; one from the east; one from the north. Three said that it flew in a straight line, while two others reported that it had made a 90 degree turn as it flew off. One witness had noticed that the small lights on the object were blinking; another noticed no lights at all. Nor could the seven agree on the searchlight's path over the ground; each felt that the light had been aimed at himself. Four heard no sound from the object as it approached, while the other three reported a sound resembling that of a small airplane. The duration of the bright light was estimated respectively as 5 seconds, 15 seconds, 30-45 seconds, a half minute, "a minute or so," a minute and a half, and 2 to 3 minutes.

One witness reported that the object sounded like a twin-engine airplane, and he said that its outline had been dimly visible after the searchlight disappeared. With this clue, the investigators went to the local Air Force base where they learned that a slow-flying twin-engine Navy plane with a powerful searchlight had taken off at 10:34 p.m. on the night of the sighting. Its southeast course went directly over the area of the sighting. An airman at the Air Force base told investigators that the pilot and copilot of the plane had been planning to pull a prank, using the plane's searchlight to "set off some UFO stories." Apparently they noticed the lights of the hunters' flashlights and took the opportunity to put their plan into effect.

Roosevelt, Utah, 1965 through 1968

A well-documented series of UFO appearances occurred over a three-year period near the town of Roosevelt in the Uintah Basin in Northeast Utah. At least 80 sightings of the UFO's occurred and were reported by Frank B. Salisbury in *The Utah UFO Display* (Devin, 1974). Witnesses reported seeing UFOs of varying shapes and sizes, some of them as large as football fields. The objects glowed with green, yellow, red or blue lights, moved in various directions as well as hovering, and emitted a humming sound.

In 1966, one witness saw "a large object, flat on the bottom with a dome on top, hovering over the house, almost appearing to balance on top of the house. It was twice as large as the house. Lights around the bottom edge were blinking on and off, giving a predominantly red impression, but also appearing at times to be green and yellow." A year later, in 1967, another witness described watching a similar UFO from a vantage point on the top of a hill: "It moved along, stayed on about the same plane, and then it broke the horizon. . . . It hovered there for a minute, and then it went almost straight again. This time when it took off, it just kind of hovered out there, and it seemed to be a little bit smaller this time, but when it left, you could see something fall away from it."

Such a long series of well-documented sightings provided a major UFO mystery that was not clarified until 1978, more than 10 years after the sightings.

UFO? No, a bug glowing in heavy electrical field. (USDA)

At that time, researchers at the USDA Agricultural Research Service in Gainesville, Florida, read reports of the Uintah Basin UFOs, and were struck by certain similarities between the reported UFOs and the characteristics of swarms of flying insects—particularly the erratic flight patterns, the large size of the UFOs, and the observed humming sounds. The researchers postulated that under certain atmospheric conditions, swarms of night-flying insects might become electrically charged and give off colored light, which would make the swarm look like a huge glowing object in the sky.

Laboratory experiments with various insects showed that in electrical fields of over 2.1 kilovolts per centimeter, these insects displayed brilliantly colored flares of bluish light from various external points of the body, such as legs and antennae. Red, green, and orange flares occurred less frequently.

These flares of colored light were corona discharged similar to the phenomenon known as St. Elmo's fire, which is often observed during electrical storms as a glow or halo on prominent points such as church steeples, ships' mastheads, and the wingtips of airplanes. Flying insects provide an excellent electrical conductor, since they are composed of a dielectric (the shell or skeleton) surrounding an electrolyte (the body fluids). Thunderheads are known to produce electrical fields far above 2 kilovolts per centimeter, quite enough to cause flying insects to give off corona discharges.

The USDA Forest Service confirmed that during the period of the UFO sightings, the Uintah Basin suffered a heavy infestation of the spruce budworm, a small swarming insect. The reported sites of UFO displays conformed closely to the areas of most intense budworm infestation, thus making it virtually certain that the UFOs were in fact insect swarms glowing in the heavy electrical fields caused by Rocky Mountain thunderstorms.

A complete analysis of this case is found in P.S. Callahan and R.W. Mankin, "Insects As Unidentified Flying Objects," *Applied Optics*, November 1, 1978, p. 3355.

Petrozavodsk, USSR, September 20, 1977

In the early morning hours on September 20, 1977, a spectacular UFO was seen by hundreds of residents in the Leningrad area. It rapidly became known as the "jellyfish UFO" because it resembled a gigantic luminescent jellyfish with long streaming tentacles hanging down to the ground. The bright point of light at its center moved northward and disappeared. TASS, the Soviet news agency, reported the incident the next day but, in line with official Soviet policy, refrained from calling it a UFO. It was merely termed "an unusual natural phenomenon." However, numerous "unofficial" Russian UFO groups were very impressed by the sighting, as were Western reporters who quickly published the story in the United States. Reports appeared stating that a beam of light from the UFO had pierced windows and drilled holes in paving stones. The UFO was also said to have caused panic in Petrozavodsk and caused vehicles to stall and go out of control. One acknowledged Russian

UFO proponent told Western reporters that the Petrozavodsk jellyfish was without a doubt a genuine UFO: "It had all the features."

Experienced UFO investigators in the U.S., however, were reminded of similar jellyfish manifestations that occurred during nighttime rocket launches under unusual atmospheric conditions. American experts, among them Allan Hendry of CUFOS, making use of U.S. information about Soviet space activities, pinpointed the supposed UFO as the launch of a Soviet Cosmos 995 spy satellite from the Plesetsk Space Center. The location, time, and direction of the launch coincided exactly with the observed reports of the jellyfish UFO. Ironically, this explanation was never published or disseminated by the Soviet press because the Plesetsk base is supposed to be top secret; TASS was therefore enjoined by security regulations from making known the real explanation for the UFO.

American UFO expert James Oberg cites this case as a particularly revealing one becauase "we are utterly certain what the so-called UFO really was. This gives us a rare standard against which we can calibrate the reliability of 'car stalling' stories, 'hysterics,' 'car chase' stories, and other 'physical evidence' which often reportedly accompany UFO incidents elsewhere."

IFOs

When UFOs are positively identified, they become IFOs, or "identified flying objects." The following selection from the historical UFO records is a group of cases which have been explained beyond a reasonable doubt:

Louisville, Kentucky, January 7, 1948
At 1:15 p.m., the Kentucky State Highway patrol received several reports of a sighting of a saucer-shaped UFO in the daytime sky. It was estimated to be 200 to 300 feet in diameter. Capt. Thomas Mantell, in an F-51 from a nearby air force base, was alerted to search for the object. He radioed that he had located the UFO; it was ahead of him and climbing. He followed it to 20,000 feet, when the control tower lost contact with him. His plane crashed, apparently when he blacked out from lack of oxygen. Investigators at first felt that the UFO might have been the planet Venus, but that

explanation was very tentative because Venus probably would not have been visible at that hour of the morning. Years later, the Air Force declassified its records of the "skyhook" spy balloons which had regularly been launched to carry automatic cameras over the Soviet Union. One of these balloons was launched upwind of the sighting area a few hours before Capt. Mantell's tragic flight and was almost certainly the mysterious UFO.

McMinnville, Oregon, May 11, 1950

A large saucer-shaped UFO appeared in the daytime sky to a married couple outside their house. Several photos of the object were snapped before it disappeared in the distance. This sighting is one of the most famous in UFO annals. The Condon Report concluded: "This is one of the few UFO reports in which all factors investigated, geometric, psychological, and physical, appear to be consistent with the assertion that an extraordinary flying object, silvery, metallic, disk-shaped, tens of meters in diameter, and evidently artificial [extraterrestrial], flew within sight of two witnesses." However, independent investigations by Philip J. Klass and Robert Sheaffer indicated that the photographs, said by both witnesses to have been taken in the late afternoon, were in fact taken in the early morning. This and other discrepancies in the witnesses' accounts led to the inevitable conclusion that the sighting was a hoax. The Condon Report photoanalyst, when confronted with this evidence, agreed that it was probably conclusive.

Fort Monmouth, New Jersey, September 10, 1951

A radar operator at the Army Signal Corps radar center picked up a high-speed UFO on his radar. He was unable to track the object on the screen, even using the radar's automated tracking system, which convinced him that the object was an unconventional craft moving at speeds over 700 mph. However, his log indicated that he had tracked the object from 11:15 to 11:18, precisely three minutes, and a comparison of this elapsed time with the radar ground track proved that the supposed UFO had actually been a conventional airplane flying at 400 mph.

Fort Monmouth, New Jersey, September 11, 1951

A radar UFO was picked up on an Army Signal Corps screen. It appeared to be changing its elevation very rapidly though remaining in the same line over the ground. The UFO flew off the radar screen at a speed in excess of 700 mph, which was the fastest speed at which the screen's automatic tracker was able to operate. It is highly probable that this was a case of anomalous radar propagation, as the weather was very favorable for that phenomenon.

Barra Da Tijuca, Brazil, May 7, 1972

A Brazilian press photographer and a reporter obtained a sequence of five photographs of a flying saucer. The case was widely hailed as one of the strongest "genuine" sightings of a UFO that ever occurred. It was claimed that analysis of the photos by the Brazilian Air Force absolutely precluded the possibility of a hoax and that the photos constitute "absolute photographic evidence that the unconventional aerial objects called UFOs are real." D.H. Menzel and L.G. Boyd, however, pointed out that the trees in the background of the photos were illuminated from the right (which would be in accordance with the position of the sun on the stated day and hour), but the UFO itself was illuminated from the left. This is an obvious impossibility that leaves no choice but to label the photographs a hoax.

Ubatuba, Brazil, 1957

A Brazilian fisherman saw a flying disc approach the shore at great speed, turn sharply, and explode into thousands of burning fragments, some of which he recovered. In many subsequent published stories, these fragments were described as samples of ultra-pure magnesium which earthly metallurgical technology was incapable of producing. Samples of the fragments were analyzed by enutron irradiation, the most sensitive analytical method available. They proved to be much less pure than magnesium produced by the Dow Chemical Company as early as 1951, thus indicating that there is no basis for assuming they were of extraterrestrial origin.

Southwestern USA, Winter, 1957

Witnesses recovered a nested pile of strange tinsel-like material which they said fell from two space ships. Samples of this metallic material were sent to a local lab for testing, where they proved to be highly radioactive and composed primarily of aluminum. Further testing at another lab by spectrographic analysis showed that the ribbons were "radar chaff," i.e., lead-coated aluminum foil that is dropped from airplanes for radar-tracking experiments. The chaff's red color-coding identified it as being manufactured by Revere Copper and Brass, Inc. in Brooklyn, N.Y.

Vandenburg Air Force Base, California, December 5, 1963

During a daytime launch of a Thor-Agena rocket, a bright object was seen passing the rocket and was recorded on a number of tracking cameras. It was thought that a UFO had been observing the launch. Further observation of the photographs indicated that the motions of the rocket and the clouds in the background might have lent an illusion of motion to the UFO, i.e., the object might have been stationary in the sky rather than "moving up past the rocket." Precise tracking analysis showed that the UFO was actually Venus; the planet was in exactly the same location as the unidentified object and had exactly the same optical qualities.

Gemini-4, June 3, 1965

A still photograph from a movie camera onboard Gemini-4 was released by NASA and widely disseminated by the press, where it was claimed by UFO writers to be a particularly convincing shot of interplanetary UFOs. The picture shows three bright points of light with luminous "tails" trailing from them; these tails were thought to be exhaust plumes from the objects' propulsion systems. The pilot of Gemini-4, Jim McDivitt, however, explained that the photograph is merely the result of light reflections on the copilot's window; he never viewed anything resembling the supposed UFOs.

Astronaut James McDivitt photographed this sun flare through the spacecraft window of Gemini 4. (NASA photo.)

Gemini-4, June 3, 1965

Astronaut Jim McDivitt sighted an object in space outside his orbiting space capsule, on a parallel course to his own. It appeared to be cylindrical, with a sort of "arm sticking out." He tried to take a picture of it through the small window of the spacecraft, but its rotation carried it into the glare of the sun before he could do so. Nevertheless, a photograph was widely reprinted in UFO publications claiming to show McDivitt's UFO; it was out of focus and appeared as a blob of light. Though McDivitt does not verify this photograph, he says of the visual sighting: "I have never been able to identify it, and I don't think anyone ever will." NASA, however, identified the object as rocket debris, probably Gemini-4's own spent booster. This identification is supported by most UFO investigators, including avowed UFO-believer J.

Allen Hynek of CUFOS, who concluded that *none* of the reported "astronaut UFOs" were truly unidentified.

Michigan, March 20–21, 1966

A highly publicized UFO flap in 1966 followed the sighting of unidentified lights on or near the ground over Michigan swampland. The lights were red, yellow, and blue-green and seemed to move from place to place as well as dimming and brightening with a gradual smoothness. These sightings were probably due to swamp gas, which rises from decaying vegetation and bursts into flame through the spontaneous exidation of phosphorus compounds. The flames are known to occur in the three colors seen by observers and to go out in one place while simultaneously springing up in another, giving the illusion of motion.

Northeastern USA, Spring, 1966

Three women and a girl observed a bright light hovering over a school parking lot. The object was red but at some moments seemed green or white. At other moments, there seemed to be three lights "playing tag" with each other. Police observers stated that the object had a more or less circular motion and was brighter than a star. This sighting was almost certainly the planet Jupiter, which at that time was in a very bright phase, eleven times brighter than a first-magnitude star. Jupiter is red, and the green and white lights were probably due to afterimages on the retinas of the observers. The object's circular motion was due to the autokinetic effect in which objects appear to move if they are stared at long enough.

Rocky Mountains, July, 1966

The pilot of an Air Force C-47 took two photographs of a UFO through the windshield of his plane. The object appeared to be flat on the underside, domed on top, with a dark band which resembled a line of windows running around the dome. Examination of the roll of film on which the slides were made indicated that the two UFO photos, which the pilot claimed were shot consecutively, were numbered 11 and 14. And both frames were shot after earlier frames which showed pictures of an October snowstorm, thus indicating that the alleged UFO shots were made after October, not in July as claimed. The inescapable verdict is that the two photographs were a hoax.

Haynesville, Louisiana, Winter, 1966

An unidentified pulsating light was observed by a man, a woman, and several children. The light was stationary and located below treetop level. It appeared reddish at first, then brilliantly white, then reddish again. The Condon Report labeled this case as unexplained, citing the "difficulty of accounting for any kind of light in the vicinity." The sighting took place in an oil field, however, where several oil wells were located. The observed light was probably due to an oil well fire; investigators found a burned area that turned out to be a "burned-over oil slick beside a pumping station."

California, Winter 1966 through Summer 1967

Mysterious aerial lights appeared for several months over towns of California's central San Joaquin valley. The lights were orange-white; they moved, hovered, disappeared and reappeared, and sometimes seemed to merge with each other. UFO investigators observed the valley from a fire tower on a nearby hill, where the "mysterious" lights could be seen rising indubitably from the runways of Castle Air Force Base in Merced. The Air Force confirmed that B-52s and tankers were making over 400 practice re-fuelling flights each month. The planes were equipped with large spotlights which they turned on and off during the operations, thus accounting for the accounts that the "UFOs appeared and disappeared."

Northwestern USA, Spring, 1967

Aerial beeping sounds of almost unvarying period and pitch were re-ported over a period of several weeks. The sounds usually began at 8 p.m. and continued until 3 or 4 a.m. There was no apparent visible source for the sounds, and they were attributed to UFOs. Several weeks after UFO inves-tigators arrived on the scene, a local farmer brought in a dead owl which he had shot the night before as it made similar beeping sounds. Tape recordings of the beeps were made at another reported locale and compared to recordings of owl calls. The "UFO" beeps proved identical to those of the saw-whet owl, a small bird about six inches long.

Ohio, Summer, 1967

A 50-year-old handyman snapped pictures of a UFO which he claimed had been 60 feet in diameter. The pictures showed a saucer-shaped craft with windows or ports on both its upper and lower surfaces. Examination of the photos showed that to achieve the sharp focus of the UFO in the photos, the camera lens would have to have been focused at infinity; objects in the foreground of the picture are in sharp focus, however, a contradiction that indicates that the "UFO" must have actually been a pie-pan sized object suspended by a thread 5 to 10 feet from the camera.

Northeastern USA, Summer 1967

Witnesses in four locations observed six to sixteen bright lights ap-pearing and disappearing in the night sky. The lights were seen between 9:15 and 9:45; they were in a horizontal line and seemed to move together. Investigators were informed by the Strategic Air Command that sixteen ALA-17 flares had been dropped from a B-52 in the same area at the same time as the reported sightings. The dropping of the flares was part of an aircrew training program; the flares were released at controlled intervals and burned with a brilliant light that was visible at distances over 30 miles.

North Central USA, Fall, 1967

A state trooper reported seeing a brilliantly glowing flying saucer as he was driving at night. The saucer seemed to be hovering on the highway, and the trooper came within 40 feet of it. When he did so, the object took off straight upward at high speed. Psychological testing of the trooper indicated that he was psychopathic or schizophrenic, manifesting a tremendous need for attention and for appearing to be important. With such deeply impaired credibility, the trooper's sighting must be viewed with a grain of salt. It was probably a fabrication, perhaps bolstered by hallucination or the common phenomenon of "road hypnosis."

Leary, Georgia, January 6, 1969

Jimmy Carter, then governor of Georgia, was waiting outside the Lions Club in the small town of Leary at 7:15 p.m. when he saw a light in the sky, "as bright as the moon," that seemed to approach and recede repeatedly. It was in the western sky and was judged by Carter to be at an angle of roughly 30 degrees above the horizon. He made out a handwritten report of the incident four years later and mailed it to the International UFO Bureau in Oklahoma City. Various investigators who have considered the case since then have quickly concluded that the UFO was in fact the planet Venus, which on the night of the sighting was a bright evening star. At 7:15 p.m., its location was in the west-southwest at an altitude of 25 degrees, which is so close to the estimated position of the supposed UFO as to be conclusive.

New Zealand, January, 1979

An aerial UFO was filmed off the coast of New Zealand by an Australian camera crew and was shown on television news programs around the world. Eyewitnesses described it as a large yellowish globe or an "illuminated ping-pong ball." The UFO was almost certainly the planet Venus. The UFO rose off the New Zealand coast for over a week in the early morning hours; Venus at that time was a very bright morning star. Observers agreed that it ascended slowly into the sky, where it "resembled a star," which is exactly the behavior of Venus.

Hard-Core UFOs

These are "classic" UFO cases; if UFOs are actually of extraterrestrial origin, it is these cases which will demonstrate the fact. These cases have mystified observers, including government agencies investigating UFOs; most of them are termed 'unexplained' by the Air Force's Project Blue Book and the University of Colorado's Condon Report. Possible explanations for these sightings have been propounded by various authorities, however, eliciting a great deal of controversy from observers in the UFO field. The most persuasive of these possible explanations have been noted below.

Further information on these cases may be found in most UFO literature. The following sources are especially complete and are perhaps the most important titles in the UFO field. These books are referred to in the following pages according to the name of the author.

J. Allen Hynek, *The Hynek UFO Report*, Dell, 1977

Philip J. Klass, *UFOs Explained*, Random House, 1974

D. Menzel and E. Taves, *The UFO Enigma*, Doubleday, 1977

Edward U. Condon, *Scientific Study of Unidentified Flying Objects*, Bantam, 1969 (known as the Condon Report)

Lakenheath, England, August 13, 1956

This famous radar/visual case was dismissed by Project Blue Book as anomalous radar propagation, but this explanation was unsatisfactory and the later Condon Report stated that this was "the most puzzling and unusual case in the radar/visual files."

On the night of August 13, 1956, the Radar Air Traffic Control Center (RATCC) at Lakenheath received a call from the Skulthorpe Air Force Base (50 miles away) reporting a UFO traveling west at terrific speeds. The Skulthorpe tower had seen the object pass directly over the landing field, and radar operators had estimated its speed at 4,000 mph. The pilot of a C-47 flying at 4,000 feet reported seeing the object streak by below his plane; he reported that it appeared as a blurred light.

Lakenheath-RATCC set its radar scopes at ranges varying from 10 to 200 miles and picked up a stationary target on the scopes about 25 miles southwest of Lakenheath; this was unusual in itself, as the radar screens usually eliminated all targets that were stationary or moving at speeds under

45 knots. The object then initiated a series of maneuvers that lasted several hours, moving up to 25 miles in various directions at a speed of 600 mph. An RAF interceptor aircraft sent up from a base near London made visual contact with the object and had the object in its gunsight. Then the object executed a swift maneuver and appeared behind the plane, following it closely and defeating all the pilot's efforts to shake it. The object ceased its chase only when the plane got low on fuel and returned to base. The UFO disappeared to the north at 3:30 a.m.

The Condon Report concluded that, although natural explanations could not be ruled out, the "probability that at least one genuine UFO was involved appears to be fairly high."

Menzel and Taves, however, have postulated an explanation for the Bentwaters-Lakenheath sightings. They explain them as a combination of an observed meteor fireball from the Perseid meteor shower and a case of anomalous radar propagation on the Lakenheath screens. See *The UFO Enigma* for a complete analysis.

Mississippi/Texas, Fall, 1957

This famous and complex sighting took place during the training flight of an RD-47 over Mississippi and Texas. The plane was cruising at an altitude of approximately 30,000 feet when one of the plane's radar operators detected a radar signal which he at first assumed originated at a ground-based radar installation. The signal, however, seemed actually to be originating from the Gulf of Mexico, where no radar transmitters were located. The radar blip moved upward on his screen, not downward in the usual manner.

The plane's pilot and copilot then observed a very bright light approaching from the southwest. The glowing object crossed the RB-47's flight path and disappeared to the north. The plane's radio informed them that a visual sighting had also been made from the ground. The radar operator tried to pick up the object again. After 20 minutes, he succeeded in picking up a similar signal, and 10 minutes later the pilot sighted a huge glowing light at a level of about 5,000 feet below the plane.

At that point, the radar blip split in two. Several minutes later, the two blips recombined, then separated again. The RB-47 by this time had enlisted the help of the Duncanville, Texas, air-defense radar station, which confirmed the presence of the unidentified object 10 miles northwest of Dallas. Shortly thereafter, the object disappeared from the plane's visual field and from both the air and ground radar screens. The pilot executed a long turn, wondering if he had perhaps overshot the object, and a minute later, a signal reappeared on the plane's radar screen. Neither the pilot nor the copilot could obtain a visual sighting, however, before the plane ran low on fuel and had to return to base.

The Condon Report failed to find a convincing explanation for this sighting, and UFO groups cite it as a "clincher" in the case for UFOs as extraterrestrial spacecraft. Klass, however, offers a point-by-point explanation of the sighting, concluding that it was in fact a complex case of multiple sightings involving radar malfunction and other radar anomalies, as well as the triple visual sightings of a large meteor, the brilliant star Vega, and a commercial airplane landing at Dallas Airport.

Great Falls, Montana, August 15, 1950

In this famous case, the manager of a Great Falls baseball team and his secretary were at an empty ball park at 11:25 a.m. when, in broad daylight, they saw two very bright objects moving in tandem across the sky. The objects appeared as rounded spheres of light and seemed to bear no resemblance to ordinary aircraft. The manager, Nicholas Mariana, happened to have his 16-mm movie camera with him at the time and shot approximately 16 seconds of film of the two objects. The lights had a bright, clean, "aluminum" quality, like "two new dimes in the sky," and they made a whistling or whooshing sound.

This film is the most impressive and well-known UFO moving-picture footage ever shot. In this case, the question of a hoax has never arisen, both because of the witnesses' probity and because photographic analysis strictly upholds the footage's authenticity; moving pictures are much more difficult to fake than still photographs.

The initial Air Force investigation of this sighting concluded that the two UFOs were F-94 jets coming in for a landing at the Great Falls Air Force Base, which was only three miles from the location of the baseball field where the sightings were made; the extraordinary brilliance of the objects was attributed to reflections of sunlight, a mirror-like effect that could have dazzled the observers. Two F-94 jets did indeed land at the air base two minutes after the sighting.

The Condon Report, however, noted that the witnesses reported observing the jets themselves immediately after the UFO sighting, thus implying that the filmed UFO's must have been something else. An independent investigation by Dr. Robert Baker of the Douglas Aircraft Company (see *The Journal of the Astronautical Sciences*, January-February, 1968) concluded that "on the basis of the photographic evidence, the images cannot be explained by any presently known natural phenomena."

Other investigators, however, question this conclusion. Why, they ask, were two brilliant objects in a noonday sky seen by only two observers? Menzel and Taves, as well as Klass, conclude that the objects probably *were* the two F-94s and that the sunlight reflected off their fuselages was only visible if viewed from a particular direction. Klass cites other instances in which brilliant reflections off airplane fuselages created similar blob-like effects. The investigators further noted that the witnesses did not notice the two F-94 aircraft until *after* the UFOs had disappeared; thus it is possible that the two planes might have first appeared as the brilliant UFOs and then, when they moved out of range of the sun's reflection, been recognizable as ordinary aircraft.

Mansfield, Ohio, October 18, 1973

This incident, described as "the best UFO case of 1973," remains one of the most puzzling, if not *the* most puzzling, in UFO annals. An Army helicopter piloted by Captain Larry Coyne (with three other crew members) reportedly nearly collided with a UFO. At about 11 p.m., a bright red light was observed to the east of the helicopter; it maintained a constant angle and seemed to be pacing the helicopter. Then it grew larger and brighter, and the crew chief warned the pilot that it was converging on a collision course. Captain Coyne estimated that the luminous object was approaching the helicopter at a speed in excess of 600 knots. Coyne put the helicopter into a steep descent to avoid a collision, and when the UFO still seemed headed for the aircraft, he put the helicopter into a 2,000-feet-per-minute dive.

At that point, the UFO suddenly stopped dead overhead for two or three seconds. Coyne described it as "approximately 50 to 60 feet long, about as big as our aircraft. The leading edge of the craft was a bright red light. The trailing edge had a green light, and you could delineate where the light stopped and the gray metallic structure began. You could see because there were reflections of the red and green off the structure itself." Coyne estimated that the UFO was about 500 feet above the helicopter. The object then disengaged the helicopter, headed west and disappeared.

Coyne was then astonished to find that the helicopter was at an altitude of 3,500 feet and climbing at a rate of 1,000 feet per minute: "We were supposed to be going down, but we were going up!" It seemed that the UFO had somehow reversed the helicopter's dive and pulled the craft upward in a sort of anti-gravity vortex. When the crew tried to contact airport control towers in the vicinity, the helicopter's instruments appeared to be malfunctioning and the radio to be dead.

This case has aroused more controversy among UFO investigators than any other in recent memory. Philip J. Klass propounded a possible explanation by theorizing that the glowing UFO was actually a meteor fireball, but it is then difficult to explain how the crew could have perceived the UFO as hovering stationary over the helicopter, even for only two or three seconds. The "dead" radio, on the other hand, was readily explainable by reason of the helicopter's low altitude: nearby hills blocked transmission. Captain Coyne even tested the radio at the same location on another night and confirmed this. The astonishing rise of the helicopter to 3,500 feet Klass explained as an unconscious action of the pilot's part to prevent crashing into the ground; at the low point of its dive, the craft was only 400 feet from the ground, and the pilot may have pulled the helicopter into an ascent as a reflex action to avoid a crash.

Although it is impossible to pinpoint exactly how many minutes the sighting lasted, any duration longer than a minute or two would make the meteor hypothesis untenable, for fireballs do not last in the sky longer than that period of time. Captain Coyne first estimated the sighting at "about a minute," but reconstruction of the event by CUFOS investigators puts it closer to five minutes. The meteor hypotheses is also at variance with the crew's report of seeing a sharly defined object above the helicopter. Nighttime sightings are notoriously prone to misconceptions, but in this case the four crewmen are quite consistent in their accounts.

Colusa, California, September 10, 1976

Bill Pecha, 39, a heavy-machine mechanic living on a farm with his family, went outside to check a circuit breaker when his TV and air conditioner went off shortly after midnight. Looking up, he saw a flying saucer hovering over his barn. He estimated its width as about 150 feet. The UFO was glowing and had a dome; "The dome was vertically ribbed with concave sections like a lemon-juice squeezer. . . . Both the dome and its base had a dark silver-gray appearance, like porous slag. The upper body of the saucer was like porcelain, while the outer rim was like stainless steel. The rim was seen to rotate in a clockwise direction, in contrast to the central area of the white, flat underside, which rotated counterclockwise. A large-diameter light source occupied the center of the underside, emitting a dim light while hovering, and a bright light when accelerating. There was a large, red light in front, two retractable sidelights, like clusters of cubes mounted on curved tubing, six dangling cables with frayed ends, and two hook-like arms."

As he watched, the UFO suddenly sped to the west (Pecha estimated that it covered 20 miles in several seconds). Soon after, it abruptly zoomed back to Pecha's property. At that point, panicking, he roused his sleeping family, and they drove off in Pecha's pickup truck. The UFO followed them. Pecha drove to a neighbor's house and pounded on the door. The neighbor came to the door and also saw the saucer, which he similarly described as domed and illuminated. The UFO then zoomed into the west, made a turn toward the south, and disappeared.

Pecha's sighting was confirmed by the accounts of three other witnesses, each of whom reported to the Colusa County Sheriff's Office that they had seen a bright object manoeuvering in the night sky. Their reports of the UFO's movements matched Pecha's closely.

Investigators were not able to find any natural explanation for Pecha's UFO. Nearby radar units had detected no unidentified objects in the sky, and no illuminated balloons had been launched in the area. The dangling streamers from the UFO sounded suspiciously like exhaust plumes from a rocket launch, but nearby Vandenburg Air Force Base confirmed that no rocket had been launched on the night in question. Pecha had felt an immense charge of static electricity in the presence of the UFO, which led investigators to wonder whether ball lightning (see *Ball Lightning*, p. 155) might have been involved, but this rare phenomenon would not have been consistent with the large size of the UFO.

A CUFOS investigation was unable to come up with any definite explanation of Pecha's sighting and rated the probabilities of four possible explanations: hoax, 1 percent; misperceived aircraft, 4 percent; exaggerated fantasy, 35 percent; genuine UFO, 60 percent.

Boianai, Papua New Guinea, June 26–27, 1959

This extraordinary sighting was witnessed by 38 witnesses, including Father William Melchior Gill, an Anglican priest who made detailed notes during the period of the sightings. On the night of June 26, shortly after eating dinner, Father Gill stepped outside and noted a bright white light in the sky somewhat above Venus, which at that time was an evening star. The object then seemed to come closer, appearing as a huge saucer-shaped disk. Other, small luminous objects seemed to accompany it, at times ascending and descending through the cloud cover. The object hovered below the clouds and illuminated them as it did so. And then, as Father Gill recorded it: "As we watched it, men came out from this object and appeared on the top of it, on what appeared to be a deck on top of the huge disc. There were four men in all, occasionally two, then one, then three, then four: we noted the various times the men appeared."

A second sighting occurred the next night. "We stood in the open to watch. Although the sun had set (behind the mountains), it was quite light for the following fifteen minutes. We watched figures appear on top—four of them—there was no doubt that they were human. . . . Two smaller UFOs were seen at the same time, stationary, one over the hills, west, and one overhead. Two of the figures seemed to be doing something in the center of the deck—they were occasionally bending over and raising their arms as though adjusting or setting up something. One figure seemed to be standing, looking down on us."

The Air Force Project Blue Book labeled this sighting as "stars and planets," but several points seem to argue against this: (1) the fact that the UFOs were observed to pass up and down through the clouds, and (2) that on the second day of the sighting, Father Gill's notes indicate that the UFOs first appeared at 6:02 p.m., when neither stars nor planets, including Venus, would yet have been visible in the sky. At various times, it has also been suggested that the UFOs were secret craft being tested by the U.S. Air Force, but the Air Force has never supported this notion, nor would it be consistent with the fact that the UFOs seemed to openly acknowledge the signals of the observers on the ground.

It is true that the planet Venus was a bright evening star at the time of the sightings and that it set at about the same hour that Father Gill's UFO disappeared from the sky, but Gill insisted that the object did not gradually set but remained visible above the horizon. The Center for UFO Studies concluded about this case: "We feel confident that the sighting was generated either by an extraordinary UFO or by Venus distorted in size and shape by amazing atmospheric conditions."

Abductions and Their Explanations

The most spectacular cases in UFO literature are the stories of people who claim to actually have been abducted by extraterrestrials and taken aboard alien spacecraft. There are well over 200 documented accounts of such abductions. Many of the abductees have suffered severe emotional traumas following their experiences.

Unlike other UFO cases, however, abductions are not open to verification by confirming witnesses. The only evidence in an abduction case is provided by the abductee himself, and the truth of the experience must rest entirely on the abductee's credibility. UFO skeptics are thus often inclined to dismiss abduction cases out of hand. UFO supporters, however, point to the fact that many abductees, under hypnosis, do not change their stories or reveal anything that would cast doubt on their veracity.

The following accounts are related as they were told by the abductees.

Barney and Betty Hill, shown holding a copy of the book about their trip into space. (UPI photo.)

Barney and Betty Hill, Whitfield, New Hampshire, September 19, 1961.
This is probably the best known and most extensively documented abduction case ever to have occurred in the United States. Barney and Betty

Hill were driving home along Route 3 in northern New Hampshire late at night on September 19, 1961. Their attention was caught by an erratically moving light in the sky. The light seemed to be following them, and Barney stopped the car to view the object through binoculars. He saw a large circular object outlined by a double row of windows. He entered the car again and resumed their trip. The aerial craft still followed the car, and the Hills, now badly alarmed, felt the car begin to vibrate to the accompaniment of a series of beeping sounds. They lapsed into a sort of drowsiness, and when they regained alertness, they found that a lapse of two hours had occurred. Furthermore, they found themselves on the road 35 miles south of the place where the beeping sounds had started.

The Hills did not immediately relate the incident in public, but they were plagued by nervous disorders and frightening dreams of being aboard an alien spacecraft. Finally, over two years later, Barney was forced to seek psychiatric help. Under hypnosis, he began to reveal the story of what happened that night on Route 3. Later, Betty was also hypnotized, and her story agreed in most material points with his.

The dual accounts revealed that the Hills were accosted by a group of abductors when the beeping sounds ceased. Their car was stopped and they were dragged out. The humanoids were small, under five feet, with triangular heads and gray skin. Their eyes were large and slanted, but they had hardly any noses and small slit-like mouths. They spoke an unknown language which was somehow translated into English in the Hills' minds.

Barney and Betty were placed on tables in separate brightly-lit "examination" rooms. They were medically examined, and samples of hair and toenails were taken. Barney's false teeth were inspected, and Betty had a "pregnancy test" that included the insertion of a long needle into her navel.

The Hills were then returned to their car and told that they would forget the incident. Investigators have not been able to either prove or disprove the Hills' story.

Charles Hickson and Calvin Parker, Pascagoula, Mississippi, October 11, 1973.

This highly publicized incident involved two shipyard workers who claim to have been abducted while fishing in the Pascagoula River on the night of October 11, 1973. Charles Hickson, 47, and Calvin Parker, 19, heard an odd "buzzing or zipping sound" and noticed a rounded craft hovering several feet above the ground. Hickson described it as being 8 to 10 feet wide and about 8 feet high, though on later occasions he said it had been more like 20 or 30 feet long. The craft was emitting a flashing blue light.

213

Three creatures emerged from the hovering object and floated toward the two men. Hickson noted that they were about five feet tall, with long arms and lobster-like claws. Their legs never separated when they moved; they merely "floated." They had gray wrinkled skin, "like an elephant," and no necks. On their heads were small fleshy cones in place of noses and ears, a "hole" for a mouth, and slits in place of eyes.

The two men were "floated" into the craft. Parker fainted and was unconscious through the entire incident. Hickson noted that the craft had no door; an opening "just appeared," and the two men were taken into a very bright room. A large round object floated back and forth over Hickson's body while he was maintained in a horizontal position. He could not move. He described his feeling as one of total paralysis.

After the examination, Hickson was floated back out of the craft, where Parker also reappeared and regained consciousness. The creatures reboarded the craft and it disappeared into the night sky.

Travis Walton, Snowflake, Arizona, November 5, 1975.

This famous incident was selected by the *National Enquirer* as the best UFO case of 1975. Travis Walton was a member of an Arizona lumbering crew working in the Apache-Sitgreaves National Forest. He and six other members of the crew were riding in a truck when they became aware of a saucerlike object hovering near the ground about 100 feet away from the road. Walton got out of the truck and approached the object. It emitted a "high-pitched, buzzing sound," and when he attempted to get closer to it, a beam suddenly emerged from the bottom of the craft and knocked him senseless. At the moment of impact, he felt a "kind of electric shock." The six other men in the truck abandoned Walton to his fate and sped away in the truck as fast as they could.

Walton woke up in an all-metal "hospital" room. He was watched by three humanoids who had pale whitish skin, small features, and bald heads. They were no more than 5 feet high. Frightened, Walton tried to overpower them, but they left the room unharmed. A "human" then entered the room. He was about 6 feet tall, with brownish-blond hair, golden-hazel eyes, and was wearing a "clear, bubble-type helmet." He did not speak but led Walton down a hallway, where three other similar creatures fitted a clear plastic mask over his face. Walton passed out.

The next thing he remembered was waking up alongside a highway. The alien spacecraft "disappeared straight up" as he watched. He called his family from a phone booth along the highway and learned that five days had elapsed since his disappearance. He said that he believed he had been in the saucer for that entire period, though he had been conscious for only a few hours at most.

"Jim," Oklahoma, October 18, 1976.

A 16-year-old high school student whose last name was withheld from publication began having nightmares about being watched and abducted. He felt vaguely that these dreams had some connection to a UFO but could not pinpoint the connection. Finally, put under hypnosis at the University of Oklahoma, he related the story of an abduction aboard an alien spacecraft.

As Jim remembered it, he was preparing for bed when he looked out his bedroom window and saw "a light going around in the sky . . . making a wavy pattern, near [the star] Polaris." The light then split into two halves, and he was aware of something in the yard outside his window. The thought occurred to him that it might be a peeping Tom, but he dismissed the idea because the dogs didn't bark.

A humanoid then appeared outside his window. "I just froze there, looking at it. It had two eyes . . . a long way from each other. Then I felt a numbness go over my body." Two more of the aliens approached, and Jim felt "something electrical" pulse through him. One of the creatures pinioned him while another put a light to his forehead. Jim had a sensation as if he were dying and passed out.

He woke up as he was being dragged along the ground to the alien ship. He underwent an examination inside the craft, lying on a hard table with a light above it that scanned his body. After the examination, he was taken outside the craft. One of the aliens placed the strange light to his forehead again and communicated to him, in an unknown manner, that he would remember nothing of the experience. He blacked out again and woke up normally in his bed the next morning.

The above cases have received particularly intense scrutiny from UFO investigators. Continuing exploration of the evidence has thrown new light on each of them and upon the phenomenon of abduction cases in general.

The Travis Walton case, for instance, almost from the moment it was first reported was treated with suspicion by many UFO investigators, despite the fact that Walton and his six witnesses were awarded a cash prize from the *National Enquirer* for "the best UFO case of the year." Walton and the six others underwent several lie-detector tests which appeared to indicate that they were telling the truth, but further investigation by Philip J. Klass, a UFO skeptic, established that the tests were so inadequately structured and administered that their results really revealed very little about the supposed abduction. Further, Klass provided evidence that Walton had failed his first, unpublicized lie-detector test. Klass concluded that the case was an elaborate hoax, and several pro-UFO organizations (NICAP and Ground Saucer Watch) agreed that his evidence was convincing.

The Pascagoula abduction has also been accused of being a hoax, notably by Klass in *UFOs Explained*. Klass notes a number of inconsistencies in Hickson's story and provides suggestive evidence that the lie-detector test that Hickson took—and passed—was inadequate, unreliable, and inconclusive. Dr. James A. Harder of the University of California at Berkeley, a prominent UFO investigator, however, felt that Hickson's and Parker's account was convincing. In The APRO Bulletin, Harder stated: "There was definitely something here that was not terrestrial. . . . Where they come from and why they were here is a matter of conjecture, but the fact that they are here is true, beyond a reasonable doubt." J. Allen Hynek, of CUFOS, also investigated the case, and endorsed Hickson and Parker, though in somewhat more qualified terms: "There is no question in my mind that these two men have had a very terrifying experience."

The question of a hoax has never arisen in the Betty and Barney Hill case, not only because the two witnesses substantiated each other's accounts but also because no evidence of a hoax was revealed under hypnosis. This has not, however, prevented the Hill case from being called into question. Investigators point out that neither husband nor wife made much of the incident immediately after it occurred. Only months later, by gradual degrees, did they begin to wonder whether "something had happened" on the night of September 19. This suggested to researchers that the tale of the abduction might be in reality a self-induced fantasy on the Hills' part. Such a fantasy would, to the Hills, be indistinguishable from reality. Under hypnosis, they would be telling the "truth" as they perceived it.

There is, of course, no way of proving or disproving conclusively the truth of the Hill case, and it continues to be the most hotly debated abduction case ever reported. Barney Hill died in 1969, but Betty Hill continues to monitor New Hampshire skies for UFOs. An investigator from CUFOS accompanied Mrs. Hill on one of her nightly vigils in 1977. She claims to see up to eight UFOs a night landing in the New Hampshire mountains. The investigator later reported: "Obviously Mrs. Hill isn't seeing eight UFOs a night. She is seeing things that are not UFOs and calling them UFOs. On the night of April 15, 1977, she was unable to distinguish between a landed UFO and a streetlight."

The possibility that many, if not all, abduction stories may be hallucinations, whether involuntary or self-induced, has received support from several scientific sources. One theory, put forward by M. A. Persinger of Laurentian University in Ontario, proposes a geophysical basis for various hallucinations, including UFO-related hallucinations. Persinger hypothesized (in *Zetetic Scholar*, 1978, vol. 1) that local electromagnetic disturbances may arise as a result of tectonic disturbances of the earth's crust. These electrical disturbances "could induce currents sufficient to produce paralysis or unconsciousness. The stimulation of electrically unstable portions of the brain, such as the hippocampal formation, could allow the person access to rich imagery of the epileptic, aura-like form. Such imagery could be intense and indistinguishable from reality."

An even more suggestive area of research concerns the similarity between abduction stories, near-death experiences, and drug-induced hallucinations. Researchers at California State University have found striking similarities between these three phenomena, thus leading to the possibility that there is "some sort of common matrix in the mind" that stimulates these visions. The researchers conducted an experiment (reported in *Science News*, February 17, 1979) in which the testimony of four UFO abductees was compared with that of four college volunteers who had undergone "imaginary abductions" carried out under hypnosis. Both groups described remarkable similar experiences. And the UFO abduction stories bore a striking resemblance to the stories told by people who have had a "death experience" where they had almost died yet recovered. The experimenters found that normal subjects, under hypnosis, could describe death experiences almost identical to those of their "real" counterparts.

Several common threads run through UFO abduction accounts, near-death experiences, and drug-induced hallucinations. According to the California State University researchers, the victims commonly report one or more of the following:

1. Seeing a bright light.
2. Hearing a humming sound.
3. Floating, especially floating out of one's body.
4. Moving through a tunnel or tube.
5. Approaching a door or other sort of border.
6. Encountering some type of being, frequently haloed or floating.
7. Experiencing telepathic or unspoken communication with the being.
8. Experiencing a rapid review of events in one's life ("seeing your life flash before your eyes").

9. Undergoing an examination.
10. Being given a message (in the case of a UFO abductee, often being told to forget the experience).
11. Returning to "real life."
12. Undergoing some kind of personality or emotional change.

It is of course impossible to ascertain with certainty whether most, or any, UFO abductions are actually products of the subconscious mind prompted by some sort of stimulus. The proponents of this theory are the first to admit that it leaves certain things unexplained. For example, several UFO abductions have involved multiple witnesses, and it strains the limits of probability to propose that the witnesses were victims of simultaneous group hallucinations. Nevertheless, all UFO abduction accounts must be approached warily, no matter how trustworthy or credible the witness. As Persinger states: "We just can't trust the senses in this experience."

Ufology

A number of pro-UFO groups feel that the study of unidentified flying objects is not taken as seriously as it should be by the scientific establishment. These UFO proponents insist that the study of UFOs should properly be considered a science—a science which has come to be known as "ufology." The most prominent pro-UFO experts, notably J. Allen Hynek of the Center for UFO Studies (CUFOS), accuse the scientific establishment of shunning ufology in a sort of reflexive refection of new and unconventional ideas. The UFO proponents see themselves as modern-day Galileos, prophets of a new science which is treated as heresy by their more traditional colleagues.

Is ufology a science? This question is at the heart of the controversy, and unfortunately it is not amenable to any easy solution. One basic problem is that the actual objects which the science seeks to consider—the UFOs themselves—are not physically present for examination, nor are the manifestations by which they supposedly reveal themselves easily examined or even confirmed.

The theoretical underpinnings of ufology are on even shakier grounds, due to the persistent refusal of most UFO theorists to abide by the accepted rules of scientific procedure. In particular, the pro-UFO camp often insists on shifting the burden of proof to the skeptics, in clear violation of all accepted tenets of scientific thought. In effect, they say: "Prove that UFOs *don't* exist."

The ufologists claim that, out of the many thousands of reports of UFO encounters, at least *some* must represent true visitations by extraterrestrial aliens. This line of reasoning is, however, scientifically unacceptable, and ufology cannot be considered a legitimate branch of science while standing on such a shaky foundation. Scientist Hudson Hoagland wrote in *Science* in 1969: "The basic difficulty inherent in any investigation of phenomena such as . . . UFOs is that it is impossible for science ever to prove a universal negative. There will always be cases which remain unexplained because of lack of data, lack of repeatability, false reporting, wishful thinking, deluded observers, rumors, lies, and fraud. A residue of unexplained cases is not a justification for continuing an investigation after overwhelming evidence has disposed of hypotheses of supernormality, such as beings from outer space. . . . Unexplained cases are simply unexplained. They can never constitute evidence for any hypothesis."

Ufologists are often accused by their critics of having a credulous and haphazard attitude toward evidence. Many, though not all, ufologists, accept UFO reports without making adequate attempts to verify their authenticity or reliability. The pro-UFO camp has been traditionally inclined to accept UFO reports at face value and to leave rigorous analysis to the skeptics, a situation which has unfortunately led repeatedly to the discrediting of the ufologists.

If the claims of ufologists are eventually vindicated, i.e., if UFOs are proven to be of extraterrestrial origin, it will be a major scientific breakthrough, perhaps the most extraordinary of the century. If not, then the UFO movement will be something quite different: the most powerful and long-lasting public delusion of our time.

Who's Watching?
A Listing of Active UFO Groups

Center for UFO Studies (CUFOS), 1609 Sherman Suite 207, Evanston, Illinois 60201. CUFOS is a clearinghouse for worldwide data on UFOs. The director, J. Allen Hynek, is perhaps the most well-known UFO proponent currently active. CUFOS investigations of reported UFO sightings are carried out by researcher Allan Hendry, or under his direction. CUFOS issues two publications: *CUFOS Quarterly Bulletin and International UFO Reporter*.

Aerial Phenomenon Research Organization (APRO), 3910 E. Kleindale, Tucson, Arizona 85712. Formed in 1952, APRO is the longest lived UFO organization currently active. The group has representatives in 50 countries. The co-directors are Jim and Coral Lorenzen. One publication: *APRO Bulletin*, 12 issues/yr.

Ground Saucer Watch (GSW), 13238 North 7th Drive, Phoenix, Arizona 85029. This is a professional organization in which membership is by invitation only. GSW has been in the forefront of the movement for the release of formerly classified U.S. government documents. APRO is dedicated to applying rigorous scientific standards to UFO investigations. Quarterly journal free with membership.

Project Starlight International (PSI), P.O. Box 5310, Austin, Texas 78763. This organization has probably the most advanced array of scientific equipment for the detection of UFOs of any of the groups listed. PSI also attempts to communicate with UFOs. An irregular bulletin is issued in exchange for cash donations.

UFO Subcommittee of the Committee for the Scientific Investigation of Claims of the Paranormal, 1203 Kensington Avenue, Buffalo, New York 14215. This is the principal active organization of UFO skeptics, dedicated to tackling "unexplained" cases which have stumped other investigators. Reports on the subcommittee's activities are included regularly in CSICP's publication, *The Skeptical Inquirer*, 4 issues/yr.

National Enquirer Blue Ribbon Panel of UFO Experts. The *National Enquirer* has offered a prize of one million dollars for convincing proof of a UFO of extraterrestrial origin. The publication's panel of experts votes yearly on the best UFO case of the year, and small cash prizes have occasionally been awarded. Send UFO evidence to UFO REWARD, National Enquirer, Lantana, Florida 33464.

STRANGE BELIEFS AND PRACTICES

Biorhythm

According to the biorhythm theory, a person's physical, intellectual, and emotional states are governed by the fluctuations of three cycles that begin on the person's date of birth.

The three biorhythm cycles move in smooth repeating curves, following a sine-wave pattern. The cycles occur simultaneously, not one after the other. The first half of the cycle is the "up" phase, when the curve is positioned above a center or average line. The second half of the cycle is the corresponding "down" phase, a mirror image of the first phase, with the cycle moving below the center line. The physical cycle of 23 days is the shortest cycle of the three (11½ days on the "plus" side and 11½ of the "minus" side). The emotional cycle lasts 28 days, and the intellectual cycle is longest with 33 days.

You can calculate your own biorhythms or look them up in one of the numerous books or newspaper columns devoted to the subject. To do it yourself, compute the number of days that have elapsed since your birth, adding an extra day for each leap year. Divide that figure by the number of days in the particular cycle you are interested in. The remainder represents the number of days that have elapsed since the beginning of your current cycle. (The beginning of each cycle is considered to be the point where it crosses the center line on the upswing.) If you were born shortly before midnight, some biorhythm theorists hold that you are actually biorhythmically closer to the following day and that your cycles should be adjusted accordingly. Similarly, if you were born shortly after midnight, you should take the preceding day as your birth date.

Proponents of the biorhythm theory believe that the three cycles govern a person's physical vitality, emotional well-being, and intellectual acuteness. The "up" side of the cycles are favorable, the "down" side unfavorable. Thus, the plus side of the physical cycle is particularly appropriate to activities demanding stamina, strength, or coordination. During the minus side of the cycle, such activities may be less successful. The emotional cycle's up days are conducive to positive thinking, cheerfulness, and the ability to get along easily with others. The down side may be a time of increased moodiness or withdrawal. On the up side of the intellectual cycle, a person will be more creative and mentally acute than on the down side. Believers in biorhythms attempt to schedule important activities for "favorable" days and to exercise caution on "unfavorable" days.

The day the cycle passes from the plus side to the minus side or vice versa is known as a "critical" day and is thought to be particularly significant. Especially, critical days on the physical and emotional cycles are supposed to be days on which one is accident-prone. (Critical days on the intellectual cycle are less ominous.) Double critical days, in which two cycles are simultaneously crossing the center line, occur about once every two months and are particularly dangerous. A triple critical day, which occurs once a year, magnifies the effects ever further. Other dangerous days occur when a critical day on one cycle coincides with a peak or trough in either or both of the other cycles.

The biorhythm theory dates from the early years of this century. The joint fathers of the theory are considered to be Dr. Hermann Swoboda of the University of Vienna and Wilhelm Fliess, a physician in Berlin, although certain elements of the theory can be traced as far back as the 1880s. Swoboda in 1904 and Fliess in 1906 published their findings concerning the physical and emotional cycles. Alfred Teltscher, an Austrian engineer, formulated the intellectual cycle in the 1920s. A good account of the biorhythm theory's history can be found in M. Gardner, "Mathematical Games," *Scientific American* (vol. 215, 1966, p. 108).

Since those beginnings, the biorhythm theory has found numerous adherents. Several national newspaper syndicates carry daily biorhythm information, and myriad books and guides have appeared on the subject.

The burgeoning interest in biorhythms has spawned a large number of studies which have attempted to prove or disprove the theory. The overwhelming weight of the evidence is on the side of the skeptics: there is no scientific evidence that biorhythms really work. The results of at least 25 different scientific studies have been published over the past 50 years (most since 1970), and none have supported the biorhythm thesis. For example, a Workmen's Compensation Board of British Columbia study in 1971 examined 13,285 accidents and concluded that they were no more likely to occur on critical days than on any others. A 1974 study of Army aviation accidents and a 1975 study of civilian and military aviation accidents found no biorhythm effects. A 1977 University of Florida study failed to find any correlation between biorhythms and the performance of various athletic teams, and other studies published in various scientific journals have shown that biorhythms have no significant effect on either mood or intellectual performance. A review of all of these studies may be found in Terence Hines, "Biorhythm Theory," *Skeptical Inquirer*, Summer, 1979, p. 26. Hines also points out that studies which have purported to support the biorhythm theory have been either undocumented or based upon unscientific statistical methods.

It should be understood, however, that there *are* many documented biological cycles in nature—the best known is the menstrual cycle—but these cycles are quite variable, both within a particular person and from one person to another. None of these natural cycles approaches the fixed, mechanical, mathematically exact character of the biorhythm cycles.

For those interested in biorhythms, detailed discussions of the cycles are to be found in George S. Thommen, *Is This Your Day?* (Avon, 1973); and Bernard Gittelson, *Biorhythm: A Personal Science* (Warner, 1977).

The Shroud of Turin

The Shroud of Turin is a linen cloth believed by some to be the 2,000-year-old burial cloth of Christ.

The 14-foot shroud has been the property of the dukes of Savoy since 1452. It can be traced back a century earlier, to 1353, when it came into the possession of Geoffrey I de Charny, in Lirey, France, but its earlier history is uncertain. The Savoy family turned the shroud over to the Archbishopric of Turin in Italy for safekeeping, and in 1694 a special chapel adjacent to the Cathedral of Turin was built to house it. The delicate cloth has been displayed publicly only five times—in 1898, 1931, 1933, 1973 (for a tele-

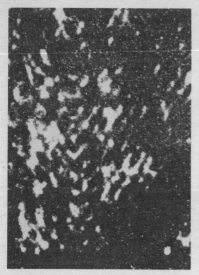

Enlargement of the Shroud (left), and of the Pontius Pilate coin (right); (UPI photo)

vision audience only), and in 1978. When it is not on display, it is kept folded, wrapped in red silk, in a silver box on the altar of the chapel.

The shroud carries the front and back images of a crucified man, elbows flexed and hands crossed, with a wound in the right side of the chest, and pierced wrists. The face shows signs of bruises and the back appears to have been lashed. The image is thought by believers to have been imprinted on the shroud while Christ's body lay in the tomb.

The image on the cloth is negative, i.e., with reversed areas of light and dark, much like an actual photographic negative. This fact was not realized until 1898, when the shroud was first photographed, and the negative yielded a much clearer image than could be seen on the cloth itself or on a regular positive photographic print.

Scientists have so far been unable to account for the manner in which the image was imprinted on the cloth. After tests of the shroud in 1978, researchers reported (in *The New York Times*, October 13, 1979) that the image could not have been painted because it had not actually been absorbed into the cloth fibers. Nor was it produced by a heat process, because that would have scorched the fibers.

The shroud's authenticity has been called into question repeatedly, beginning in 1389, when the Bishop of Troyes in France called the newly-displayed relic a fake. He said that the image on the cloth had been painted and that the artist had confessed the hoax to the previous bishop. The recent tests on the shroud, however, in finding no evidence of paint or painting, would seem to discredit this story.

The 1978 tests did not prove conclusively either that the shroud was genuine or that it was a hoax. Dr. John Jackson, one of the members of The Shroud of Turin Research Project which conducted the tests, said that the image on the cloth had been produced by a body shape under the cloth, but whether it had been an actual body could not be proved. Another of the researchers, Dr. Raymond Rogers of the Los Alamos Laboratory, stated that the project team examined every conceivable method of faking the shroud and had not been able to conclusively prove any of them.

Donald Lynn of the Jet Propulsion Laboratory in Pasadena stated (in the *Washington Post*, September 22, 1978) that the shroud could probably not be duplicated by modern science, even using up-to-date techniques. He

Turin, Italy: an estimated 140,000 persons file through Turin San Giovanni Cathedral to see the length of linen (displayed on wall in rear) believed by many to be the burial shroud of Jesus, during its first two days of public display. (UPI photo.)

said that if the shroud was a forgery, it was an extraordinarily sophisticated one: "We don't know how the image got on the cloth. There is nothing comparable to it."

Previous attempts have been made to duplicate the shroud but have not been successful. Proponents of the cloth's authenticity have suggested that the image was created by a reaction between body chemicals and the linen fabric which had been impregnated with spices, in accordance with burial practices of early Christian times. Attempts to reproduce such a process, however, have never succeeded.

The age of the shroud has not been established. Members of The Shroud of Turin Research Project say that newly developed carbon dating techniques would help pinpoint its age, but the Turin authorities have so far refused to allow carbon tests (as well as ultraviolet and X-ray tests) on the grounds that they might damage the delicate fabric.

New evidence has added further credibility to the "Shroud of Turin." The Shroud can be dated by the imprint of a coin issued by the procurator who sentenced him to death, said the Reverend Francis Filas, S.J., in a copyright 7,000-word report released June 29, 1980. Pilate is the Roman procurator of Judea who passed the crucifixion death sentence around 33 A.D. The imprint was found over the right eye of the "Man of the Shroud", and fits the supposition that a coin had been placed on the eyes of the dead man to keep them closed, said Filas, a theology professor at Loyola University. Explanation of the photo enlargements of the coin in existence and the imprint on the Shroud: actual Pontius Pilate coin—15mm in vertical dimension; "lituus" or astrologer's staff visible in its middle, 12mm from base to the crook. Notice to the left of the staff, ascending along the rim are the letters IOU; all other letters of this coin happen to have been eaten away by centuries of burial. Notice from 1:30 to 3:30 on the coin a definite clipped area interrupting its curve. The enlargement of the area on the right eye of the "Man of the Shroud", representing a photographic negative of the markings on the Shroud cloth. It is suggested that the photo be held at arm's length in case the high degree of enlargement prevent a viewer unfamiliar with this material to locate the staff and the UCAI at once. More discernible is a clearly outlined apparent chepard's staff-figure, slightly off the center of this panel. From 9:30 to 11:30 o'clock the curving and angled letters can be easily made out: UCAI. The length of the staff on this photo when adjusted to lifesize dimensions of the Shroud approximates 12 mm, the same as the staff on the actual coin.

Even if the shroud were dated accurately to the first century A.D. and its body image proved to have been the result of some sort of natural process, it would still be necessary to establish that the body wrapped in the shroud had actually been that of Christ. Given the shadowy history of the cloth prior to 1353, this cannot be considered a likely possibility. The Roman Catholic Church itself takes no position on the shroud's authenticity, although it encourages its veneration.

For further information, see Ian Wilson, *The Turin Shroud* (Gollancz, 1978); Peter Rinaldi, *It Is the Lord* (Warner, 1973); and John Walsh, *The Shroud* (W. H. Allen, 1964).

Freemasonry

The Freemasons are a secret fraternal order with autonomous branches in many parts of the world.

According to fairly recent estimates, upwards of four million men in the United States, and another two million abroad, belong to the various Masonic orders which comprise Freemasonry. Related orders enroll large numbers of female relatives of Masons, and millions of boys and girls.

The widely scattered branches of the order throughout the world share a common ancestry in Great Britain, but the character of the different national groups and of the different rites even within a country, varies considerably.

Modern (or speculative) Freemasonry can be traced back at least to early 17th century England and Scotland, when upper-class people began to be admitted into the lodges of freemasons and cathedral builders, which had flourished in the late Middle Ages.

The original freemasons had been trained as architects as well as skilled workmen. Their lodges possessed a body of legend, recorded in special documents, tracing the history of geometry and masonry from the civilizations of Babylon and Egypt to the supposed granting of the first freemason charter in 10th century England.

These documents, later called Gothic Constitutions, also contained moral teachings that stressed brotherly love and mutual assistance, honesty, and loyalty to king and church. The knowledge and values of the builders were also conveyed through colorful, symbolic rituals.

After the decline of cathedral building during the Reformation, and the decline of the guild system, in general, nonoperative, or accepted members were admitted to the lodges, possibly to boost membership. Some of these new members were adept at Hermetic philosophy, the unorthodox tradition of magic, mysticism, and pre-Christian thought that flourished during the Renaissance and Reformation periods. Such men may have been attracted by the secrecy of the Masonic lodges, or by their claims to ancient symbolic wisdom; they left their own mark on Masonic ritual and lore.

The first grand lodge, or association of lodges, was formed in London in 1717. During the next half century, the movement spread with unprecedented speed throughout the European and colonial world, by emigration or imitation. Independent grand lodges were established in many countries.

The varieties of rites and degrees proliferated, especially in the United States, and various charitable institutions were founded. Among the prominent organizations (some of which restrict membership to those with high degrees in other orders) are: Craft or Symbolic Rite, Royal Arch or Capitular Rite, Royal and Select Masters or Cryptic Rite, Knights Templar or Chivalric Rite, Scottish Rite, Shrine, Grotto, Veiled Prophets, and Tall Cedars of Lebanon. The Order of the Eastern Star is the major women's group; the Order of de Molay is for boys, the Order of Job's Daughters is for girls.

Freemasons have often been the victim of persecution or harassment by religious or political authorities, and has been charged with fomenting political or religious disloyalty. Nevertheless, it would be misleading to ascribe any particular set of political or cultural views, or any political interest at all, to Freemasonry as a whole. This conclusion is borne out by the disparate nature of Freemasonry's enemies, which have included, at times, Roman Catholic authorities, Russian Czarists as well as Communists, Nazis and other fascists and U.S. anti-slavery agitators. The only features that its persecutors may have shared were claims to a monopoly or political power or religious truth, and a tendency to believe conspiracy theories.

The movement acquired a reputation for dissidence during the 18th century, when some Enlightenment rationalists were attracted to its nonsectarian creed. The English grand lodge has always been headed by a peer of the realm, often a member of the royal family, while the American colonial lodges included many prominent patriots, including George Washington.

In Roman Catholic countries, the Masons often attracted anticlericals, and in Russia, pietist reformers were drawn to its ranks. On the other hand, some of the German lodges, which were persecuted by the Nazis, were themselves anti-Semitic and in the United States lodges have been accused of religious discrimination.

For further information, see: Francis A. Yates, *The Rosicrucian Enlightenment* (Rutledge and Kegan, 1972).

The "Dream People"

The "dream people" are the Temiar, part of the Senoi, a group of agricultural peoples living in the interior of Malaya, whose culture gives an unusually central role to dreams.

The Senoi, numbering some 30,000 in all, are divided into several groups, of which the Temiar and the Semai have been studied by Western anthropologists. The Temiar were first studied in the 1930s, and again in the early 1950s; the "Dream People" label is also sometimes used to describe the Semai.

According to these studies, the Temiar rely on dreams to help them make group and individual decisions, such as choosing a place to fish, or finding a bride. They claim to have discovered useful inventions in dreams, such as fish traps or medicines. Much of their creative life—music, songs, poetry, dances, decorative patterns and even complicated puzzles—is dream-inspired.

A Temiar shaman (witch-doctor) gets his calling through dreams, when a spirit called a *gunig* comes to him and teaches him a song-dance-costume combination and gives him practical advice.

But even non-shamans are visited in dreams by spirits who may appear in various disguises. A dreamer is permitted to kill members of his own family in a dream if they attack him, or may have incest with them in a dream if they seduce him, since it is presumed that the relative is a spirit in disguise.

Children are encounraged to discuss their dreams with parents, who guide them on the proper dream behavior. The child is encouraged to be aggressive in his dreams, and to struggle against and master whatever spirit frightens him. Once mastered in the dream, the spirit's powers can be used by the dreamer.

A child is told that if he dreams that he is flying, or falling, he must not attempt to stop, since the dream indicates that his soul is on a journey.

Both the Temiar and the Semai are said to be singularly nonviolent and to have an aversion to interfering in other people's lives, even in ways which seem noncoercive to an outsider.

The Semai rarely resort to child-beating. When asked why, they ask in reply, "How would you feel if the child died?" When asked why they refuse to strike an adult during a dispute, they respond, "What if he hits you back?"

When a personal dispute occurs among the Semai, the parties to the dispute resort to nasty rumors until one of them leaves for another settlement.

However, both the Temiar and the Semai have no qualms about killing outsiders during warfare and at least one blood feud, resulting in two deaths, was reported among the Temiar. Furthermore, the anthropologist H. D. Noone, who was the first to study the Temiar, was himself killed by two of the tribesmen. An active dream life and full awareness of it may not be a guarantee of utter peacefulness.

For more information, see: Robert Knox Dentan, *The Semai* (Holt, Rinehart & Winston, 1968); Richard Noone, with Dennis Holman, *In Search of the Dream People* (Morrow, 1972); and Richard Noone, *Rape of the Dream People* (Hutchinson, 1972).

Eggs

Eggs have long been used as symbols for some of mankind's basic emotions and beliefs. They figure in the mythology and legend, the folklore and religions of almost every culture of the world.

From dim antiquity, eggs have been associated with fertility, birth, life, white magic, black magic, death, resurrection, immortality, dreams, divination, demonology, witchcraft, sacrifice, the origin of the earth and the fate of the human species.

The Arabs in Palestine described the egg as having "neither foot nor head, nor tail" and as "neither living nor dead." The Egyptians regarded the egg as the seat of the soul; the sun was born of Chaos Goose, and then Ptah, Lord of Truth, emerged from the egg. The Hindus of India believed that Brahmin produced a golden egg floating on the water, and that this egg contained wisdom, power, and death in the shapes of the gods Brahma, Vishnu, and Siva, the Hindu trinity.

Hawaiians believed their islands came from an egg laid on the water by a great bird. The Japanese believed the world came from a cock's egg, from which emerged a giant, who conquered heaven and made woman. She then mated with a crocodile to become the mother of the human race.

In Ancient Greece an egg was used to purify the ship of Isis. After Greeks finished eating eggs, they smashed the shells to prevent sorcerers from using them. Like the Greeks, the Romans carefully destroyed the shells of eggs they had eaten so that they would not be harmed by any magic worked upon them.

The Druid priests of ancient Britain proclaimed their high office by wearing gold-encrusted serpentine eggs, the size of apples, suspended from their necks by chains. Other Britons of antiquity never ate eggs because they thought it was sinful to destroy the vital life principle in the embryo.

Eggs were also used in divination. In Scotland, the future was told by dropping the white of an egg into water and then studying the shapes it assumed. Suetonius, the Roman historian, said that Livia, a Roman empress, in trying to divine the sex of her unborn child kept an egg in her bosom until there emerged a chick with a cockscomb, indicating a boy.

Eggs were associated with burial rites: The Khassia of Assam put an egg in the navel of a corpse; the Maori buried their dead with a moa's egg held in one hand; the Jews of Galicia ate eggs upon returning from a funeral.

In fact, the egg has been associated with both life and death. In the Swiss Museum of Folklife, a costume of Death is hung with wreaths of eggshells, connecting the egg with both death and resurrection.

Another concept of the egg views it, on the one hand as the pure, sacred bearer of new life and, on the other hand, as the dark secret "inside" from which anything could come. In Albania, at the turn of the century, no one dared set an egg for hatching without first making the sign of the cross over it, lest some monstrous creature come creeping out.

Eggs figured in fertility rites, both human and agricultural. In 17th century France, when a bride entered her new home, she broke an egg to ensure her fertility. Slavs and Germans smeared plows with a mixture of eggs, bread, and flour on the Thursday before Easter, to guarantee a rich harvest.

Eggs have been used to cure disease. Germans believed that jaundice could be cured by feeding a hen an egg containing the blood of the patient. Rhinelanders treated jaundice by placing a thread across the patient's stomach and tying it around a fresh egg which was laid in hot ashes. If the egg jumped out of the grate, the jaundice would leap out with it.

Eggs explained dreams. In the past, the blacks of the southern part of the United States believed that a dream about a good egg meant good luck, while a dream of a broken egg was a warning that lovers were about to quarrel.

Eggs symbolized spring and resurrection. In the Harz Mountains, in Germany, on Midsummer Eve, fir trees were decorated with flowers and red and yellow eggs, and then the people danced around them. In Bohemia, boys

231

rolled red eggs downhill on Easter Monday, and the boy whose egg rolled the fastest won all the other eggs.

Cock's eggs have always held enormous importance in the popular mind. At Basel, in 1474, legal proceedings were actually taken against a cock for having laid an egg. The prosecution maintained that it was the work of the Devil and that a cock's egg gave enormous power to a sorcerer. It was finally concluded that the cock was possessed by evil spirits and it, together with its egg, was solemnly burned at the stake. Sir Thomas Brown, in his *Vulgar Errors*, describes the belief that a "basilisk" or "cockatrice" comes from a cock's egg hatched under a toad or a serpent. A basilisk was believed capable of killing a human being merely by looking at him.

Cannibalism

Cannibals eat the flesh of other human beings. The practice takes place under many different conditions, and societal cannibalism—in which cannibalism is an established social custom—is very different from nonrecurrent cannibalism which takes place under conditions of starvation.

The ritual practice of cannibalism has been reported since the dawn of recorded history. Certain Asian tribes in the fifth century B.C. were reputed to eat the flesh of their dead ancestors. In the modern era, reports of cannibalism began with Columbus, who, on landing on the island of Hispaniola, was warned about man-eating Caribs on nearby islands. The Spanish under Cortez accused the Aztecs of butchering and eating their victims and feeding the remains to animal menageries. Henry M. Stanley, the famous explorer of Africa, claimed that he had been surrounded by cannibals as he trekked to find Livingstone. Relatively recently, anthropologist Margaret Mead reported the cannibalistic habits of the primitive Mundugumor tribe of New Guinea.

These cannibalistic societies were motivated principally by aggression, i.e., their cannibalism was a way of demonstrating their superiority over their victims. Other types of cannibalism are also known, principally the form which is based upon reverence for ancestors. Here flesh eating represents not aggression but the pious desire to partake of the good qualities of one's forebears—and also in some cases to give the soul of the dead ancestor a new life in a living body.

Cannibalism occasionally takes place in non-cannibalistic societies, particularly when people are in extreme situations and cannibalism is the only alternative to starvation. Such instances of flesh-eating are known to have occurred during the retreat of the French army from Moscow in 1812; aboard the raft of the frigate Medusse, which drifted for weeks following a shipwreck off Senegal in 1816; among members of the Donner party, marooned in the Sierras in 1847; and in the Andes in 1972 following the crash of a Uruguayan airplane.

Though ritual cannibalism in primitive societies seems to be well documented, William Arens, an anthropologist at the State University of New York at Stony Brook, has stated in *The Man-Eating Myth* (Oxford University Press, 1979) that all such instances of cannibalism have actually been reported only at second- or third-hand. Arens' contention is that most of these reports are probably inaccurate and that cannibalism may never have existed anywhere as a regular custom.

In Arens' hypothesis, cannibalism is essentially a myth perpetrated against primitive societies by societies that considered themselves civilized. The myth originates in the tendency of primitive tribes to accuse their neighbors of cannibalism. Thus, the Arawak Indians told Columbus that the Caribs were cannibals; similarly, the Arapesh said the same thing to Margaret Mead about the Mundugumor. Arens feels that these reports were the result of exaggeration, resentment, or misunderstanding, and were repeated erroneously as fact by their hearers. Columbus and the Spaniards in the Americas then went on to use these accusations of cannibalism as justification for colonialism and the slave trade. Columbus wrote, for instance, that the more "cannibals" could be sent to Spain the better.

In the case of the Aztecs—who purportedly practiced a well documented cannibalism—Arens believes that Western observers have confused human sacrifice with cannibalism. The Aztecs undoubtedly sacrificed human victims, but the actual eating of human flesh is not thoroughly documented. Arens attributes the reports of cannibalism to the opportunism of the Spanish conquistadors: they needed an excuse for destroying the Aztec civilization, and so they accused the Aztecs of cannibalism. (The Aztecs also accused the Spaniards of cannibalism—a common result of the collision of two cultures, according to Arens.)

The orthodox view of cannibalism is treated in M. Harris, *Cannibals and Kings* (Random House, 1977); and R. Tannahil, *Flesh and Blood: A History of the Cannibal Complex* (Stein and Day, 1975).

233

Psycholunology

Psycholunology is a branch of cosmobiology that maintains that the phases of the moon affect human behavior. The full moon, especially, is associated with fertility, with the menstrual cycles of women, with murder and suicide, with births, with epilepsy, and with violence and madness.

The first practicing psycholunologist is A. L. Lieber, a Florida psychiatrist, who believes that the moon affects the human body in much the same way it affects the tides: "Like the surface of the Earth, man is about 80 percent water and 20 percent solids. . . . The gravitational force of the Moon, acting in concert with the other major forces of the Universe, exerts an influence on the water in the human body . . . as it does on the oceans of the planet. Life has . . . biological high tides and low tides governed by the Moon. At new and full moon these tides are at their highest—and the Moon's effect on our behavior is its strongest." (See *The Lunar Effect: Biological Tides and Human Emotions*, by A. L. Lieber, Anchor Press/Doubleday, 1978.)

There is a widespread, semi-folkloric belief that certain forms of behavior are intensified by a full moon. Nurses in maternity wards often expect more births at that time. Emergency-room attendants frequently expect to see an upsurge of cases having to do with violence and bleeding. Policemen, firemen, and ambulance drivers are reported to be on the alert for increased violence. In his book, Lieber even cites the case of a justice of the peace in Georgia who believes that more marriages take place on the full of the moon, and of a Massachusetts congressman who receives more crank phone calls during the same periods. In past ages, the full moon was also associated with episodes of lycanthropy, or werewolfery.

Many studies have been done to try to determine whether these lunar effects actually do exist. The question of the moon's influence on the birth rate has received the most study. Results have been somewhat contradictory. A study at the Tallahassee Memorial Hospital between 1956 and 1958 seemed to support the hypothesis that the full moon affects births: 401 babies were born within two days of the full moon, while only 320 were born within two days of the first quarter. A New York City study of 510,000 births during the years 1948–1958 indicated that the birth rate was one percent higher during the two weeks following the full moon than before. A second study in 1973, however, showed precisely the reverse. And a third study of the years 1961–1963 showed an excess of births *centered* on the time of the full moon. Two other studies—one in Danville, Pennsylvania, (1957) and the other at UCLA Hospital in Los Angeles, covering 1974 through 1978—revealed *no* correlation between phases of the moon and births.

Lieber analyzed cases of murder in Dade County, Florida for the 15-year period, 1956 through 1970, using a complicated computer method of converting regular solar time into lunar time. His findings indicated that homicides peaked at the time of the full moon and rose again during the new moon. A similar study for Cuyahoga Country, Ohio showed a peak three days after the full and new moons, a result Lieber attributed to Cuyahoga's more northerly latitude.

Other studies have not supported the connection between violence and the full moon, however. In all of these studies—including a study of homicides in Texas between 1959 and 1961 and again between 1957 and 1970; a 1969 analysis of suicide in Erie County, New York; and a 1968 study of mental hospital admissions—there was no statistical evidence of the moon's effect on human behavior. Thus, there seems to be no absolute proof of the power of the full moon. It may simply be that people remember those occasions when spectacular occurrences coincide with the full moon but forget those other times when nothing at all happens. This can lead to the belief that the moon is influencing human affairs when in fact, statistically, no reliable link exists.

Flat Earth

The belief that the earth is flat did not end with Columbus. Flat earth societies exist today in several countries, notably Canada and Great Britain, whose members still believe that the earth is a flat plane with four corners.

The belief in a flat earth was an article of faith in medieval times, because the Catholic Church interpreted the Biblical reference to "the four corners of the world" to mean that the earth was literally a flat object with four corners. Actually, the ancient Greeks had realized that the earth is round and had even calculated its diameter, but this knowledge was forgotten during the Dark Ages. The voyages of Columbus and particularly of Magellan—

who circumnavigated the globe in 1519—put a general end to the medieval view of the world. Isolated groups of fundamentalists continued to believe in the flat earth, however.

During the first half of the 20th century, for instance, Zion, Illinois, was the home of a fundamentalist sect called The Christian Apostolic Church of Zion. The group was ruled by the eccentric Wilbur Glenn Voliva, who made it part of the clan's orthodoxy that the earth was flat—not a four-cornered plane, however, but a round one, shaped like a pancake. Voliva considered the North Pole to be at the center of this circular earth and the South Pole to be distributed around the circumference. Before he died in 1942, Voliva made several lecture tours around the world to popularize his ideas.

Modern flat earth societies range from deadly serious believers to more tongue-in-cheek adherents. The Canadian Flat Earth Society listed some of its aims as follows:

"To restore man's confidence in the validity of his own perceptions. For more than fifteen hundred years man has been blinded by metaphysics and coerced into denying the evidence of his senses. The Flat Earth Society stands for a renewed faith in the veracity of sense experience.

"To combat the fallacious deification of the sphere, which ever since the deceptions of Eudoxus has thwarted Western thought.

"To spearhead man's escape from his metaphysical and geometrical prison by asserting unequivocally that all science, like all philosophy and all religion, is essentially sacramental and therefore all reality, as we verbalize it, is ultimately metaphorical."

The members of the society say that their stand regarding the flatness of the globe is not their main point but that they are using it to dramatize their desire to "keep our God-given senses from being numbed by technology." Among other things, they state that globes are pernicious objects because they breed prejudice, making the people who live on the underside feel inferior.

Hollow Earth

Belief in a hollow earth goes back to the 17th century, when Sir Edmund Halley first proposed the idea. Today several hollow earth societies exist.

They maintain that the Earth is composed of several concentric hollow spheres, and that advanced civilizations live inside the Earth.

In 1683, Halley, who discovered Halley's comet, proposed that the earth was composed of three concentric hollow shells enclosing a solid core. The outermost shell, he said, was 500 miles in diameter, while the two inner shells were the diameters of Mars and Venus respectively. The solid inner core was supposed to be as big as Mercury. Halley also believed that each of the three spheres supported life. This was possible, he said, because they received light from their luminous atmospheres. The aurora borealis was supposed to result from the escape of glowing gas from these luminous atmospheres that existed in the earth's inner spheres. Since it was known that the earth was slightly flattened at the poles, Halley proposed that the outer crust would be thinnest at those points, thus allowing the aurora to escape.

The idea that there were openings in the earth at the two poles was first proposed by John Cleves Symmes, a retired American Army captain, in the early 19th century. Symmes claimed that the ocean flowed in and out of these openings (which came to be known as Symmes Holes). He also assumed that the interior of the earth was inhabited. Symmes died in 1829, but various groups carried on his ideas. Well into the 20th century, a society led by Marshall B. Gardner in Illinois enthusiastically proselytized for the idea that holes at the poles led into the interior of the earth. Gardner's group rejected as "absurd" Symmes' dogma of the interior concentric rings. Gardner maintained that the earth was composed simply of one sphere and that the interior was lit by a tiny sun about 600 miles in diameter.

Cyrus Reed Teed of Utica, New York created a powerful new orthodoxy in the 1860s by declaring that the earth was indeed hollow but that we are living on the inside. He postulated that the reason that no one could see to other side of the sphere was that the atmosphere was opaque. He said that the sun was a half-light-half-dark ball at the center of the earth and that its revolving gave the illusion of night and day. The stars and planets were supposed to be merely reflections of light. Teed adopted the pseudonym Koresh and the new movement came to be known as Koreshanity.

Teed's ideas received their most serious consideration in Nazi Germany. Under the leadership of Peter Bender, a German aviator, Teed's hollow earth beliefs gained a considerable following. In April 1942, the Nazi admiralty sent a naval expedition to the island of Ruegen in the Baltic with the purpose of taking pictures of the British fleet by aiming their cameras upward and shooting across the center of the hollow earth.

Today, believers in a hollow earth tend to see the interior of the globe as the site of various subterranean civilizations. One of these is known as "the sacred territory of the Agartha," who are supposed to be "hidden masters" with god-like powers. (See *Science Digest*, November 1972, p. 62.) It is regularly alleged that flying saucers come not from outer space but from the interior of the earth. They enter and exit through the Symmes Holes at the poles.

Hollow earth believers claim that Admiral Byrd actually did discover the holes at the poles but that the government is covering up the discovery. It is also claimed that in 1870 President Grant sent the *U.S.S. Polaris* to the North Pole, where it sailed into the interior of the earth and explored the unknown civilization that existed there. The government, they claim, has never revealed the results of this expedition for fear of alarming the populace.

CULTS

Cults of all kinds proliferated throughout the 1960s and 1970s, and today some of them have achieved semi-religious status, with hundreds of thousands of followers and large sums of money at their disposal. The public attitude toward cults is mixed and often contradictory, being shaped on the one hand by sensational media accounts of occasional cult violence and on the other hand by a tendency to trivialize cults by labeling their followers with colloquial nicknames such as "Moonies" or "Jesus freaks." The emergence and proliferation of cults is, however, an important social phenomenon, and the cults themselves are the first to insist that they should be taken seriously by the establishment.

Experts in the field believe that the growth of modern cults is due to a feeling of dissatisfaction or frustration with modern life on the part of their followers. Jose I. Lasaga, a University of Miami psychologist, in speaking of the People's Temple, noted (in *Science News*, December 1, 1979) that people attracted to the cult "were highly dissatisfied with the American way of life, either because of personal and family frustrations—like racial discrimination—or because of political idealism—people longing for a more just form of social organization."

Cults hold out the promise of a better, less stressful, life to their followers. The cult in most cases functions as a supportive unit—in many respects playing the role of a large extended family—which relieves the follower of some of the pressures of the outside world.

Almost every cult is headed by a forceful, highly charismatic figure (in almost every case a man) who leads and directs the group, formulates the cult's doctrine and establishes its rules of behavior. This cult leader often functions as a "father figure" to the cult members, making important decisions for the group and thus giving his followers a strong sense of direction and relieving them of uncertainty.

Cults proliferated during a period of turmoil that also spawned what is generally known as the "human potential movement." Various self-improvement or stress-reducing programs, such as EST, yoga, rolfing, Esalen, primal scream therapy, and many others, mirrored the same sense of social discontent that led to the formation of cults. Cults go beyond the human potential programs, however, in that they require stricter loyalty and obedience from their followers. In many cases, cults approach religious status, elevating the cult leader to divine or superhuman stature.

Most cults are small and short-lived. A few, such as Charles Manson's small band of followers, achieve momentary notoriety through violence or other means. A number of cults have, however, grown and prospered for a decade or more, becoming large successful organizations with national or international followings.

The Organization of Cults

Most modern cults are organized, to a greater or lesser degree, along communal lines. Members usually live together, and even in the case of very large sects where this is not possible, members often organize themselves into enclaves and remain in close touch with each other. Members donate money or labor to the organization, in some cases turning over all their earthly assets to the cult. The cult in turn takes care of the members' day-to-day needs, procures food, arranges employment, secures medical care, and conducts the financial affairs of the group and sometimes of individual members. Former cult members who have left their sects to return to conventional life have reported difficulties in rehabituating themselves to the ordinary minutiae of everyday life, such as shopping, using the telephone, and balancing a checkbook.

How cults attract followers. The basic attraction of a cult is that it promises a better life for its followers. For many cults, no recruitment of new members is necessary, simply because the cult's message is so attractive that a steady stream of converts is available. Other cults devote much time and effort to recruitment on new members. California has always been a breeding ground for cults, in large part because its population had a large percentage of disillusioned transplants from other states. This was fertile ground for pseudo-religious leaders and charismatic authority figures who held out the promise of a stress-free life with easy answers to complex problems.

Dr. Louis J. West, chairman of the Department of Psychiatry at the University of California at Los Angeles, describes the people who are attracted to cults: "They expect California to be a utopia. But some get disillusioned when they get here, and they get mixed up with cults, because they promise them the ties they are seeking. To lots of these people the cults look like utopia." (*The New York Times*, November 26, 1978). Most cult leaders are highly effective preachers, skilled at influencing crowds and whipping up emotion. The Rev. Jim Jones of the People's Temple was described as a particularly adept speaker: "His style was a little like Billy Graham. He would say, 'The Bible says . . . this is the way it is. . . .' It had great appeal with unsophisticated—and some sophisticated—people. In today's world, a lot of people like to hear, 'This is the way, I know where I'm going, I invite you to go with me.'" (*New York Times*, November 26, 1978.)

Another such persuasive leader was Charles Dederich of Synanon, also a California-based organization. A brilliant speaker and conversationalist, he was almost literally adored by members of Synanon. He attracted dropouts from conventional society who were looking for a better world. One of Synanon's converts described himself as a utopian: "I wanted to try a commune . . . Against the background of what we were seeing on television—the mass slaughters in Vietnam and the assassination—it (Synanon) looked pretty good. . . . It was very exciting. We were going to create a new American institution, and we'd be the leaders. There was a vision that we could create a new world." (*The New York Times*, December 10, 1978.)

Some cults adopt a more active regimen of recruitment, actively seeking out new members and sometimes using questionable means to do so. The Unification Church of Rev. Sun Myung Moon has repeatedly been charged with browbeating potential converts and in some cases of holding them against their will. The church and its affiliates hold meetings and seminars to attract new members. At one six-day seminar held at a YMCA camp in Gainesville, Florida in 1980, the local sheriff's department received a complaint from the mother of a participant who claimed that her daughter was being held against

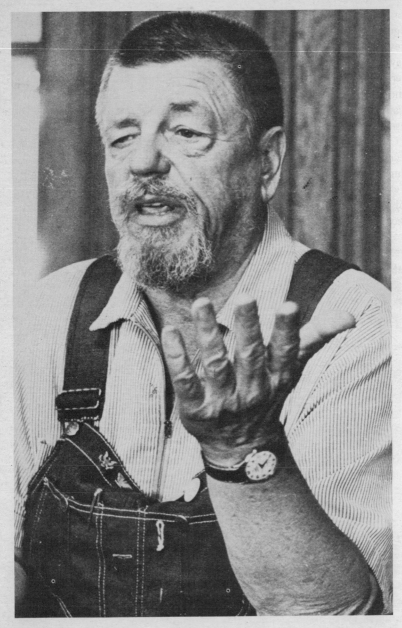

Synanon founder Charles E. "Chuck" Dederich. (UPI photo.)

her will. Police deputies confronted the seminar leaders, and after a long argument were allowed to see the young woman. She and four others said they wished to leave, telling the police that they did not "feel comfortable staying here." (See *The New York Times*, January 3, 1980.) The young people were escorted from the seminar by the police; the daughter of the woman who had lodged the complaint later stated that she harbored no resentment against the Church but that the incident had left her feeling "tired and confused."

The Rev. Jim Jones of the People's Temple is known to have used deceptive means in luring new converts into his organization. Margaret T. Singer, a clinical psychologist at the University of California in San Francisco, studied the People's Temple and reported: "The recruitment was very sophisticated. . . . Jones was a modern master of deception." (*Science News*, December 1, 1979.) Interviews with defectors from the sect revealed that

The Reverend Jim Jones picks flowers in this picture reproduced from a photo album found at Jonestown, Guyana. (UPI photo.)

Jones had developed complex and illegal recruitment scenarios. Jones' accessories would investigate potential converts (people, for instance, who had attended Jones' meetings), particularly those who seemed unsophisticated and impressionable. They would rifle the person's garbage can to glean clues regarding the individual eating habits, friends (discarded letters were especially helpful), and household habits. If necessary, two Temple members would call on the prospective target. While one of them made conversation, the other would ask to use the bathroom, where he would take notes on the contents of the medicine cabinet, kinds of medications, names of doctors, types of drugs, etc. Other valuable information was gathered by telephoning the recruit (or his relatives) and, on the pretext of taking a survey, learn such statistics as birth date and place of birth.

At the next Temple meeting attended by the prospective recruit, Jones would use this information to demonstrate his supposedly "magical" powers. At one lecture, for instance, he said that he "sensed the presence" of a 45-year-old woman who had diabetes and whose doctor was named Johnson. The listening woman was "deeply impressed."

Such underhanded tactics as this convinced impressionable people that Jones was indeed the superhuman figure he described himself to be. In many cases, they were all too willing then to deliver themselves into his hands.

How cults control followers. Many new recruits are loyal to the cult with the fanatical dedication peculiar to recent converts. In such cases, the cult leaders have to exert very little outward control over the follower, for the follower in a sense ties the knots of the ropes that bind him. Such cults remain together by force of loyalty, dedication, and admiration of the leader. Other cults choose to bind followers more tightly, using additional control methods that make it very difficult for the follower to leave the cult or even to conceive of disloyalty. Lasaga has listed seven methods by which cults can control their followers, methods which he describes as "basic techniques of political control" (in "Jones: The Deadly Hypnotist," *Science News*, December 1, 1979). These methods are:"

—Control of the follower's property and income
—Weakening of family ties
—Institution of a sociopolitical caste system
—The "no-escape" society
—Control over verbal expression
—Cognitive and emotional control of the mind
—Drugs

Control over the follower's property and income is a feature of many cults, and in most cases the cult members submit willingly, even joyfully, to dedicating all their worldly goods to the cult. The People's Temple, for instance, levied 25 to 40 percent of its members gross income. Other groups have insisted that members work only for the cult, devoting their full working day to the group. Such control over property, income, and work make the follower dependent to a greater or lesser degree upon the cult leader, "like a child in relation to his father," according to Lasaga.

The cult leader or his deputies then become the sole source of support for the follower. This sort of control was aptly symbolized in the People's Temple by the fact that many of the cult members referred to Rev. Jones as "Dad." The Unification Church of Dr. Sun Myung Moon similarly exercises a sort of familial control over its members, paying for its younger members to attend religious schools and colleges.

Actually family ties, however, are usually weakened by the cult, which demands that the loyalty once shown to spouse, parents, or children now be directed to the cult leader. The Unification Church has figured in many allegations of weaning young people away from their families, and parents have even gone to such lengths as "kidnapping" their children to get them back again. Charles Dederich of Synanon attempted to weaken family ties between married members of his group by demanding that couples divorce each other and switch to other partners.

Jones also strove to break up the relationship between husband and wife. He apparently had a neurotically intense sexual appetite and appointed one of his secretaries to arrange for female church members to sleep with him. Jones stridently insisted on being known as the most important love object in the community—to both men and women. He frequently forced Temple members to testify before the group as to his sexual powers. On occasion, he would force one member of a couple to watch while he had relations with the other member. Such actions sundered or weakened ties between cult members; the only strong tie that remained with the one that bound the follower to the cult itself. Richard B. Ulman, a professor of psychiatry at the New York Medical college, reported how one woman watched her brother's mental condition "deteriorate as he became more and more caught up in the almost hypnotic-like spell cast over him by the charismatic Jim Jones." (*Science News*, December 1, 1979.)

The sociopolitical organization of a cult is usually quite rigid. It is constructed like a power pyramid, with the leader at the top, his deputies in the middle, and the ordinary members at the bottom. The cult leader exercises a strict control over the pyramid, so that none of the regular members of the sect attain any sort of personal, social, or political power within the group. the cult may include "planning commissions," "counsels of ministers," and "courts," but such bodies are almost always mere mouthpieces for the cult leader. In this totalitarian society, cult members have no say in affairs. Lasaga notes of the People's Temple, for instance: "The common people were absolutely powerless."

In some instances, notably at the People's Temple in Jonestown, Guyana, the members of the sect come to believe that it is inconceivable to even think of leaving the group. This is Lasaga's "no-escape" society. In the Jonestown example, Jones intimidated members to the point that they were terrified to leave the compound. Other cults practice similar methods, though rarely so completely or thoroughly as Jones. Jones equated leaving the cult with treason. Anyone attempting to leave Jonestown was severely punished. Jones convinced his followers that they were under CIA investigation and that if they left Jonestown, they would be caught and tortured or imprisoned. He also warned black members that concentration camps awaited them if they left the safe confines of Jonestown.

Most cults censor their members' verbal expression. The essential rule is that criticism is not allowed. The leader of the cult, especially, is sacred and must not be questioned, either directly or indirectly. Dissent within the group is explicitly frowned upon, and members who "make waves" are quickly given to understand that such behavior cannot be tolerated. The repression of criticism and free thought increases the cult's hold over its members. The cult's control mechanisms may include a spy system that reports all instances of dissent to the cult leader. Lasaga notes: "In this type of society most people behave like little children who do not dare express their feelings because of their fear of a terribly punitive father, and this means there is no room for external dissent."

Cognitive and emotional control of the mind consists of indoctrinating the cult member with the creeds of the cult until the individual has few independent thoughts of his own. Most cults have lengthy and in some cases semi-mystical indoctrination sessions for all new members. In the Transcentantal Meditation movement of Maharishi Mahesh Yogi, recruits go through a training period in the techniques of meditation and finally through an initiatory rite called the puja ceremony that finally binds them to the organization.

In the case of the People's Temple, such indoctrination was predictably intense. Jones gave frequent long speeches or harangues, sometimes up to six hours long, in which he inculcated his doctrines in his followers. Hours each day were taken up by further talks over powerful loudspeakers. At the same time, almost all contact with the outside world ceased, thus increasing the members' dependence on the leader for information. Lasaga notes: "No outside sources of information were available to the community except those which had received his (Jones') explicit approval. Let us emphasize the tremendous psychological power of these techniques."

The final method of control over cult followers is the use of drugs. It is not practiced by all cults. Synanon, for instance, is expressly a drug-rehabilitation group, and the use of any drugs, including alcohol, is taboo. Nor in certain fundamentalist or "back-to basics" cults is drug use widespread. In others, however, drugs can provide a valuable means for the cult leader to keep his followers in a docile and easily-led state. The People's Temple made almost unlimited amounts of such drugs as Quaaludes, Demerol, Valium, morphine and Thorazine available to its members.

"Brainwashing." The control methods listed above add to to such severe cases of mind control that cults are accused of brainwashing their followers. Concerned parents who "kidnap" their children away from cults allege that the youngsters have been programmed to the point where they do not know their own minds. Members of most cults also receive such criticism from outsiders. Members of the Unification Church attending the Harvard Divinity School have been characterized by their classmates as typical "brainwashed" or "programmed" converts. (*The New York Times*, November 4, 1979.) Accusations by former cult members, psychologists, and impartial onlookers lead to continued allegations that cults deprive followers of their own free will and hold them essentially as prisoners. Representatives of the cults argue that this is nonsense, that members enter cults of their own free will and that any attempts by others to "rescue" them are impertinent and frankly illegal kidnapping attempts.

Psychologists argue, however, that the question of mind control is not a simple, cut-and-dried one. Dr. Hardat Sukhdeo, a Guyana-born, American-trained psychiatrist who has interviewed and analyzed Jonestown survivors, has stated that cult members may not realize the extent to which they are controlled by the cult leader. He details the case of one young woman (in *The New York Times Magazine*, November 18, 1979), who "never realized she was under 'mind control' until she returned. She found herself doing everything her relatives told her not to do. She would eat whether she wanted to or not. She would think: why am I eating this food? And it gradually came to her: when you're under mind control, you never really know it."

Other psychologists have compared mind control with hypnosis, arguing that a charismatic cult leader closes off the disciple's contact with the outside world, much as a hypnotist closes off his subject's sensory awareness.

Lasaga has stated *Science News*, December 1, 1979): "The hypnotist requires the subject to close all his channels of communication with the external world except one: the voice of the hypnotist. Since there are no other channels available to check the truth of the hypnotist's statements, his or her voice becomes a substitute for reality. . . . It is mass hypnosis at a social level."

Kinds of Cults

Cults are organized along various doctrinal lines that give each cult its individual character and profile. The cult's activities may apply only to one area of the lives of its followers—such as the religious or the philosophical— or they may constitute the follower's entire life style. Cults may be either "advanced," in the sense that they may advocate modern or controversial forms of self-realization or consciousness-raising; or they may be reactionary or fundamentalist, preaching a return to old ways and simpler methods. Most modern cults fall into one of six categories: religious, therapeutic, rehabilitative, consciousness expanding, fundamentalist, or military.

Religious. Most modern-day religious cults have a distinct "mission" and devote a great deal of time, effort, and money to winning new converts. They are therefore highly visible and often in the public eye. In general, they are the only cults that receive steady and lasting media attention.

The best example of a modern religious cult—and probably the most successful in terms of winning converts and attracting donations—is Moon's Unification Church. Moon was born in Korea, but has based the church in the United States. It claims over two million members throughout the world, most of whom are young men and women between the ages of twenty and thirty. The church owns large parcels of real estate, particularly in the United States, including the church headquarters and seminary in Tarrytown, New York and over one hundred church centers scattered over the country. Moon himself lives in a large mansion. Estimates of his wealth center around $15 million, but the church claims that this does not represent personal wealth but is instead the property of the church. *The Washington Post* has estimated that the Moon church receives $6 million a year in donations from its members and followers. Moon himself is not just an evangelizer but also sits on the boards of corporations in South Korea and Japan.

Moon is a self-ordained preacher who was born a Presbyterian. According to his own testimony, Christ came to him when he was 16 years old

Reverend Sun Myung Moon at the 8th Annual Conference of the Sciences in Los Angeles. (UPI photo.)

and commissioned him as a prophet. He claims to have discovered "the process and meaning of history, the inner meanings of the parables and the symbols in the Bible, and the purpose of all religions." He began his preaching mission at the age of 26 and brought his message to the new world in 1972, arriving in New York and obtaining a permanent resident visa.

The Unification Church considers itself a form of christianity, though it has been characterized in *Time* (September 30, 1974) as a mixture of christianity and "occultism, electrical engineering, Taoist dualism, pop sociology and opaque metaphysical jargon." The church's principal premise is that Jesus was the first Messiah but that a second Messiah was born in Korea in 1920 (the year of Moon's birth). The church believes that Jesus accomplished mankind's spiritual salvation but did not complete man's physical salvation. The movement's doctrine is contained in *Divine Principles*, a 536-page book containing Moon's collected writings. Members of the church say they do not see a contradiction in the idea of a Christian awaiting another Messiah, but the National Council of Churches of Christ has denied membership to the Unification Church because it does not accept Jesus as the only Messiah.

The majority of "Moonies" describe themselves as converts to the true faith. Many have broken family ties and spent long hours working for the church, raising funds or studying the writings of Moon. A small minority of followers have left the movement; some of them have claimed that they were subjected to tactics that broke down their personality or were tormented by lack of sleep and poor diet. The church has been the repeated target of accusations that it brainwashes its followers. Numerous attempts have been made to "deprogram" young members who have been allegedly subjected to such psychological conditioning. A psychiatric social worker who interviewed more than one hundred former members of the Moon church charged, at hearings in Washington, D. C., that half of them were either schizophrenic or borderline psychotics.

The church maintains its own seminary, the Unification Theological Seminary, in New York State. The Board of Regents of the State of New York has twice turned down its request for accreditation, however, largely because of the church's unsavory reputation for breaking family ties, for engaging in questionable fund-raising methods, and for its alleged involvements in South Korean politics. The church as been paying the tuition of its followers to attend major accredited schools such as Harvard, Columbia, Yale, Fordham, as well as Toronto and Swansea in Wales.

Therapy. Therapy cults are aimed at improving their followers' mental and physical health. In this sense, they are similar to other segments of the

"Moonies" at Harvard. (Ira Wyman, *The New York Times*.)

"human potential movement." The therapy cults, however, are usually much more closely-knit and formally-organized than such human-potential movements as EST, Arica, or Esalen.

The best known group in the therapy area is the Church of Scientology. The Scientology movement was founded in the 1950s by L. Ron Hubbard, a former fiction writer. Scientology is in part based on, and incorporates details of, Dianetics, a counseling method that the church describes as therapy for certain mental and psychosomatic illnesses and which seeks to improve its followers' mental and emotional outlook by ridding the subject of ingrained "engrams" that hamper complete development. The church describes itself as an "applied religious philosophy which believes that man is a spiritual being who is basically good," and, through the church's counseling, "can better deal with his own life and take responsibility for the world around him."

The church claims 6½ million worldwide members, although outside observers have estimated that total membership is somewhat lower. The church has been involved, almost from its inception, in a long struggle with various government agencies over matters such as the church's tax status and governmental scrutiny of church activities. The church has described the government's actions in these instances as a "sordid 28-year attempt to annihilate our religion." The President of the church, Rev. Kenneth Whitman, has protested against "the cover-up and nonprosecution of Government agency criminal acts and conspiracy against our church. . . ." The church has also objected to statements by several medical organizations, including the American Medical Association, which were critical of the church's Dianetics program.

In 1979, suit was brought against the church for conspiring to steal Government documents relating to the church. Evidence was submitted that church members had stolen files from Interpol, the IRS, and the Justice Department, as well as bugging IRS offices. Five of the Church's members were sentenced to jail terms for their part in the affair.

Rehabilitation. Rehabilitation cults resemble therapy cults in that they attempt to ameliorate their followers' life situations. The rehabilitation groups specifically aim at curing members of drug addictions or alcoholism.

One of the most successful ventures in this field has been that of Synanon, the acclaimed drug-rehabilitation program founded in California in 1958 by Charles Dederich, a former salesman and reformed alcoholic. The Synanon program was credited with curing thousands of drug addicts. It received millions of dollars in donations and acquired large parcels of real estate in California where large communal villages were built. Branches were also established in Malaysia, the Philippines, and West Germany. Synanon's assets have been estimated at $50 million by government agencies. Membership in the organization numbered at least 20,000 in the early 1970s but had dropped to around 1,000 in 1978.

Synanon promised members a utopian community. "The Synanon I joined was so beautiful," one former member stated (see *The New York Times*, December 10, 1978). Dederich was described as a charismatic leader and brilliant conversationalist: "People adored him; that was the only word for it."

The heart of the Synanon experience was a group-participation encounter known as "The Game." This was a no-holds-barred verbal combat among a dozen to 15 members in which savage attacks helped the participants to a more realistic self-awareness. These rough encounter sessions were presumably instrumental in helping members lick their drug addiction.

Many Synanon devotees, however, came to distrust "The Game," realizing after a time that they were losing their self-respect. "'The Game' is an incredible instrument for manipulating human behavior," said David Gerstel, a former Synanon member (see *The New York Times*, December 10, 1978, p. 20.) Members found themselves becoming increasingly dependent upon the Synanon community, and especially Dederich, for support, and they became increasingly less confident about their ability to return to the outside world.

In 1973, Synanon's strict rules against physical violence were broken by Dederich himself, and thereafter according to former Synanon members, more violent episodes occurred. (See *The New York Times*, December 10, 1978.) Dederich began requiring all Synanon members to take part in jogging exercises and required all overweight members to reduce. He also ordered female members to shave their heads. Dederich's later policies included forced vasectomies for men, mandatory abortions for women, and a "change partners" rule in which 230 married members were ordered to divorce and switch spouses.

Synanon sued *Time* magazine over a 1977 *Time* article in which Synanon was criticized and labeled "a kooky cult." The American Broadcasting Company was also sued over a report on Synanon; a Synanon member attended ABC's 1978 shareholders' meeting and told the company chairmen: "There is great danger for you, your wives and your families."

Los Angeles attorney Paul Morantz won a $300,000 default judgment against Synanon in which he represented a couple who claimed they had been kidnapped, imprisoned, and "brainwashed" by Synanon. Thereafter, Morantz was bitten by a 4½-foot rattlesnake which had been placed in his mailbox.

Two Synanon members were arrested in 1978 in connection with the rattlesnake attack, and Dederich himself was arrested on a warrant that charged him with conspiracy to commit murder and solicitation to commit murder. Dederich was taken to the Mojave General Hospital where a 25-minute hearing took place before a judge. The judge declared Dederich mentally incompetent to be arraigned for trial. This judgment was reversed in 1979, however, and Dederich was ordered to stand trial with two other Synanon members. He pleaded no contest and received a $5,000 fine and a five-year sentence of probation (he was not sent to prison because of his deteriorating health).

In 1979, 41 of the 44 allegations in Synanon's suit against *Time* magazine were dismissed by a Superior Court judge. The suit proceeded to trial on the basis of the remaining counts, principal of which was the alleged "innuendo" that Synanon had abandoned its charitable purposes.

Consciousness Expansion. Cults in this category are variously based on programs of meditation, yoga, expanded consciousness, or "cosmic consciousness." Their teachings are mystical rather than practical. The cults are headed by leaders who claim to have achieved degrees of enlightenment beyond those possible to ordinary practitioners.

The largest and most well known organization of this sort is the Transcendental Meditation movement, a worldwide organization under the leadership of Maharishi Mahesh Yogi, an Indian of the Kshatriya (warrior) caste by birth and of indeterminate age. Transcendental Meditation is usually thought of by the general public as a non-religious, nonsectarian meditation technique, but it has in fact, in a 1977 New Jersey court case, been determined to be an actual religion, specifically Hinduism.

Maharishi Mahesh Yogi in the early years of this century was a disciple of Guru Dev, a leader of Vedantic Hinduism (India's main religion) and one of India's most influential holy men. From him, Maharishi learned the techniques of yoga which he later simplified and recast as "Transcendental Meditation." The techniques of TM, as it is often called, are designed to offer several benefits to the follower, including complete development of one's mental potential, excellent physical health, and "naturally correct" social behavior. World peace is indicated as a fourth benefit of TM.

Disciples undergo a training program under the supervision of an instructor. Inductees are instructed in yoga technique and assigned a personal mantra (a Hindu word used in meditation). They also undergo the puja ceremony, an initiatory rite conducted in Sanskrit.

According to R. D. Scott, a former TM instructor who left the movement, TM is actually a religion, regardless of what the movement's leaders

Maharishi Mahesh Yogi. (UPI photo.)

may say to the contrary. (See *Transcendental Misconceptions*, R. D. Scott, Beta Books, 1978.) Scott claims that the religious side of TM has been played down in an effort to win scientific acceptance for TM techniques. He indicates that the mantras are actually the names of Hindu gods and that the puja ceremony involves overt acts of worship. Transcendental Meditation was taught for a time in certain New Jersey public schools, but a court case brought by concerned parents established that it was in fact religious in nature and thus in violation of the First Amendment, which requires the separation of Church and State.

As for the claimed benefits of meditation itself, numerous scientific studies have so far proved inconclusive. Meditation has unquestionably been shown to lead, in many cases, to health improvements of a purely physical nature (such as a lowering in a practitioner's blood pressure). But no studies have found conclusively that meditation alters basic personality or leads to discernible changes in self-image.

Transcendental Meditation Mantras

Age of Individual	Mantra
10–12	*Eng*
12–14	*Em*
14–16	*Enga*
16–18	*Ema*
18–20	*Aeng*
20–22	*Aem*
22–24	*Aenga*
24–26	*Aema*
26–30	*Shiring*
30–35	*Shirim*
35–40	*Hiring*
40–45	*Hirim*
45–50	*Kiring*
50–55	*Kirim*
55–60	*Shyam*
60–65 and older	*Shyama*

Fundamentalist. These sects are usually small, self-contained units preaching a "back to basics" philosophy which is often predicated on a strict interpretation of the Bible. Chastity and/or sexual seemliness are stressed. The role of women is downplayed; women are assigned to traditional functions like cooking, sewing, cleaning, and keeping house. Such sects often run their own schools, feeling that ordinary public schools are contaminated by new-fangled teachings. Rigid fundamentalist schools rarely teach science or any subject that isn't "necessary."

The Yhwhhoshua Assembly, a small Colorado movement, is a good example of this type of young, developing, highly-individualized sect. The Assembly is a highly religious group of predominantly young people. The name of the cult, Yhwhhoshua, is itself a religious term, a combination of the Hebrew words for Jehovah and savior. (It is pronounced Ya-way-ho-SHOO-ah.) Members of the Assembly believe that this is the only name for God; they efface from their books any other names for the diety, such as God, Lord, etc.

Their fundamentalist beliefs include an unwillingness to use the names of the days or months because these names derive from pagan deities, i.e., Wednesday comes from Woden's Day and August is named for Augustus Caesar, a deified Roman emperor. The sect opposes all displays of indulgence or personal luxury, including alcohol, drugs, haircuts, jewelry, dancing, neckties, and dating. Holidays such as Easter and Christmas are not celebrated. All forms of medicine are avoided, including doctors, hospitals, and Medicare.

The sect believes that all art, even religious art, is blasphemous. Drawings, paintings, and photographs are all taboo. Art in any form, the sect preaches, leads to thoughts of lust. (Assembly members all wear heavy loose robes to guard against the temptations of the flesh.) Members of the sect have refused to have their picture taken in order to obtain drivers licenses, holding that even this form of "art" is blasphemous. The court battle over this position led all the way to the Supreme Court, which refused to hear the Assembly's appeal. Laycher Gonzales, the cult's leader, stated that if their driver's licenses were revoked, "we'll just go with horse and buggy." (See the *New York Times*, October 21, 1979.)

Military. Avowedly military sects are probably the rarest form of cults, although most cults arguably have militant overtones to one degree or another. These sects are usually located in underdeveloped countries, particularly those with either weak or totalitarian governments.

The House of Israel of Georgetown, Guyana (which has no relation to the former People's Temple of Jonestown, Guyana) is the largest cult of the military type. It is headed by Edward Emanuel Washington, a self-proclaimed rabbi. Washington claims that the mass suicide at Jonestown in 1978 was a "blessing," bringing publicity to him and to Guyanese cults in general, and increasing membership in the House of Israel to more than 8,000.

Like the late Jim Jones, Washington preaches that he is God. "When you pray tonight," he says to his followers, "you pray to me." He also tells

Rabbi Emmanuel Washington, leader of the controversial House of Israel sect, George-town, Guyana. (UPI photo.)

his followers that they must be prepared to die for the cult, although he has also stated that he is fervently opposed to the idea of suicide. Disciples of the cult turn over all their possessions to the House of Israel and pledge allegiance to Washington. Washington rules the group absolutely. Members of the cult may not marry, date, or seek outside employment without his express permission. Major decisions are discussed with the group's seven "ministers of state," but Washington has stated that "I think it is safe to say that I am the first and the last word." (See *The New York Times*, October 21, 1979.) Members who infringe rules or otherwise disappoint the cult's leader are punished by a court of three judges who dispense penalties two nights a week.

The House of Israel is both religious and military in nature. Most of its adherents are young men who must, according to Washington, be ready to defend themselves in a race war which Washington sees beginning in Guyana in the near future. The cult leader has stated that there have been numerous attempts on his life and that his headquarters, the Central Synagogue, has been bombed.

The cult has been accused by critics of having been involved in the slaying of a Jesuit priest in Georgetown in 1979 and of having attacked demonstrators at anti-government rallies in Georgetown. One critic, Eusi Kwayana (quoted in *The New York Times*, October 21, 1979) has accused Washington of running a "pseudoreligious cult that has little to do with religion. It's merely a pseudomilitary arm of the ruling party."

Washington himself is a fugitive from American justice. He was known in the United States as David Hill and has a police record as far back as the 1940s. He jumped bail in Cleveland in 1971 after being convicted of corporate blackmail; he was later convicted *in absentia* on two counts of larceny.

People's Temple (Jonestown, Guyana)

The People's Temple, led by the Rev. Jim Jones, rose to grisly prominence on November 18, 1978, when more than 900 of its members died in the Guyana in a mass suicide/murder. The People's Temple contained elements of the religious, fundamentalist, and therapy cult types, based upon a grab-bag doctrine established by Jones. It was, in a sense, the quintessential modern cult.

Since the cult was largely the creation—almost the embodiment—of Jim Jones, any assessment of it must be an assessment of him. He was born a poor country boy in Indiana in 1931, son of an invalid father and a nagging mother who wanted the child to "make something" of himself. In the late

Jonestown, Guyana: hundreds of bodies are visible from the air near the community hall of the People's Temple. (UPI photo.)

1950s, he became a preacher at the Disciples of Christ Christian Church, a middle-of-the-road Protestant denomination. The People's Temple began as an affiliate of the Disciples of Christ, and in 1967 Jones, declaring to his congregation that the world was about to be engulfed by a devastating nuclear war, moved the group to an isolated rural setting in northern California.

At this time, Jones did not display the paranoic qualities that he was later to display. A county judge who knew him personally described him as follows (*The New York Times*, November 26, 1978): "He was a very bright, humanistic person. He didn't seem to be a socialist. They were nice, concerned people. Their most significant characteristic was that they wanted to come to the aid of anyone in trouble. Jones wasn't a fanatic when I knew him, although people were emotionally dependent upon him. The people in his community built their lives around Jones and his church."

The emotional dependence of the congregation on Jones snowballed in later years, fed by Jones's creeping paranoia. A few Temple members later acknowledged that they privately questioned the need for Jones's marathon sermons, his insistence that they spend all their time working, and his increasing preoccupation with sexual matters. It was at this time that Jones instituted his so-called "catharsis sessions," in which members were ridiculed, harangued, and sometimes beaten.

Jones's paranoia took the form of a persecution mania. He became convinced that the CIA was "out to get him," and he had newcomers and visitors searched before they were admitted to the People's Temple site. One member explained: "He hated everybody—the President—but he said he liked Hitler and Lenin." He reserved his particular hatred for defectors from the Temple. At least one such defector, Christopher Lewis, was murdered in San Francisco in 1977, although the crime was never officially connected to Jones or the People's Temple. Two other defectors, Al and Jeannie Mills, were found murdered on February 27, 1980 in Berkeley, California. Again, the crime has not definitely been linked to the People's Temple, although the police admitted that they were investigating that possibility.

When Jones's persecution mania reached unmanageable proportions, he moved the cult to a location in the Guyanese jungle and named the site Jonestown. He considered this move a response to what he considered to be "dark forces that were out to shut down his experiment in communal living."

According to University of Miami psychologist Jose I. Lasaga, "Jonestown was a mini-totalitarian state ruled by the primitive mind of a paranoic." Jones demanded complete loyalty from his followers. Most the the cult members were characterized by psychiatrists as dissatisfied, vulnerable, and

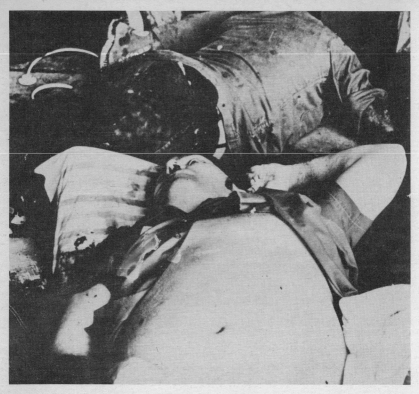

Reverend Jim Jones, leader of the People's Temple cult, lies shot to death in his agricultural retreat, Jonestown, Guyana. (UPI photo.)

impressionable, who sought to "merge with their idealized omnipotent leader in hopes of overcominq their lack of . . . self-esteem." (Richard B. Ulman of the New York Medical College, quoted in *Science News*, December 1, 1979.)

Jones kept his followers in a vulnerable state by overworking them and doling out unlimited supplies of drugs. He became obsessed with the idea of dying for "the cause." When relatives of Temple members lodged complaints, Jones replied in a letter: "We must develop the courage of dying for a cause. We likewise affirm that before we will submit quietly to the interminable plotting and persecution of this politically motivated conspiracy, we will resist actively, putting our lives on the line if it comes to that." He held "suicide rehearsals," rousing his followers in the middle of the night and distributing glasses of red liquid.

A series of complaints and warnings to various U.S. government agencies led to a Congressional investigation of Jonestown led by Rep. Leo

J. Ryan of California. This was the final move that precipitated Jones's suicidal mania. Convinced that the Temple was surrounded by enemies who intended to destroy it, he decreed a "white night" of sacrifice, and the suicide rehearsals became real. Shortly after a shootout at the Jonestown airstrip that left Congressman Ryan dead, 912 People's Temple members (including 276 children) were fed punch laced with cyanide.

A tape recording of the voice of Jones was found after the mass suicide: "We are not committing suicide. It's a revolutionary act." Most of the cult members apparently took the poison willingly. One woman, Bea Orsot, who was absent from Jonestown at the time of the deaths, later stated: "If I had been there, I would have been the first one to stand in that line and take that poison and I would have been proud to take it." (*The New York Times Magazine*, November 18, 1979.)

Several books about the Jonestown experience have been published, among them *The Strongest Poison*, by Mark Lane (Hawthorn, 1979) and *White Night*, by John Peer Nugent (Rawson Wade, 1980.)

Cults and the Law

Perhaps nothing is more indicative of the marginal status of cults than their frequent encounters with the law. Suits and court cases are a recurring note in their existence. Cults have received the scrutiny of the Justice Department, the IRS, and the Supreme Court, as well as having numerous encounters with state and local courts and law-enforcement officials. Aside from relatively straightforward cases involving civil disobedience, violence, or libel suits, several areas of indistinct usage have arisen in relation to the activities of cults.

Perhaps the most crucial, as well as the most argued, is the matter of "brainwashing." Mind control is notoriously difficult to prove or even define, and the real question is how far can law enforcement officials and private individuals go to "protect cult members from themselves?" Following the Jonestown suicidal mania, there was a public outcry that the government should have done something to prevent it. Warnings to officials that something was seriously wrong in Guyana began as early as 1977. On June 22, 1978, James Cobb, a former member of the People's Temple, filed a suit against Jim Jones in which he charged that Jones was planning "mass murder" that "would result in the death of minor children not old enough to make voluntary and informed decisions about serious matters of any nature, much less insane proposals of collective suicide." (See *The New York Times*, November 26, 1978, p. 20.)

Two government inquiries following the Jonestown events reprimanded several Federal agencies for having ignored warnings of potential trouble in Jonestown, and the State Department criticized itself for poor handling of information and other lapses in the matter of the murder of Congressman Ryan. However, both government inquiries concluded by declaring that no one could be held accountable for the tragedy. And impartial observers have to agree that, under the First Amendment mandate that separates church and state, the government would have had little justification for interfering substantively in Jonestown affairs.

Only when cults perpetrate clear infringements of the law is government intervention clearly justifiable. Such intervention was not possible in the case of Jonestown, but in numerous other instances, government agencies are bringing cults to court on a variety of offenses. For instance, several cult "executioners" and "hit men" (according to *The New York Times*, November 15, 1979) have been brought to trial for various murders and beatings. And a landmark Oregon court decision awarded $2 million to a former cult member who endured "anguish and emotional distress" from cult harassment.

Other government inquiries into cults have languished, however. A Congressional subcommittee requested that the Justice Department consider investigating the Unification Church for alleged violations in the fields of banking, taxation, currency, immigration, and arms export, but no action has been taken. And numerous civil suits are on the books against cults, many of them yet undecided. 685 claims have been filed against the People's Temple by relatives of the dead—amounting to a total of $1.7 billion—charging the People's Temple with complicity and responsibility for the deaths of its members. The judge in whose district these cases are to be tried has said, however, that these claims can simply not be satisfied, for the bank accounts of the People's Temple, even if they are all traced and repatriated, would not contain even 1 percent of the amount of the claims. (See *The New York Times*, November 18, 1979).

In all cases involving cults, the courts have made it clear that the only admissable cases are those involving violations of criminal law. In other words, the question of religious freedom is not at issue. The courts have admitted certain cases involving questions of mind control, on the grounds that they are concerned with mental health and not with religious freedom, but this is a highly inexact area, and the cults themselves have argued vociferously to have such cases thrown out of court. There is currently no legal consensus on the question and it promises to be the epicenter of all legal debate involving cults for a number of years to come.

This leads to a wider question with both legal and social implications: Are cults religions? This question is intimately tied in with the legal position of cults, for it impinges broadly on their tax-exempt status. Most cults argue that they are religions, for organized religions are tax-exempt. The IRS has a thorny problem in deciding which organizations are legitimate religions, for many self-styled religions have incorporated themselves in an effort to achieve tax-exempt charitable status.

An interesting and outstanding exception to this policy was the case of the Transcendental Meditation movement, which has tried to shun religious status. The movement attempted to gain scientific acceptance for its meditation techniques, and, to a larger extent, to attempt to spread its doctrine through the medium of governmental agencies, particularly schools. It presented its teachings as a therapeutic technique without religious overtones. But this attempt proved futile, as TM was held in court to be patently religious in nature and thus in conflict with the First Amendment.

What is the future of cults? As long as unstable, confusing world conditions prevail—conditions in which appreciable number of people are led to seek refuge from their besetting problems—cults will flourish. The attractions of an authoritarian organization that relieves the follower of decision-making and promises personal fulfillment are irresistable in such a climate.

Cults are especially attractive in environments where traditional religion has lost its hold. Statistically, many people have abandoned churches, but a large percentage of these have not actually lost their spiritual needs. It is these people who are inclined to gravitate to cults. Two University of Washington sociologists concluded (see *Science News*, January 19, 1980) that there is a direct relationship between the weakening of traditional religion and the proliferation of cults. Cults have been shown to thrive particularly in those areas where church membership is statistically low; conversely, cults languish in areas (such as Utah) where churches retain their congregations.

It is questionable, however, whether any cults will eventually become as large as regular organized religions. Part of the attraction of cults is that they are small and select. The charismatic personality of the cult leader—an important part of the appeal of nearly every cult—functions more powerfully in small groups; the leader's charisma loses effect if his personal contact is diluted by too large numbers of followers.

Further, many cults are predicated on a paranoic basis, i.e., the cult believes that the outside world is plotting against or otherwise oppressing its members. If the cult becomes too large and "successful," such beliefs are obviously ridiculous, and the cult will not survive. These cults have, therefore, a certain built-in self-destructive mechanism.

Sociologists have concluded that most of the people who have drifted away from organized religions have done so because the churches have made claims that science has disproved, thus weakening their credibility. However, many of the cults into which such unchurched people have drifted are more mystical than the abandoned churches. The implication is that many cult followers will eventually drift away from the cults, too.

In the shorter run, however, cults are well entrenched. Their protection under the First Amendment seems assured, and a great deal of irregularity appears to be tolerated both by the government and the public under the umbrella of religious freedom. Whether this religious freedom is abused by cults is a moot point. In the words of a *New York Times* editorial (November 15, 1979): "Unless this dilemma is confronted, not just by the government but also by individuals . . . , the cult phenomenon that exploded in Jonestown may ignite more—and larger—disasters."

PSYCHIC PHENOMENA

Psychic Archeology

Psychic archeology is the exploration of the past through the use of ESP. Proponents of this method claim that psychics can discover facts about earth's prehistory which are unavailable to conventional archeologists.

There are several forms of psychic archeology. One is the location of archeological sites by psychic means; this, broadly speaking, is archeological dowsing. Another is the prediction of artifacts to be found at any particular archeological dig. A third form of psychic archeology is the interpretation of artifacts by psychic means; this is known as psychometry or "object reading" in which a psychic person obtains facts about the history of an artifact, including the people who made it and the environment they lived in.

Psychic archeology began in 1907, when Bligh Bond, an English ecclesiastic, enlisted the aid of a psychic in investigating the history of Glastonbury Abbey in England, a ruined shrine used both by prehistoric Celts and early Christians. Under Bond's guidance, the psychic, who practiced automatic writing, produced floor plans of the ancient, still-unexcavated parts of the abbey. When excavation was finally undertaken, several structures were unearthed that bore a resemblance to the psychic's predictions.

When Bond published his experiences with psychic archeology in the *Gate of Remembrance* (Blackwell, 1918), they created such an adverse reaction in scientific circles that Bond was dismissed as a phony and a crank, and all excavations at Glastonbury Abbey were abandoned.

In the mid-20th century, Stefan Ossowiecki, a Polish psychic, initiated the practice of psychometry, which consists of reading details of archeological objects and implements. Given a spear point from the collection of the museum of the University of Warsaw, for example, Ossowiecki handled it for ten minutes and then proceeded to give investigators from the University a detailed account of stone-age life in an encampment from which he said the spear point derived. Ossowiecki made further descriptions of stone-age life which were reported by A. Borzmowski in "Experiments with Ossowiecki," *International Journal of Parapsychology,* Summer, 1965, 7:259. Among Ossowiecki's observations were the supposed facts that Paleolithic inhabitants of Europe (in what is present-day Belgium) lived in round semisubterranean huts, that they had succeeded in domesticating the dog, and that they cremated their dead.

Edgar Cayce, probably the best known psychic of the 20th century, revealed the existence of a cosmic hall of records—containing the entire history of the earth, man, and civilization—which he called the Akashic records. He claimed that he had the ability to read and consult these records while in trances. Cayce appeared to focus most strongly on past ages where he himself claimed to have lived a former life. He gave detailed reconstructions of ancient Egyptian life, for instance, noting that pre-dynastic Egyptians seemed to be predominantly Negroid rather than Caucasian and that early Egyptians were already experienced farmers. These readings have been partially confirmed by recent archeological findings. Other readings of Cayce concerned the legendary lost continent of Atlantis. His archeological reconstructions are contained in E. Cayce, *The Outer Limits of Edgar Cayce's Power* (Harper & Row, 1971); J. Furst, *Edgar Cayce's Story of Jesus* (Coward McCann, 1960); and G. D. Kitter, *Edgar Cayce On the Dead Sea Scrolls* (Paperback Library, 1970).

None of the claims of Bond, Ossowiecki, or Cayce made much of a dent in orthodox archeological methods. Bond's floor plans of Glastonbury Abbey were put down to coincidence or even to fraud, and Ossowiecki's and Cayce's reconstructions of the life of past epochs were inherently unconfirmable and thus tended to be dismissed by the scientific establishment.

After Cayce, psychic archeology entered a period of eclipse that ended with Jeffrey Goodman's Arizona excavations from 1973 to 1975. Goodman was an archeology student at the University of Arizona who used psychic methods in conducting his own archaeological dig near Flagstaff, Arizona. Goodman published the results of his work in *Psychic Archaeology: Time*

Machine to the Past (Berkley, 1977), a book which refocussed attention on psychic archeology.

Goodman felt that there were a number of anomalies in the conventional anthropological view of the settlement of the New World. In particular, he felt that the continent must have been inhabited by *Homo sapiens* much earlier than is currently believed. Most professional archeologists believe that the New World was settled by Asians who crossed the Bering Straits about 10,000 to 13,000 years ago. Goodman theorized that man must have been present on the American continent 100,000 years ago.

During the summers of 1973 and 1975, he excavated a 27-foot-deep shaft at a site to which he was directed by a psychic. The psychic predicted, among other things, that Goodman would find stone tools at the 4-foot level (corresponding to a date of about 3,000 B.C.); potsherds and shreds of cotton fabric at depths of 7 to 12 feet (7,000 to 8.000 B.C.); and skeletons of early humans at the 20-foot level (100,000 B.C.).

It was Goodman's contention that "archaeology is undergoing a revolution where ESP is replacing the spade as archaeology's primary tool." He claimed results at the Flagstaff dig were astonishing. In his first season at the site, he found presumed stone artifacts at the 15-foot and 20-foot levels that, he claimed, pushed back the date for the entry of ancient man into America to over 25,000 years ago. further excavations at a deeper level convinced him that man had actually been present 100,000 years ago, "at dates far, far earlier than archeological texts have dared to speculate about."

Critics of Goodman's work point out that his initial propositions were ill-founded, his methodology poor, and his discoveries dubious. In particular, Goodman found none of the artifacts that the psychic assured him he would find—potsherds, cotton cloth, or human skeletons. His only substantial discoveries were a small number of alleged stone tools that most trained archeologists claim are not tools at all, but merely stones with sharp edges created by natural abrasion and frost action.

One of Goodman's critics, D. R. Barker of the University of Virginia, in a review of Goodman's book in the *Journal of the American Society for Psychical Research* (April, 1978), concluded: "In short, Goodman found no undisputed evidence of Paleolithic human activity anywhere in his test shaft."

Goodman went on to postulate that the presumed early settlers of the New World were refugees from the legendary lost continents of Atlantis or Lemuria, an assertion that led most serious archeologists to dismiss his work as dubious and unreliable.

Few actual scientific tests of psychic archeology have yet been made, although several other archeologists beside Goodman have begun to use psychics in archeological projects under controlled conditions. Controlled experiments in archeological dowsing have yet to be done, but regular dowsing experiments in Great Britain, Canada, and the Soviet Union have exhibited extremely selective, variable, and unreliable results.

Psychic Photography

The process of photography involves the imprinting of an image on a sensitive film when the film is exposed to light. Psychic photographers claim to produce pictures on photographic film by the power of mind alone, without exposing the film to light.

The history of psychic photography began in Boston in 1842, about 20 years after the process of photography had been invented. William H. Mumler, an engraver and amateur photographer, discovered odd and inexplicable results in portrait photographs he had taken of his family. Some of the shots showed the portraits of Mumler's dead relatives alongside of the "normal" portraits. Mumler's spirit portraits caused a considerable stir in photographic and spiritualistic circles, and they were the subject of several investigations. A judge for the U. S. Court of Appeals, John Edmond, investigated Mumler and, in a letter to the *New York Herald* on August 6, 1853, declared Mumler's authenticity. Skeptics, however, claimed that Mumler's spirit portraits were merely cleverly faked double exposures.

Psychic photography continued to be practiced throughout the 19th century, particularly in Great Britain. Beginning with Frederick Hudson in 1872, a long line of spiritualists obtained portraits of dead relatives and friends—even, in some cases, portraits of people they claimed never to have known while they were alive. The most well known and prolific of the spirit photographers was probably Mrs. Emma Deane, who produced hundreds of portraits of deceased people.

Many of these psychic photographers were investigated by reputable scientists, such as the famed naturalist Dr. Alfred Russel Wallace, but the test conditions under which the experiments took place were never stringent enough to prevent skeptics from crying fraud. The most complete documentation of this phase of photographic spiritualism is probably F. W. Warrick's *Experiments In Psychics* (E. P. Dutton, 1939).

The validity of psychic photography in the twentieth century has repeatedly been questioned by investigators. Even the former president of the

Parapsychology Foundation, Eileen Garrett, has been on record as believing that all cases of psychic photography were fraudulent.

The invention of Polaroid film gave rise to a new kind of psychic photograph—one imprinted directly on sensitive paper without being first developed as a negative. Double exposure is difficult on Polaroid film, as the film is very light-sensitive and no negative is available. Most psychics who work with Polaroid film do not produce exposures in which portraits of deceased persons are found along side of portraits of those who actually sat for the photograph. Usually the Polaroid exposures show single images, often of an object or a physical scene.

The psychic photographer Ted Serios uses Polaroid film to produce images of scenes seen by him in out-of-body experiences. Serios claims to be capable of astral projection, in which he leaves his own body, visits a distant place, then returns to his physical body and records his impressions of the place on unexposed Polaroid film. His photographs have appeared in several magazines of popular photography and also in *The World of Ted Serios*, by Colorado University professor Jule Eisenbud. Serios' credibility has been damaged by repeated and convincing allegations of fraud, however. No tests have been made of his ability under stringent conditions, and he is not currently taken seriously by impartial observers.

The most prominent modern psychic photographer is probably Masuaki Kiyota, an 18-year-old Japanese who underwent a rigorous series of tests in London in 1978. Masuaki claimed the ability to project mental images onto unexposed Polaroid film. His talent is known in Japan as "nengraphy" and is often called in the West by the colloquial term "thoughtography." Prior to the London tests, Masuaki had produced a number of famous psychic scenes. The most impressive were several aerial shots of the Statue of Liberty in New York, supposedly made from angles that would have precluded any cheating.

The London tests were designed to be quite strict and to provide an accurate assessment of whether psychic photographs could really be produced by the power of the psychic's mind alone. They were conducted under the control of Professor John Hasted of Birkbeck College and Christopher Scott of the Society for Psychical Research. A television crew was also present during most of the duration of the expeirment. The tests were designed to start informally and progress to successive levels of difficulty, involving tighter controls.

On the second day of the tests, Masuaki showed two photographs: one of a shadowy, indistinct scene that resembled Trafalgar Square in London which presumably showed a section of Nelson's Column; and the other an

The "Trafalgar Square" photo. (Mike Hutchinson, *The Skeptical Inquirer*)

even more blurry photograph said to show six guardsmen in file. It was established, however that the camera and film had been with Masuaki overnight, and while experts from the Polaroid Corporation could not tell whether the film pack had been tampered with, the two photographs could not be held as evidence of Masuaki's ability, as they had not been proved to have been made in the laboratory.

During the course of the experiments, Masuaki produced additional photographs: a representation of several square and triangular shapes that was dubbed "The Matterhorn" because the triangular shapes resembled mountains; and an impression of the Eiffel Tower with a lamppost in the foreground. These photographs were produced after Masuaki had had both camera and film in his possession, away from the laboratory, for at least two hours.

Masuaki made numerous attempts to produce psychic photographs in the laboratory, but they all ended in failure. He also tried to make exposures on the film during a small party in his hotel room, with the television crew present, but this attempt also had no results.

When one of the Polaroid experts said that it might be theoretically possible to take a Polaroid film pack apart, expose several exposures, and

Image of Royal Albert Hall exposed onto Polaroid film by Mike Hutchinson without a camera, using a color transparency and a "pinhole projector". (*The Skeptical Inquirer*)

put the pack together again—all without leaving tell-tale traces of manipulation—several of the experimenters then attempted to test this theory by taking apart a film pack and reassembling it. They found that the film pack could be unloaded in conditions of near darkness, unwound, and exposed by means of a crude "pinhole projector" using an ordinary slide viewer. The film could then be reinserted into the pack and replaced in the camera without it being obvious that the pack had been tampered with. The experimenters succeeded in making photographs by this method which achieved much of the same blurry, grainy quality of Masuaki's photographs.

Two of the investigators, Christopher Scott and Michael Hutchinson, reported the results of the tests in *The Skeptical Inquirer*, Spring 1979. As Masuaki had failed to produce psychic photographs in the laboratory under conditions which had been acceptable to him, the conclusion was that his alleged psychic ability was suspect: "Under fairly tight conditions Masuaki Kiyota was unable to fulfill his claim to project mental images onto film. The only time he achieved any success was after the film had been in his possession—and not under any control—for at least two hours." The presumption was that the photographs were produced by fraudulent means.

A modern treatment of psychic photography is Hans Holzer's *Psychic Photography* (McGraw-Hill, 1969).

Psychic Crime-solving

Police investigators make use of psychics who claim that their extraordinary powers can help solve baffling cases.

Such psychic crime-solving has until recently been more common in Europe than in the United States. The exploits of several European psychics have been extensively documented, particularly Gerard Croiset and M. B. Dykshoorn. Croiset works primarily through psychometry, or handling objects associated with a crime. Dykshoorn uses a small bent wire like a dowsing rod to assist him to "see" events connected to a crime. Both men are highly regarded by police detectives, with whom they work closely, Croiset in the Netherlands, Dykshoorn all over Europe and Australia and recently in the United States. Croiset's exploits are chronicled in J. H. Pollack, *Croiset, The Clairvoyant* (Doubleday, 1964), Dykshoorn's in his autobiography *My Passport Says Clairvoyant* (Hawthorne, 1974).

The most extensive tests of psychic crime-solving have been conducted in Los Angeles, where the Los Angeles Police Department has enlisted the aid of psychics in a number of difficult cases. The LAPD also pioneered the use of hypnosis as an investigative technique. One of the most conspicuous successes of psychic crime-solving occurred in the case of the South Gate killings, the murders of three boys in the community of South Gate, California. Police investigated the case for two years, with no results. They finally turned to a local psychic, who envisioned a particular face and helped police artists reconstruct it on paper. Using this clue, police arrested an acquaintance of one of the murdered youths three weeks later.

Dr. Martin Reiser, director of the behavioral science laboratory of the Los Angeles Police Department, then undertook an extensive investigation of the possibilities of psychic crimesolving. In a controlled experiment in 1978, eight professional and four amateur psychics were provided with information about two solved and two unsolved crimes. The tests consisted of two parts. First, the psychics were given sealed envelopes containing evidence related to the crime and asked to try to predict what the envelopes contained. After the envelopes were opened, the psychics examined the evidence and tried to obtain clues to the crimes.

One crime involved an 89-year-old church historian who had been murdered. One of the psychics determined that the crime had occurred around a church and stressed that a church played an important role in the crime. In another crime, a woman with two children was murdered by car thieves who were trying to steal her car. Five of the psychics predicted that an automobile played a significant role in the crime. Three of them also mentioned that children were involved.

The published results of the survey included an example of the type of responses the psychics gave. One psychic, for instance, gave the following account: "I get a man, black. I hear screaming, screaming. I'm running up stairs and down. My head . . . someone bounces my head on the wall or floor. I see trees—a park? In the city, but green. Did this person live there? What does the number '2' mean? I get a bad, bloody taste in my mouth. The names 'John' or 'Joseph' or something like that. I am running on the street like a crazy. This is a very serious crime. I can't hold the envelope in my hand." (See M. Reiser et al, "An Investigation of the Use of Psychics in the Investigation of Major Crimes," *Journal of Police Science and Administration*, March 1979).

Although several psychics occasionally produced interesting clues, the results of the experiment in general were disappointing. To quote Reiser: "A psychic may generate relatively accurate information on one case, but be totally incorrect on another; a correct information may be generated only in parts of each case; all information from some psychics may be incorrect; a psychic may have picked up correct information about one case, but may have reported it for another case (displacement); a psychic may be more accurate on one day as opposed to another . . . Overall, little, if any, information was elicited from the twelve psychic participants that would provide material helpful in the investigation of the major crimes in question. There was a low rate of psychic congruence and accuracy among the responses elicited in this research. We are forced to conclude, based on our results, that the usefulness of psychics as an aid in criminal investigation has not been validated."

This conclusion does not mean that psychics do not have the ability to learn details of a crime through paranormal means—only that their results are so variable that police departments cannot rely on them in a standard way.

Details of alleged crime-solving by psychic means are contained in the following books: F. Archer, *Crime and the Psychic World* (William Morrow, 1969); G. Frank, *The Boston Strangler* (New American Library, 1966); and P. Tabori, *Crime and the Occult* (Taplinger, 1974).

Psychic Surgery

Faith healing has long had a worldwide following. Psychic surgery is a form of faith-healing in which the healer, possessed by psychic powers, actually performs surgery on the subject.

Several techniques may be involved in psychic surgery. In some cases, the psychic surgeon believes he is possessed by the spirit of a dead doctor; he mimes an operation while in a trance, guided presumably by the spirit doctor. Other psychic surgeons perform actual operations, making incisions, usually without anesthesia, and cause instantaneous healing of the wound.

Psychic surgery must not be confused with psychosurgery. Psychosurgery is a standard medical technique involving brain surgery. According to Willard Gaylin of the Hastings Institute of Society, Ethics and the Life Sciences, it is "surgical destruction of certain portions of the brain for purposes of treating psychiatric conditions." Psychic surgery, on the other hand, is surgery performed through paranormal means; it involves operating on any part of the body, not on the brain.

The most widely known and well documented psychic surgeon of recent times was a poorly educated Brazilian peasant known as Arigo, who practiced during the 1950s and 1960s. Arigo claimed to be possessed by the spirit of "Dr. Fritz," a German doctor who he said practiced in Estonia between 1914 and 1918. Dr. Fritz told Arigo that he had made several serious mistakes as a surgeon and that he had sworn to continue his practice after death, as penance. Arigo performed his surgery in a sort of trance, speaking with a German-accented voice.

Arigo was investigated by several medical teams, including one from the United States in which Dr. Andrija K. Puharich, a doctor from Northwestern University and a believer in psychic phenomenon, witnessed several of Arigo's procedures. Arigo saw patients twice a day—early in the morning and late in the afternoon—when he was not working at his regular job in the government welfare office. For many patients, Arigo simply made a quick examination, then wrote out a prescription that he claimed would alleviate the illness or malady.

When actual surgery was required, Arigo usually used a rusty penknife. He did not clean the knife or use any antiseptic procedures. Nor did he anesthetize his patients. His operations usually came under the medical category of minor surgery—cysts, tumors, cataracts, etc. In one operation witnessed by Puharich, Arigo operated on a man with an eye ailment. According to Puharich's account, he simply plunged the 4-inch knife into the man's eye, under the lid, and began scraping violently between the eyeball and inside of the eyelid. The patient showed no reaction at all. Arigo finally withdrew the knife, telling the man: "You will be well."

Arigo eventually came under scrutiny both by the Catholic Church—which claimed he was practicing black magic—and the Brazilian government, which charged him with practicing medicine without a license. He spent over a year in jail before his death in 1971.

Arigo evidently believed in what he was doing and had no doubt that "Dr. Fritz" was actually the entity that performed the operations and wrote the prescriptions. Hundreds of Brazilians who consulted him testified to the efficacy of his cures. But impartial observers noted that Arigo's success at psychic surgery might be explained by a combination of semi-hypnosis and crude untutored medical knowledge. For instance, Arigo's supposed medical acumen and knowledge of prescription drugs could have been picked up, consciously or unconsciously, at his job in the welfare office, where doctors often treated patients in his presence.

It is true that he used a dirty knife, that he did not tie off blood vessels, and that he did not use stitches. But it is also true that his operations were minor ones—and no follow-up was performed on most patients to see whether complications ensued. Many of Arigo's patients were reputable professionals such as scientists and executives, but most of them were admitted believers in parapsychology and the occult. Arigo may actually have performed a kind of hypnosis upon them—again, it may have been unconscious—in place of anesthesia.

The Philippines have been another center of psychic surgery, where several healers, notably Tony Agpaoa, have been active. Agpaoa, like Arigo, uses no anesthetic, but unlike Arigo, he uses no knife either. He appears to make an incision with his bare hands. Diseased tissue is then removed with his hands or snipped away with unsterilized scissors. After the operation, Agpaoa passes his hands over the incision, which appears to heal instantly, leaving no scar.

Filmed records have been made of Agpaoa at work. Skeptics such as Milbourne Christopher, a professional magician, believe that feats of psychic surgery are actually cases of clever conjuring. (See M. Christopher, *Mediums, Mystics, and the Occult*, T. Y. Crowell, 1975). It is claimed that operations of Agpaoa's type can be faked. For instance, if the healer palms a small quantity of blood and a piece of animal tissue, he can then pinch the skin of the patient to make it appear as if an incision has been made. After the "operation," the blood is wiped away, making it appear that the incision has been miraculously closed. If an actual cure follows such an operation, it would be the result of suggestion—the placebo effect, in reality.

Because most instances of psychic surgery have taken place in backward regions under controlled conditions, there is no scientific proof that psychic surgery works or even is a genuine phenomenon. The medical establishment does not endorse the practice, nor do parapsychologists support the procedure. Anyone who submits to psychic surgery does so at his or her own risk. The purported benefits may seem small in comparison to the risks involved.

Documentation of psychic surgery is contained in: J. G. Fuller, *Arigo: Surgeon of the Rusty Knife* (T. Y. Crowell, 1974); H. Sherman, *Wonder Healers of the Philippines* (De Vorss, 1967); and T. Valentine, *Psychic Surgery* (Henry Regnery, 1973).

PARAPSYCHOLOGY

The Psi Phenomenon

Modern exploration of the paranormal began in 1930, when Dr. Joseph Banks Rhine began his now famous series of experiments at the Parapsychology Laboratory of the Psychology Department of Duke University in North Carolina. Since that date, parapsychology has come under increasing scientific scrutiny as researchers attempt to gather evidence of the four main parapsychological processes: clairvoyance, telepathy, precognition, and psychokinesis.

Clairvoyance, also known as second sight or remote viewing, is the ability to see in the mind's eye an object or event which is not actually visible to the eye. Telepathy is mind-reading, the ability to transmit or receive mental messages across large distances. Precognition is the ability to see or predict the future. Psychokinesis is the faculty of moving inanimate objects using the power of the mind alone; it is often referred to as the "mind over matter" process. Clairvoyance, telepathy, precognition, and psychokinesis are grouped together under the common heading of "psi" phenomenon.

The 50-year history of research in the paranormal has had its share of ups and downs. The ups have consisted of experiments whose results provide suggestive evidence of the reality of psi. The downs consist of numerous instances of fakery, as well as the steady opposition of the scientific establishment, which is reluctant to accept parapsychology as a legitimate scientific

Dr. J. B. Rhine. (UPI photo)

discipline. Nevertheless, research into the paranormal continues to expand, becoming more sophisticated in the process.

The existence of ESP is already accepted by a large proportion of the general public. An increasing number of scientists are also coming to accept ESP as either a proven fact or a strong possibility. Dr. Mahlon Wagner, a psychologist connected with the State University of New York at its Oswego

West Duke Building, Dr. Rhine's laboratory. (Duke University News Service)

campus, conducted a poll of 2,100 professors at universities and colleges across the United States. The results of the survey, quoted in *The New York Times* (January 29, 1980), established that of the scientists who responded to Dr. Wagner's questionnaire, 9 percent believed that extrasensory perception was "an established fact" and 45 percent felt that ESP was "a likely possibility." The implication is that a majority of the scientists in the United

States is now prepared to take parapsychology seriously, a dramatic change since 1930, when parapsychology was dismissed by most scientists as pseudoscience or quackery.

Rhine and the Duke University Parapsychology Laboratory are credited with conducting the first scientifically-controlled research on psi. The late Dr. Rhine was the first to use statistics and mathematical methods in psi testing. Throughout the 1930s and 1940s, Duke University was the leading center for psi testing. Several famous experiments, particularly the Pearce—Pratt experiments of 1933–34 and the Pratt-Woodruff experiments of 1938–39, stood for many years as the best evidence for the existence of psi.

In 1955, G. R. Price launched a hard-hitting attack on these and other psychic experiments. (See *Science*, August 26, 1955). He accused parapsychologists of fraud, alleging widespread collusion between agents and subjects. He also claimed that psi experiments were poorly controlled and conducted, with many instances of clerical or statistical error, as well as the possibility of subtle, unintentional clues passing between agent and subject. In 1972, however, Price retracted some of his accusations, stating: "I have had some correspondence with J. B. Rhine which has convinced me that I was highly unfair to him in what I said."

C. E. M. Hansel continued the attack on parapsychology in his book *ESP: A Scientific Evaluation* (Scribner, 1966). He charged that the security measures of the Duke University experimenters denied that any misconduct had taken place during the experiments, but Hansel's accusations made scientific observers wary of the Duke results. As long as the *possibility* of fraud exists, the established rules of scientific experimentation say that the results of an experiment must be viewed with skepticism.

The Soal-Goldney-Shackleton Experiments

The Soal-Goldney-Shackleton card-guessing experiments were conducted between January 1941 and April 1943 and have probably received more attention than any other single piece of research in the field, before or since. They were tests for telepathy; the subject was the psychic Basil Shackleton.

The experiment had presumably stringent precautions against fraud—observers were selected, witnesses were asked to sign the score sheets, and signed copies were sent to third parties. One of the observers, C. D. Broad, professor of philosophy at Cambridge University, stated: "The precautions taken to prevent deliberate fraud or the unwitting conveyance of information by normal means . . . (are) seen to be absolutely water-tight." and "There can be no doubt that the events described happened and were correctly reported; that the odds against chance-coincidence piled up to billions to one. . . ." Rhine termed the experiment "one of the most outstanding researches yet made in the field . . . Soal's work was a milestone in ESP research." The experiment was thoroughly documented; the published report is more detailed than that for any other ESP experiment and copies of the records are still available at the Society for Psychical Research for study.

The experiments were conducted with subject and agent seated in different rooms, out of sight of each other. A third person, the experiment supervisor, sat across from the agent at a table. They were separated by a screen with a small circular hole at eye level. At the beginning of each run, five cards were placed face down in a row in front of the agent; each card had the picture of a different animal on its face. The supervisor was not allowed to see the placement of the cards. The supervisor would then pick a number from a random number table—any number from one to five—and hold up a card bearing that number before the hole in the screen. The agent, on the other side of the screen, would observe the number and pick a corresponding card—termed the "target card"—from the row of five in front of him. For instance, if the number the supervisor held up was four, the agent would pick up the card in the fourth position in front of him. He would concentrate for a moment on the animal pictured on the card, then replace the card face down in its place. The supervisor would then signal the subject in the adjoining room to make his choice.

A run consisted of fifty trials, which meant that, statistically, Shackleton had one chance in ten of guessing right. The final tabulation yielded a strange result. Shackleton achieved poor results in identifying the target card. But he achieved striking success in identifying the card which came up two cards *after* the target card. In a total of eighteen sittings, he scored numerous successes. In one series, he obtained 439 hits where chance would dictate only 321 hits. The odds against such a chance occurrence are 100 billion to one.

For many years, the Soal-Goldney-Shackleton experiments were considered to be the best evidence of the existence of ESP. Skeptics had a few quibbles, but nothing conclusive. Hansel for instance complained that Shackleton was able to obtain his spectacular results only in this particular set of experiments, and, in other experiments with different agents, he was never able to score above chance. Such results seemed suspicious, although psi investigators pointed out that such "on-again-off-again" results were common in ESP experiments. In 1956, G. R. Price, an avowed skeptic, asked to look at the original handwritten score sheets of the experiment and was informed by Soal that they had been lost in 1945. Copies remained, though not in the original handwriting. Price implied that such a "convenient" loss was suspicious.

In 1960, Soal and Goldney admitted that Mrs. Gretl Albert, who had participated as an agent in two of the runs of the Shackleton series, had claimed at the time that she had seen Soal altering the figures during the experiment. She had reported this to Goldney, who had been unable to find any evidence of cheating but who had kept all the records for possible further use. The basic accusation was that Soal had tampered with the set-up of the runs or had doctored the score sheets, changing ones into fours or fives. This hypothesis was subjected to a remarkably rigorous statistical analysis by C. Scott and P. Haskell and reported *in Proceedings of the Society for Psychical Research*, October, 1974. Scott and Haskell found overwhelming evidence that the results of Sittings 8 and 16 and the first three sheets of Sitting 17 had been doctored. They concluded that the results of these sittings could not be accounted for either in terms of chance or of ESP "operating in a direct or straightforward manner;" cheating was therefore indicated. Most parapsychologists now admit that the Soal-Goldney-Shackleton experiments are of doubtful authenticity. Even though evidence of cheating was found in only three out of the forty sittings, observers admit that these three instances throw the rest of the series into doubt. As Scott and Haskell conclude: "It seems unlikely that any significant proportion of the results in the Shackleton series was obtained by extrasensory perception."

The Taylor Experiments

This is an example of a series of experiments that *failed* to find any evidence of psychokinetic effects. The experiments were scientifically important, however, because they shed light on how psi experiments can go awry.

John C. Taylor, a mathematician at Kings College in England, reported the experiments in *Nature* (vol. 276, p. 64). The experiments were intended as tests for the electromagnetic nature of psi phenomena but offered insights into psychokinetic experiences as well. Taylor's tests involved large, "macroscopic" effects in contrast to Jahn's and Curry's "microscopic" effects.

At first, the results of the experiments seemed astoundingly impressive. In one test—a needle rotation experiment—subjects were asked to move their hands back and forth around a cylinder containing a needle suspended by a thread. The object was to try to cause the needle to turn. The initial results indicated that each subject had produced an average 60 degree rotation of the needle.

In a second test, a short section of a drinking straw was placed on a piece of plastic floating in a glass of water under a glass dome. Subjects were instructed to try to rotate the piece of straw while sitting quietly in front of the dome—and without bringing their hands near the dome. Again, the preliminary outcome was impressive. The subjects succeeded in rotating the straw up to 20 degrees.

When the researchers made a close examination of the conditions under which the experiments had been conducted, however, they found several problems that demolished the seemingly impressive results.

In the needle rotation experiment, Taylor discovered that the observed effects were caused by a static charge induced on the needle from the outer surface of the cylinder. When he rubbed anti-static ointment over the outside of the cylinder, the successful results immediately vanished. In the drinking straw experiment, it was eventually discovered that warm air from an electric heater behind the subject caused a convection current within the glass dome and caused the drinking straw to rotate. When the experiment was repeated with the heater turned off, none of the subjects was successful in causing the straw to rotate.

These experiments have pointed up the necessity for very carefully controlled conditions during psi testing.

Machine Testing for ESP

G. R. Price in his famous 1955 article, "Science and the Supernatural," called for new experimental methods using automated electronic equipment. He implied that this would be the only way to eliminate the problems of human error and fraud that had plagued previous experiments.

Dr. Helmut Schmidt, currently a physicist at the Mind Science Foundation in San Antonio, designed the first machine for testing ESP. It was a fully automated random target generator based on the decay of radioactive material, considered one of the most random processes in nature. (Radioactive decay is the process by which a radioactive material gives off radioactive particles and eventually turns into a non-radioactive substance. The decay or uranium into lead is a good example.) The machine automatically recorded the subject's guesses and hits, thus eliminating the need for supervisors or agents. The subject was alone with the machine; there was no chance that the presence of another person could provide cues, either intentionally or unintentionally.

Various versions of the Schmidt machine have been used by other researchers. All operate on the principal of random radioactive decay. The machine's radioactive core delivers electrons randomly to a Geiger counter. A pulse generator sweeps simultaneously over an array of target-choice possibilities. When an electron reaching the Geiger counter flips a switch that controls one of the target choices, a lamp on the target display board lights up. Since the process is completely random, each lamp has an equal probability of being the next target; if there are four lamps on the board, each has a 25 percent chance of being illuminated.

In experiments with these machines, the subject is essentially trying to guess which lamp will be lit up next. The subject registers his choice by pushing a button on the console. Feedback is immediate; the glowing light tells him whether he has guessed right or not. Guesses are recorded automatically on tape by a keypunch machine.

Most modern experiments in parapsychology are now conducted with these machines. They are thus tests for either precognition (guessing which light will be illuminated next) or psychokinesis (influencing the radioactive decay process itself). Indeed, most researchers do not differentiate between precognition and psychokinesis in these tests, since presumably it would be impossible to say with certainty which method the subject was actually using.

Parapsychology and the Media

Television, newspapers, magazines and radio have a seemingly insatiable appetite for ESP stories. Unfortunately, the media often slant their reporting in favor of sensational or "positive" accounts of extrasensory experiences. Stories supporting the existence of ESP are common; those reporting negative evidence are less numerous.

Occasionally, the media go to some lengths in their search for a good story. In 1978, for instance, a Baltimore television station accepted Mark Stone's offer to predict the outcome of the World Series. Stone was a stockbroker and part-time "mentalist." Two days before the World Series began, he sealed his predictions in a metal box and turned them over to the station's sportscaster. When the box was opened after the final game, Stone's preductions were astonishingly accurate.

Stone was back in a few months to predict the results of the Super Bowl game. This time, however, seasoned onlookers caught him tampering with the sealed box that contained his predictions. It became obvious that he had used the old "jammed lock ruse,' well known to magicians, to insert his "predictions" into the box *after* the game had been played.

Commentators criticized the TV station for its gullibility and its lack of responsibility in checking Stone out carefully before giving him such prominent exposure on a news program. A columnist for the Baltimore Sun wrote: "When you stoop to putting on charlatans with impossible sports predictions—and thus give them the credence of being associated with a "news' broadcast—you pass the level of comedy and sink to the level of dangerous ridiculousness." Another columnist wrote: "Surely the time taken up by Stone's appearance could have been used for something else—real news, for instance."

It is an open question as to who is really responsible for biased or sensationalized reporting—the media or the public. As long as the public retains its appetite for ESP stories, however poorly documented, the media will continue to play them up. The media position can be summed up by the old excuse: "We're only giving the public what it wants."

The credulousness of at least a proportion of the news-consuming public is almost unlimited. A spate of feature stories appeared in 1977 featuring Lee Fried, a student at Duke University. According to the stories, Fried had predicted the March 27, 1977 airplane collision in the Canary Islands. Fried had made a written prediction one week before the crash; the prediction was inserted into a small box and sealed in the safe of the president of Duke University and only opened after the event. The prediction read: "583 Die in Collision of 747s in Worst Disaster in Aviation History."

Fried then revealed himself as an amateur magician. He frankly admitted having planned the prediction as a stunt. Fried had written the supposed "prediction" *after* the airplane crash and inserted it into the box, by sleight of hand, as the box was being removed from the safe. He said: "I don't claim to have any supernormal abilities, ESP or anything like that. I don't claim to have any of these things. I've been a performing magician for some time." Yet many news features on Fried neglected to mention this fact, and Fried himself stated later that he had been confronted by people who refused to believe that his prediction was faked.

The question of the media and ESP is considered at length by James Randi in "The Media and Reports on the Paranormal" in *The Humanist* (July-August, 1977).

Parapsychology Today

Despite the problems of fraud, media misrepresentation and scientific skepticism, parapsychology continues to grow as a field. The body of statistical evidence relating to parapsychology is huge. Parapsychologists themselves are largely convinced that the existence of ESP is by now a proven fact. For the most part, they have given up trying to convince the skeptics, preferring to devote their time to refining current knowledge of the paranormal. The research frontier today consists of three main thrusts: (a) defining the conditions which lead to or encourage psi, (2) describing what actually happens in psi, and (3) formulating hypotheses for a possible scientific basis for psi.

Modern Psi Experiments

Modern psi experimentation is no longer solely the province of "psychically-oriented" organizations. Of course, a great deal of statistical inquiry still goes on at these centers. But more traditional centers of science and learning are also becoming involved in psi research. One of the most impressive modern experiments, the Jahn/Curry psychokinesis tests, was conducted at Princeton University; Dr. Robert G. Jahn is dean of the University's Engineering and Applied Science department. Such a broadening of the base of parapsychological research is an indication of how far parapsychology has come in enlisting the support of the traditionally skeptical scientific establishment.

Difficulties of Psi Experimentation

Explorations into the paranormal are hounded by certain difficulties which are peculiar to the field of parapsychology and do not normally appear in experiments in other fields of science.

Psi tests involving human subjects are often so complex that they cannot be controlled as easily as ordinary laboratory experiments. Especially in the case of clairvoyance or telepathy tests, which may involve subjects, agents, and supervisors in several separate locations, experiments may be open to all sorts of inadvertent lapses or cases of human error—or even of fraud. Such control problems may go unnoticed by the experimenters, not out of carelessness but simply because of failure to provide adequate safeguards at every point of the experiment.

Modern testing methods involving machines have evolved largely in response to objections such as these. Experiments with Schmidt-type random event generators are an attempt to bring psi experimentation into the laboratory and subject it to unimpeachable scientific methods.

The Decline Effect

One of the most distressing problems in the field of psi research is the inability of experimental subjects to maintain high test scores after a successful series of runs. Even gifted subjects in time seem to lose their ESP ability. There is currently no convincing explanation as to why these subjects should simply seem to "run down," like a dying battery.

Charles Tart has noted in "Drug-Induced States of Consciousness," *Handbook of Parapsychology* (Van Nostrand, 1977): "One of the major problems in attempting to study and understand paranormal (psi) phenomena is simply that the phenomena don't work strongly or reliably. The average subject seldom shows any individually significant evidence of psi in laboratory experiments, and even gifted subjects, while occasionally able to demonstrate important amounts of psi in the laboratory, are still very erratic and unpredictable in their performance."

J. B. Rhine has elaborated on this problem by noting that psi is an as yet imperfectly understood function. In *The Reach of Mind* (Wm. Sloane, 1947), he noted: "Psi is an incredibly elusive function! This is not merely to say that ESP and PK have been hard phenomena to to demonstrate, the hardest perhaps that science has ever encountered . . . Psi has remained an unknown quantity so long . . . because of a definite characteristic of elusiveness inherent in its psychological nature . . . A number of those who have conducted ESP or PK experiments have reported that they found no evidence of psi capacity . . . Then, too, experimenters who were once successful may even then lose their gift . . . All of the highscoring subjects who have kept on very long have declined. . . ."

Actual cheating, as opposed to casual misrepresentation, has unfortunately been fairly common in psi experimentation. In any modern experiment, if even the *possibility* of cheating exists, the results of the experiment are likely to be disregarded by both scientists and parapsychologists. Carefully controlled procedures and rigorous laboratory methods are the only safeguards against cheating.

The cheating problem has been most widespread in the cases of skilled magicians posing as "psychics." Even sophisticated scientists have been taken in by such performers. Uri Geller's presumed clairvoyant and psychokinetic powers were "verified" by two Stanford Research Institute physicists; but Geller has since been exposed as a skilled magician and is considered a dead issue by most parapsychologists. (Probably the most complete exposure of Geller's fraudulent practices is "Tests and Investigations of Three Psychics," by James Randi, *Skeptical Inquirer*, Spring/Summer, 1978). Other frauds have occurred and continue to occur. Examples are Margery Crandon and Eustasia Palladino (who have been exposed as fraudulent mediums), Ted Serios (whose alleged ability to create psychic photographs on Polaroid film are highly suspicious), and a group of Russian women who claimed to be able to "see" with their fingers (M. Gardner explained the fraud in *Science*, vol. 151: 654, 1966).

Cheating is both more serious and more deplorable when it takes place among actual psi researchers. In 1974, Dr. Jay Levy, an MD who was widely considered to be the heir apoarent to J. B. Rhine at the Institute of Parapsychology at Duke University, was caught by several of his assistants tinkering with his test results. Levy confessed his guilt and resigned, and all of his work at the Institute has since been called into question. (See J. B. Rhine,

"Second Report on a Case of Experimenter Fraud," *Journal of Parapsychology*, [December 1975].

The Levy affair illustrates some of the pitfalls and temptations of psi experimentation. At the time he resigned, Levy explained to Rhine that he had been obtaining successful results on his experiments for some time but that these results had begun to deteriorate. He said that he doctored his data in an effort to keep interest in his field of experimentation alive. Dr. Theodore Barber of the Medfield Foundation in Massachusetts has attributed this and other instances of data "fudging" to the heavy pressure in the scientific and academic world to obtain positive results. (See "Pitfalls in Research: Nine Investigator and Experimenter Effects," in *Second Handbook on Research and Teaching*, [Rand-McNally, 1973]. Rhine himself stated that cheating is characteristic of young disciplines: "Fifty or more years ago, there were notorious cases of experimenter fraud in physics, biology, and medicine, among other fields."

Rhine also accused scientific skeptics of being too eager to cry fraud, without any real basis for doing so. (See "Security Versus Deception in Parapsychology," *Journal of Parapsychology* [vol. 38, 1974]). Rhine charged that the last gasp of skepticism is the charge of fraud. When more legitimate criticisms, such as those of methodology, have failed, detractors are led to attack the honesty of the experimenters.

Ganzfeld Technique

ESP research took a large step forward in the 1960s when the concept of altered states of consciousness began to receive public attention. Psi researchers discovered that altered states of consciousness, such as dreaming, meditation, and deep relaxation, facilitated psi performance.

Charles Honorton, director of research at the Parapsychology Division of the Maimonides Medical Center in Brooklyn, New York has pointed out that psi is a weak and tenuous phenomenon that occurs only under favorable conditions. When the mind is being bombarded with the usual stimuli of everyday life, psi functioning is often completely obliterated. For psi communication to occur at its optimum levels, some of these extraneous sensory distractions must be blotted out.

The ganzfeld ("whole field") technique is a sensory-deprivation method that simulates the floating state of sleep without leading to actual unconsciousness on the subject's part. During a ganzfeld session, the subject is isolated in a soundproofed room. He or she reclines in a movable chair while listening to "white noise," an unobtrusive semi-hypnotic sound that tends to sedate the brain. The room is lit by a dim red lamp. The subject is able to open his eyes but sees only a diffuse rosy glow. After only a brief time in this ganzfeld environment, the subject is unable to tell whether his eyes are open or closed. His mind is in a totally relaxed psi-conducive state.

Clairvoyance

The classic modern tests of clairvoyance are the Puthoff-Targ experiments of 1976, conducted at the Stanford Research Institute (SRI) in Menlo Park, California. They were acclaimed originally as nearly perfect experiments, but they have recently been subjected to ingenious and damaging criticism. Nevertheless, they will stand as probably the best modern demonstrations of clairvoyance.

Harold Puthoff and Russell Targ conducted several series of interconnected experiments, including more than fifty complex tests with nine subjects. The tests demonstrated the ability of some of the subjects to "see" places and objects at great distances. The results of the experiments were published in the *Proceedings of the Institute of Electrical and Electronic Engineers* (March 1976), which was a landmark in the publication of paranormal research in established scientific journals.

The Puthoff-Targ experiments followed complicated procedures and adopted complex scoring methods, all with a view toward lessening the possibilities of unintentional error. Subjects for the tests included both experienced psychics (including Ingo Swann) and untutored "learners."

In Puthoff's and Targ's first series of tests, a subject was isolated with an experimenter. At the same time, a "target team" consisting of from two to four other experimenters picked at random a "target location" from a list of 100 locations in the Menlo Park area. The list consisted of various locations with strong identifying traits, such as a swimming pool, a tennis court, and a playground.

After picking the item from the list, the target team then drove to the named location. All locations were within a 30-minute drive from SRI, and when those 30 minutes had elapsed, the subject was asked to guess where the target team was. The subject described his impressions (they were recorded on tape) and made drawings of the site (these were carefully preserved). The subject had fifteen minutes to "view" the site and record his impressions. When the fifteen were up, the test ended: the subject left the test room and the target team returned from the test location.

Each subject completed either eight or nine tests. A research analyst was given the subject's sealed packets and asked to rank each packet on a scale of one to nine according to how well the packet described each site.

The results were impressive. In the evaluation of one subject, for instance, the analyst gave seven out of the nine packets nines. Indicating that the subject had done extremely well at describing the target locations. The odds against this happening by pure chance were more than 33,000 to one. Another subject received five packets in the first rank and four in the second. A third subject had three packets ranked first and three ranked second (out of eight). All of these results gave statistical odds significantly higher than those predicted by chance. A fourth subject's test results, however, did not differ significantly from chance.

Another series of tests involved what Puthoff and Targ described as precognitive remote viewing. It was designed to test whether the subjects could accurately identify a target subject *before* the target team actually arrived at the site.

Again, the procedure was complex in order to guard against contamination by chance or human error. At 10 o'clock, the target team (only one man in this case, the target experimenter) left SRI with ten sealed envelopes containing the target locations. He also carried a random number generator. At the same time, the subject was isolated in a room in the laboratory and asked to guess where the target experimenter would be at 11 o'clock. The subject again used both drawings and tape recordings to record his impressions of the test site. After driving for a half hour, during which time the subject had *already completed* his description of the target location, the target experimenter would use the random number generator to select a number between 1 and 10. He would then open the sealed packet corresponding to that number and proceed to the target location listed inside. He waited at that location for fifteen minutes, then returned to SRI.

Four tests with one subject were conducted, and three judges, working independently, were each able to match packets to target locations without error. Although the odds against this happening by chance were not astronomical, they were very conservatively estimated at twenty to one.

The Puthoff-Targ experiments were greeted with widespread acclaim from both parapsychologists and scientists in other fields, who praised their conceptual framework and careful procedures. An expanded version of the results was published by Puthoff and Targ in *Mind-Reach* (Delacorte, 1977). Some skeptics grumbled about various procedures used in the experiments, principally the method of target selection and the procedures for grading hits.

In 1978, two investigators from the Department of Psychology at the University of Otago in New Zealand reevaluated the original transcripts of the experiments, throwing new light on the results. David Marks and Richard Kammann reported their results in *Nature*, (August 17, 1978). They maintained that their work indicated that the originally successful results may have been due to improper clues contained in the transcripts used by the judges..

To cross check their results, Marks and Kammann asked two impartial judges to try to rank the test packets after all extraneous and improper cues had been removed. These judges were research psychologists and they visited the target locations exactly as the original judges had done. Without the content value of the expunged "cues," however, their rankings did not differ significantly from chance.

The end result of this investigation was to throw doubt on the Puthoff/Targ conclusion that clairvoyance does indeed exist.

Future investigators have been cautioned to make sure that judges in similar experiments are not given subtle but revealing clues that may bias the results of the tests.

Psychokinesis/Precognition

Tests of psychokinesis and precognition using random number generators are currently the most sophisticated experimental areas in the parapsychological field. These experiments can be controlled more stringently than any other kind, and their results are less open to unintentional bias. In many cases, these tests demonstrate outcomes that at first glance seem insignificant, at least to the eye of the non-scientific observer. For instance, such an experiment might yield 50.5 percent hits where chance would dictate only 50 percent. But over the course of literally thousands of trials, even this one-half percent difference takes on a huge significance. Parapsychologists and scientists alike consider this field the most exciting and productive in psi research today; if indubitable statistical proof of psi is to be found, it is probably in this area that it will be discovered.

The Schmidt Experiments

Helmut Schmidt of the Mind Science Foundation in San Antonio, the developer of the random event generator, has been responsible for the most sophisticated tests in the field of psychokinesis. The Schmidt experiments are probably the *single most impressive* tests of psi phenomena that have ever been done. Schmidt reported the results of his observations at a symposium of the American Physical Society in 1979; the results were reported in *The Skeptical Inquirer* (Summer, 1979) and in *Science* (February 10, 1979).

Schmidt, himself a practicing physicist, achieves results that impress even skeptics. Ray Hyman, a professor of psychology at the University of Oregon, is on record as stating: "By almost any standard Schmidt's work is the most challenging ever to confront critics such as myself. His approach makes many of the earlier criticisms of parapsychological research obsolete. The targets are randomized automatically. The data are recorded in such a way as to avoid obvious possibilities for recording errors and biases. The total number of trials per experiment are set in advance. Schmidt monitors the randomness of the generator before, during, and after each experimental run. And he always predicts the sort of result (psi-missing or psi-hitting) in advance on the basis of a preliminary experiment for each major experiment."

In one experiment, Schmidt used a machine with a ring of lights arranged like the dial of a clock; the random event generator illuminates one of the lights at a time. The subject is instructed to try to influence which light will come on. Both external and internal counters tabulate the number of flashes of each light. Schmidt's results indicate that successful subjects sometimes—though not always—succeed in effectively altering the frequency with which each light is illuminated. One typical result was 50.8 percent occurrence of the "target" light. Chance would have indicated a 50.0 percent outcome. The most successful in Schmidt's trials achieved a hit rate of 52.5 percent. This may seem rather small, but over the total run of 6,400 trials, the figure takes on great magnitude. The probability of this event being due solely to chance is so small that a meaningful mathematical figure cannot be assigned to express it.

In another experiment, Schmidt gave the subjects the same instructions, but, unknown to them, he had already determined the machine's random series of numbers the previous day. He had made electronic recordings of these numbers and stored them in a safe without examining them. The subjects believed that the machine itself was operating, rather than a recording. Astonishingly, the results of this experiment indicated that the subjects were affecting the outcome of the trials, even though the results had been pre-recorded. As Dr. Schmidt reported at the American Physical Society symposium, "The implication seems to be that the effect can work backward in time, and that is an outrageous idea from a conventional standpoint. But it may be that some quantum effects not yet understood could account for just such an outcome."

Such spectacular results have elicited both praise and blame from scientists. Paul Horowitz, a physicist and President of the American Physical Society's Forum on Physics and Society, said that Dr. Schmidt was "probably wrong. But it's important that the investigation of parapsychology be kept within the structure of science where it can be examined critically." (See *The New York Times*, [January 29, 1980]). But Ray Hyman stated: "In many ways Schmidt was the most sophisticated parapsychologist that I have encountered. If there are flaws in his work, they are not the more common or obvious ones. They must involve subtleties or hidden biases that cannot be detected from a review of his published data or from carefully interviewing him."

The Jahn/Curry Experiments

This series of experiments is currently being conducted at Princeton University and is perhaps the most scientifically respected psi research being carried on in the United States at this time. Robert G. Jahn, dean of Engineering and Applied Science at Princeton, and Carol K. Curry, an undergraduate, originated these experiments. They have since been joined by other researchers. Preliminary results were published in *Science News* on November 24, 1979. Conclusive results have not yet been published, but Jahn's and Curry's findings have been very impressive so far. An ad hoc committee at Princeton has established a charter for these experiments.

Jahn and Curry tried to eliminate all bias and random error from the tests by designing procedures in which the data would be absolutely clear-cut and open to statistical analysis.

Instead of trying for spectacular psychokinetic effects like spinning a compass without touching it or bending metal without physical contact, Jahn and Curry concentrated on much smaller phenomenon. They defined psychokinesis as "a palpable disturbance of a physical system by thought alone." In one experiment, they instructed subjects to try to raise the temperature of a thermistor a few hundred thousandths of a degree. In a second experiment, the subjects were asked to separate two mirrors in a Fabry-Perot interferometer by a hundred-thousandth of a centimeter.

The experimental conditions were as rigorously controlled as possible, to guard against fraud, self-deception, instrument error or malfunction, or statistical bias.

The preliminary results, described by Jahn at a science writers' meeting in Palo Alto, California, and reported in *Science News* (November 24, 1979), were dramatic. Subjects seemed capable, at will, of raising the temperature of the thermistor or altering the optical pathlength of the Fabry-Perot interferometer. Jahn and Curry noted, however, that the results were not completely "reproducible" in the scientific sense: they varied from person to person and from day to day. Until full results are published, Jahn and Curry prefer to treat their experimental findings as "tutorial" rather than as conclusive. They make no claim that these experiments offer proof of the validity of psychokinesis; they maintain that they should be used as models for more extensive and rigorous testing.

One interesting implication of Jahn's and Curry's preliminary results was that psychokinetic ability seemed to be trainable. Before the experiments began, the subjects were not aware of any innate psychic ability. They improved markedly, however, as the tests proceeded. Jahn attributes this to the effects of feedback. The experiments were designed to give the subjects instant feedback so that they would know when they had scored a "hit." Presumably the feedback leads to a practice-makes-perfect situation in which the subjects "learn" to sharpen their psi abilities.

Frauds

One of the thorniest problems of psi research is the question of fraudulent psychics. Much of the evidence for the existence of extrasensory perception rests on the abilities of certain gifted subjects to achieve higher-than-average results on ESP tests. In such cases, the probity of the subject is of crucial importance to the acceptance of the results. Unfortunately, impostors turn up regularly, attempting to pass themselves off as possessors of extraordinary psychic abilities. Parapsychologists, when faced with such claims, must walk a narrow line between credulity and disbelief. The psychic must not be accepted too hastily as genuine, but neither must he or she be condemned out of hand as a fake.

Prominent scientists have often been taken in by the claims of psychics who were later shown to be fraudulent. Ray Hyman, professor of psychology at the University of Oregon, explained in *The Skeptical Inquirer* (Summer, 1979) these happenings: "Training and aptitude for doing normal science does not at all prepare one for dealing with confidence men who are willing to exploit the scientist's rational and systematic approach to nature."

Most fraudulent practitioners sooner or later fade into oblivion. Uri Geller, the most prominent psychic of the early 1970s, was endorsed by scientists as well as parapsychologists. Harold Puthoff and Russell Targ of the Stanford Research Institute, two of the most prominent researchers in the parapsychological field, conducted extensive tests with Geller and declared that his psychic powers were genuine. John G. Taylor, a distinguished mathematician at King's College in London, also testified to Geller's authenticity in his 1975 book *Superminds*. Geller has since been exposed as a magician and sleight-of-hand artist whose spoon-bending and wire-bending feats were clever trickery.

In spite of the use of more sophisticated testing methods and increased wariness on the part of parapsychological researchers, so-called psychics still continue to put forward their claims.

Jean-Pierre Girard. Girard is a French pharmaceutical salesman who displays psychokinetic powers. He has received the endorsement and financial backing of officials of Pechiney, a large French corporation. Girard has taken part in experiments in which he has allegedly shifted compass needles and bent metal bars by the use of mind power alone.

Girard underwent a series of four carefully designed and conducted tests between 1976 and 1978: with Leprince-Ringuet and Trillat in 1976, Randi, Davies, and Evans in June, 1977, with B. Dreyfus in September, 1977, and with Y. Farge in January, 1978. All the operators were trained scientists (members of important scientific organizations such as the French Academy) with the exception of James Randi, a practicing magician and ESP-skeptic. The conditions of all four tests were outlined in advance so that neither side could later claim that they had been improper, unfair, or inadequate. A sepcial feature of the September 1977 experiment was the use of electronic instruments to monitor Girard's psi-power by detecting any chanqes it might make in gravitational or electromagnetic fields.

The experiments were a bit of an anticlimax. Nothing happened. In one of the tests, Girard tried to bend metallic bars paranormally. In another, he attempted to cause small objects to move on a tabletop and to make them levitate. A third was an attempt to cause realignment in needles enclosed in a glass box. In only one of the experiments did a manifestation occur: Girard supposedly accomplished the displacement of the compass needles. However, the alleged movements took place when most of the experimenters were out of the room momentarily, and the head experimenter refused to validate the occurrence unless he had seen it happen with his own eyes. It was later shown that the observed effect could easily be duplicated by the use of a small (3 mm) magnet concealed beneath a fingernail which the test instrumentation would not have been able to detect.

One of the experimenters, Jean Huvé, later wrote in Grands Articles du Mois, December 1975: "We can state that all the experiments we witnessed were fraudulent, on Girard's own admission." Girard indeed admitted that he does sometimes cheat. He had originally started his "spoon-bending" feats as a joke that would fool scientists. He now insists, however, that despite his cheating, he does possess authentic parapsychological powers. Results of the various Girard tests were printed in *The Humanist* (September/October 1977); in the French scientific journal *La Recherche* (February, 1978); the *New Scientist* (July 14, 1977 and February 16, 1978).

Suzie Cottrell. Cottrell is a 21-year-old farm girl from Meade, Kansas who claims clairvoyant and precognitive powers. She uses an ordinary deck of cards in her demonstrations. Cottrell claims to be able to name the cards in a face-down deck and gives her success rate as roughly 48 out of 52. She also claims to be "almost invariably successful" in predicting (in writing) which card an observer would select from a face-down deck.

In 1978, Cottrell offered to be tested by members of The Committee for the Scientific Investigation of Claims of the Paranormal, generally considered to be the arch-skeptics of the parapsychological world. Conditions of the tests were agreed upon which were acceptable to both parties. Cottrell was under video surveillance, from a TV camera focused on the table where she worked, during the entire duration of the experiment. In addition to members of CSICP, members of a commercial television camera crew were present, as well as two psychologists from the State University of New York at Buffalo The demonstration was conducted as follows: Cottrell shuffled and cut a deck of unused cards, shuffling as long as she chose. Then she wrote her prediction on a piece of paper which she handed to a third party to hold until the conclusion of the experiments. She then placed the full deck of cards face down on the table and spread them around in a jumble. She then asked a volunteer to pick a card from this random mass and to set it aside, still face down. After the card was chosen, she again spread around the remaining 51 cards on the table, mixing and rearranging them. The volunteer was instructed to pick up another card and put it aside. In this manner, five cards were chosen from the face-down pile on the table.

Cottrell then instructed the volunteer to line up the five chosen cards in front of him, still face down. She would then study the cards. One by one, she would point to four of the cards, thus eliminating them. She would turn over the fifth card. This card was then compared to the identity of the card written on the peice of paper which was being held by the third party.

In four trials, Cottrell was right three times. The odds against a chance occurrence of this nature are 36,000 to 1.

However, when the experimenters introduced a slight change into the procedure—cutting the deck just before Cottrell spread them on the table— Cottrell's success rate fell off to zero.

Professional magicians who had observed the experiments explained Cottrell's method. After shuffling the cards, and just before spreading them on the table, Cottrell straightened the pack and sneaked a glimpse at the top card as it fell into place. This is the card whose identity she then wrote on the piece of paper. During the next phase of the demonstration, as she arranged and rearranged the cards seemingly randomly on the table, Cottrell actually kept the crucial card under close control. She would then introduce this card to the top of the pile where the volunteer would be most likely to choose it as one of the five cards selected. She would then eliminate the other four cards and "select" the fifth as the target.

In the card-sharp's parlance, she had performed the top-peek, false three-way cuts, top-retaining shuffles, and the Schulein force. At one point in the proceeding, when Cottrell thought the videotape camera was not on, she was actually caught on tape lifting the top card of the deck to look at it. The CSICP reported the complete results of the tests in *The Skeptical Inquirer* (Spring 1979). One of the observing psychologists was quoted as follows: "On the basis of the tests, one cannot discriminate between Suzie Cottrell and a fraud."

As a result of these and similar experiences, many parapsychologists are coming to the conclusion that claimed psychics must be submitted to examination by hard-headed skeptics. Only in this way will parapsychological findings be free from taint and from accusations of fraudulence. The distinguished English author C. P. Snow has attacked the problem of fraud head-on:

> An abnormal number of all reported paranormal phenomena appear to have happened to holy idiots, fools, or crooks. I say this brutally, for

a precise reason. We ought to consider how a sensible and intelligent man would actually behave if he believed that he possessed genuine paranormal powers. He would realize that the matter was one of transcendental significance. He would want to establish his powers before persons whose opinions would be trusted by the intellectual world. If he was certain, for example, that his mind could, without any physical agency, lift a heavy table several feet . . . or could twist a bar of metal, then he would want to prove this beyond, as they say in court, any reasonable doubt.

What he would *not* do is set up as a magician or illusionist, and do conjuring tricks. He would desire to prove his case before the most severe enquiry achievable. . . . Any intelligent man would realize that it was worth all the serious effort in the world. (See "Passing Beyond Belief," *Financial Times*, London, January 28, 1978.)

Scientific Attacks on Parapsychology

Parapsychology is engaged in a running battle with the scientific establishment as to whether the field deserves to be called a science and, indeed, whether psi exists at all. Parapsychologists claim that their discipline is now so well established that such questions do not even deserve to be discussed. Scientists on the other hand point to various characterist of psi research which they say violate the most basic rules and tenets of science.

In a sense, parapsychology "came of age" in 1969 when the American Association for the Advancement of Science (AAAS), at the urging of Margaret Mead, accepted the Parapsychological Association as an affiliate. Since then, the increasing number of psi programs at leading universities and the burgeoning of grants for psi research indicate the widening acceptance of psi in scientific circles.

One of the largest and most important grants ever made for psychic research went to Dr. Peter F. Phillips of Washington University in St. Louis in 1979. The McDonnell Douglas Corporation, which manufactures the DC-10 airliner, granted $500,000 to Washington University for Phillips research in psychokinesis and spontaneous occurrences. In making the grant, James S. McDonnell, chairman of the board of the corporation, said: "Man is approaching the evolutionary point where he is beginning to realize there is a possible merging of matter and mind, and a priority item for current scientific research in the understanding of human consciousness."

Despite these indications of the wide acceptance of parapsychology, there are signs of a scientific backlash against psi research. The attack has been led by John A. Wheeler, director of the Center for Theoretical Physics at the University of Texas at Austin and one of the primary creative theoretical thinkers in the U.S. today. Since 1979, Wheeler has been calling for the AAAS to deprive the Parapsychological Association of its affiliate status. Wheeler stated that though he fully supported the right of parapsychologists to solicit grants for their work, they should be denied the right to use affiliation with the AAAS "to give those solicitations an air of legitimacy." Wheeler characterized the admittance of the Parapsychology Association into the AAAS in 1969 as only a manifestation of the permissiveness of that period and argued that standards should now be tightened up.

One of the big objections to parapsychology is that the field lacks a clearly stated conceptual framework. One of the basic tenets of science is that experiments must be designed to test a specific hypothesis. In general, parapsychological experiments do not do this. The aim of most psi experiments is simply to find out whether there is statistical evidence that a particular phenomenon, such as psychokinesis, exists. This is not a satisfactory scientific hypothesis. Scientists tend therefore to view most psi research as merely the gathering of information rather than the actual testing of theories.

Another scientific objection to psi research is that parapsychological experiments lack replicability, i.e., they cannot be repeated successfully by impartial experimenters. Replicability is another basic tenet of scientific belief. Parapsychologists argue that psi is different from other sciences in that the outcome of experiments depends to a certain degree on the attitude of the experimenter; skeptics rarely or never get good results. The view of the parapsychologist is that psi deals with unique events and is therefore a unique science. Scientists find it difficult to swallow this explanation. They point out that if any other researcher, such as a biologist or a physicist, reported results as skimpy as those presented by the parapsychologist, he would simply be ignored.

Some parapsychologists have accepted the need for replicability of experiments, recognizing that parapsychology will never wholly be accepted by traditional science until such repeatability is established. Dr. Helmut Schmidt, probably the leading researcher in the field of psychokinesis, has indicated that one of his priorities is to try to get rid of this "experimenter effect" by having his expements repeated by neutral scientists.

So far, no psi experiments seem to lend themselves to easy replicability. Most have not even been repeatable by their own experimenters. According to John Beloff ("Parapsychology and Philosophy," *Handbook of Parapsy-*

chology [Van Nostrand, 1977]): "There is still no repeatable experiment on the basis of which any competent investigator can verify a given phenomenon for himself." One of the first priorities of responsible parapsychological research is the creation of such repeatable experiments.

Does psi really exist? This is the ultimate question of parapsychological research. Psi researchers have long since been convinced that the answer is yes, but there is as yet no real *concrete* proof. There is a large body of statistical evidence relating to psi phenomena; this does not constitute scientific proof. Because extrasensory perception seems to fly in the face of so many basic physical laws, many observers find it difficult to accept psi's reality. Psychokinesis, for instance, violates the scientific principle of conservation of energy; precognition presupposes "backward causation;" and all forms of ESP seem to be independent of space and do not weaken with distance, a condition unlike that of any known physical force.

Between the credulity of certain parapsychological researchers and the knee-jerk conservatism of certain scientists, there exists an impartial middle ground. This is where most of today's parapsychologists and scientists are grouped. The openmindedness of both sides is necessary for the future of parapsychology.

As yet, there are no comprehensive theories about what causes psi and how it operates. According to Ray Hyman, professor of psychology at the University of Oregon (see *The Skeptical Inquirer* [Summer, 1979]), the ultimate explanation of psi will turn out to surprise *both* parapsychologists and traditional scientists: "Probably, in my opinion, whatever it turns out to be will differ greatly from what either the believers or the critics think is going on. I suspect that answers will have more of an impact on the philosophy of science, methodology, and the sociology of science that on the fundamental forces and laws as envisioned by contemporary physics. Even if it all turns out to be fraud or self-delusion, it is important to study because this would have other implications for what could take place in other areas of scientific inquiry."

Do-It-Yourself ESP Test

Simple parapsychological tests can be conducted with a homemade pack of fifty Zener cards. Ten cards of each of the five Zener designs should

Do-It-Yourself ESP test using Zener cards. (Oliver Williams/© 1980 by *The New York Times* Company. Reprinted by permission)

be made. The experiment lends itself to several variations. Here are the two most common:

(1) The experimenter shuffles the pack carefully and then looks at each card in turn. The subject should not be able to see the cards; he can be blindfolded, sit behind a screen, or be in another room. As the experimenter

turns each card, the subject tries to guess its identity. The experimenter records the answers as the cards are turned.

(2) The cards are shuffled carefully by the experimenter before the test begins. The subject is then asked to name each card *before* the experimenter turns it over. This experiment can be conducted with or without feedback; that is, the subject can be told after each guess whether he was right or not or the card can actually be turned face up and revealed to the subject.

One or two runs are probably not enough to provide reliable results. More accurate information is produced by dozens, or even hundreds, of runs. The odds predict that the subject has one chance in five of correctly identifying any particular card. In a pack of fifty cards, a subject would be expected to make ten correct choices, on average, by chance alone. If over a long series of runs, the subject correctly guesses more than ten cards in every pass of the deck, then some mechanism beside pure chance may be operating. The more correct guesses, the more convincing the evidence of a paranormal effect.

STRANGE PEOPLE

The Man in the Iron Mask

The Man in the Iron Mask was a mysterious prisoner of the French government—kept incommunicado and masked in black velvet—who spent the last few years of his life in the Bastille in Paris, and died in 1703.

The prisoner was brought to Paris by Benigne de Saint-Mars, in 1698, when the latter was named superintendent of the Bastille. The prisoner had apparently previously served time in the Pignerol prison in Italy and on the island of St. Marguerita near Cannes. When the prisoner died in 1703, he was buried in the cemetery of St. Paul under the name of Marchioli.

Voltaire popularized the story in his book *Siecle de Louis XIV*, published in 1751. Voltaire was probably the originator of the misconception that the mask was made of iron.

About the year 1800 a legend arose that the prisoner had been the legitimate Louis XIV, kept in captivity while the throne was being occupied by a usurper, an illegitimate son of Louis' mother and Cardinal Mazarin. Also, according to this account, the man in the mask had married and fathered a son while in captivity. The son was spirited off to Corsica and later became the grandfather of Napoleon Bonaparte.

Alexandre Dumas the Elder also wrote of the man in the mask in a book published in 1848, *Le Vicomte de Bragelonne*. He maintained that the man was either the elder brother of Louis XIV or his twin, and that he was kept in prison to preserve France from a struggle for the succession.

By other accounts, Count Ercole Antonio Mattioli, a confidential secretary of the Duke of Mantua, had been identified as the man in the mask. Mattioli had been arrested after revealing to foreign powers the details of delicate diplomatic negotiations between Mantua and France. He was imprisoned at Pignerol, moved to several other fortresses, and died in 1703. Opponents of the Mattioli theory point out that the count's original incarceration was well known, and there would have been no reason to disguise his identity behind a mask.

Much modern support has gone to the theory that the man in the mask was one Eustache Dauger de Cavoye, a valet. Dauger may have been an intermediary in negotiations between Louis XIV and Charles II of England.

One interesting version of this theory holds that Dauger was the father of Louis XIV. Though the prisoner was officially said to be only 45 years old at his death, the records in question were notoriously inaccurate.

Louis XIII, the story goes, was impotent, and a young man was employed by Cardinal Richelieu to impregnate the Queen and ensure an heir to the throne. The surrogate father was paid off and sent to a remote place, perhaps Canada, but later returned to demand more money. At this point, Louis XIV may have decided to lock up his troublesome father, and keep the whole affair as secret as possible.

The Dauger theory would explain both the extreme secrecy with which the case was treated, and the fact that the prisoner was neither mistreated nor killed, but left to die a natural death.

For additional information, see: H. R. Williamson, *Enigmas of History* (Macmillan, 1957).

The Zulu Kings

The Zulu kings were a dynasty of rulers in 19th century southern Africa who built the Zulu nation from a small clan into a major military force.

The Zulu kingdom was founded by Shaka (c. 1787–1828), an illegitimate son of the chief of the small Zulu clan, who spent his childhood and youth in humiliating exile. When he became chief in 1816, the Zulus, numbering 1,500 in all, were among the smallest clans in the region of present-day Natal province in South Africa. Shaka immediately began a career of personal revenge and then conquest.

Shaka reorganized the army. Discarding the typical lance, he equipped his men with the *assegai*, a short but long-bladed sword, which he designed himself for use at short range. This prevented his soldiers from keeping their distance from the enemy, which was the relatively bloodless custom of the time. He also had his soldiers fight barefoot for greater mobility.

The army was then organized into separately quartered regiments, together called the *impi*, based on age groups. Young boys were recruited as carriers of weapons and luggage, and doctors were employed to care for the wounded. Shaka developed a system of spies and informers, and communication by smoke signals was used.

Conscription was rigorous, and semi-military training began at age twelve. No soldier was permitted to marry until age thirty-five, and a Spartan value-system emphasizing courage was inculcated.

Shaka developed a standard battle tactic, with pincer movements and a reserve force. By the time he was murdered by two of his half-brothers in 1828, just twelve years after coming to power, the Zulu kingdom had become the dominant force throughout the area.

Shaka, by all accounts, ruled as a cruel, ruthless, and absolute dictator. The slightest opposition was met with execution. Any woman in his harem of 1,200 who became pregnant was executed. Shaka himself left no offspring. Upon the death of his mother, Shaka killed about 7,000 subjects out of grief, as well as thousands of cows. No crops were planted for a year, and any woman found pregnant was executed with her husband.

Shaka's harsh policies, while effective at the time, proved disastrous in the long run for the Zulus and other blacks of South Africa.

His initial campaigns started a chain reaction of wars of extermination as terrified, disposed clans and tribes migrated and fought back and forth over all of Natal and beyond. About two million people were killed in the 1820s, leaving much of the region depopulated and unable to resist the Boer "Great Trek" and mass settlement of the 1830s. But Shaka's kingdom survived his death, in reduced circumstances, despite incursions by the Boers and the British, and despite two mediocre successors, Dingane (ruled 1828–40) and Mpande (ruled 1840–72).

The last independent Zulu king was Cetewayso (c 1826–1884), sometimes spelled Cetshwayo, who ascended the throne in 1872. In the tradition of his uncle, Shaka, Cetewayso himself was an outstanding soldier, handsome, tall, and muscular, and skilled in the use of the assegai. The Englishmen he encountered all ascribed to him great dignity, intelligence, and force of character, although he, too, was charged with incidents of cruelty.

Cetewayo's military and political abilities led to a revival of the kingdom's strength, but his army of 40,000 was an obstacle to British ambitions.

The Zulus were defeated by the British at great cost in 1879, and Cetewayo was deposed.

After a sensational visit to England and an interview with Queen Victoria, Cetewayo was restored to the throne of a much-reduced kingdom over local opposition, but he died soon after.

By the 1970s the Zulus numbered over four million people, all descendents of the various clans united by Shaka. They lived throughout the Republic of South Africa.

Some 12,000 square miles of land in Natal Province, divided into a series of enclaves, have been set aside by the white South African government as a semi-autonomous area, Kwazulu, that is eventually to become independent. But the large majority of Zulus live outside Kwazulu, and many of them oppose the plan, including Chief Gatsha Buthelezi, the elected chief minister of Kwazulu.

For more information, see: C. T. Binns, *The Last Zulu Kings* (Longmans, 1963) and R. Fourneaux, *The Zulu War* (Lippincott, 1963).

Kaspar Hauser

Kaspar Hauser (1812[?]–1833) was a mysterious teenager, found by the police wandering the streets of Nuremberg, Germany, on May 26, 1928.

Although normal in physical appearance, Hauser had the psychological development of a three-year-old child—he could not feed, dress, or clean himself. He was found carrying two letters addressed to the captain of the local cavalry regiment (which later turned out to be forgeries). He told the police a confused story about having been raised in a dark room and fed on bread and water.

Under the care of Georg Frederich Daumer, an educator, he began to learn, and his intelligence developed with amazing speed. In 1829, Hauser wrote his autobiography. In 1832, the Earl of Stanhope took responsibility for his education and the famous jurist, Anselm von Feuerbach, became his patron.

Hauser was wounded in 1829, allegedly by an assailant. Then in 1833, while he was working as a court clerk, he suffered fatal stab wounds in a mysterious attack.

The last year of Hauser's life and the mysterious circumstances of his death stirred up an intense controversy and political recriminations. Some

Kaspar Hauser. (lithograph by F. Fiessler/New York Public Library Picture Collection.)

claimed he was an imposter and a fake and that his wounds had been self-inflicted.

O. Flake, in his book *Kaspar Hauser* (Kessler Verlag, Mannheim; no date), claimed Hauser was the hereditary Prince of Baden who had been imprisoned as part of a plot to put another claimant on the throne and that he was the victim of premeditated murder. Flake stated that everything about Hauser was improbable, including his death, and that he was "a man pursued throughout his life by evil forces." As evidence, Flake cited an autopsy of Hauser's wounds which, he argued, proved they could not have been inflicted. The *New International Encyclopedia*, however, argues that the fatal wound, as well as the earlier injuries, were self-inflicted because Hauser craved attention. In respect to Flake's opinion that Hauser was the hereditary Prince of Baden, the *New International Encyclopedia* notes that the theory "has persisted, despite the publication of the official record of the baptism, the autopsy, and the burial of the heir in question."

Cagliostro

Count Alessandro Cagliostro was an 18th century alchemist, clairvoyant, and necromancer, sometimes called the "Prince of Quacks."

Born June 2, 1743, in Palermo, Italy, Count Cagliostro, accompanied by the Countess Cagliostro, made his first recorded appearance in 1776, in London. He came with considerable funds and generously employed and aided strangers who came to him for help. Unfortunately, many of the beneficiaries of his generosity swindled him out of great sums, a pattern that repeated itself throughout his career. In one instance, he predicted a winning lottery number for a certain Captain Scott, who, as a measure of his gratitude, offered Cagliostro a gambling partnership. When Cagliostro, who was an ascetic and opposed to gambling, refused, Scott began a harrassment campaign to persuade him to change his mind. Eighteen months later and 3,000 guineas poorer, Cagliostro left England.

However, during his stay, Cagliostro had joined the Esperance Lodge of the Order of Strict Observance and became a freemason. Although the lodge's activities were chiefly philanthropic and social rather than occult, it gave him access to occult circles all over Europe.

Cagliostro next surfaced in March 1779 in Russia. He had already evolved his own system of freemasonry, Egyptian Masonry, which main-

Cagliostro (New York Public Library Picture Collection.)

tained that all people possess psychic powers. He styled himself the Grand Cophta of Egyptian Masonry. He announced that he had divined, through clairvoyance, the location of buried treasure, but refused to dig it up because it was guarded by evil spirits. In St. Petersburg, he conducted a seance that turned out to be rigged. In Poland, he boasted of his prowess in alchemy, but made a quick exit when he attracted the attention of knowledgeable alchemists who exposed his pretense.

Cagliostro surfaced next in Strasbourg, France, in 1780, and remained in France for the next five years. He confined himself largely to healing and clairvoyance, for which he seemed to have a genuine flair. He dispensed quack medicines, one of which was the *Elixir Vitae* (elixir of life), supposedly discovered by alchemists to prolong life. Another potion, the Wine of Egypt, was purported to have rejuvenating powers. According to an apocryphal tale related by W. R. H. Trowbridge in *Cagliostro* (Gordon Press, 1910), a maid who drank a whole vial of her mistress' potion appeared to be thirty years younger the following morning.

In his supposed feats of clairvoyance, Cagliostro used a medium, always a child about five years old. If a boy, he was called a pupille and, if a girl, she was a colombe. In one instance recounted by Trowbridge, Cagliostro anointed the head and left hand of the pupille, the son of the Marshal von Medem. Cagliostro and the pupille then led the gathering in prayers and hymns. The marshall requested that the pupille see his daughter, the pupille's sister. The pupille had a vision of the daughter putting her hand over her heart and kissing her brother, the pupille's older brother. The marshall said this was impossible because the older brother was far away. But when he sent for his daughter, he discovered his son had come home unexpectedly and that his daughter had had heart palpitations before his arrival.

The upswing of his career during the five-year stay in France came to a sudden end when Cagliostro along with his protector, the Cardinal of Rohan, was implicated in the Affair of the Diamond Necklace (1875–1876), a farcical affair in which a jeweller was persuaded to give up the valuable necklace on the assumption it was for Marie Antoinette. Though both Cagliostro and Rohan were innocent and were acquitted, they incurred the wrath of the French Court, which was embarrassed to see them become martyrs and public heroes. Cagliostro was forced to flee France and was never again able to reestablish himself. Though he was popular with the Republican forces in Europe, he suffered persecution at the hands of the supporters of the French monarchy.

At this same time, in 1876, a French royalist agent claimed to have discovered Cagliostro's true identity—a Guiseppi Balsamo, an adventurer born in Palermo. Although the Count denied that he was Balsamo, most historians have accepted the story on the basis of considerable circumstantial evidence. Cagliostro's own account of his life seems to have been fabricated to demonstrate the antiquity of Egyptian Masonry.

After leaving France, Cagliostro's wanderings finally brought him to Rome where, in 1791, he was convicted by the Inquisition for spreading freemasonry and was sentenced to death. The sentence was later commuted to life imprisonment in the prison of San Leo where he died in 1795.

During his career, Cagliostro's standing changed dramatically. In Paris, he had a few thousand followers who venerated him as the Grand Coptha of Egyptian Masonry. A much larger number of people considered him a curiosity because of his meteoric career. Generally, the public was amused by his pretentiousness and regarded his success in impressing the upper classes of France as a sign of their decadence. During the Diamond Necklace Affair, he was a laughing stock. However, when he fell victim to the Inquisition, he ceased to be the clownish mascot of the wealthy aristocrats and became a martyred hero in the cause of liberty.

Judge Crater

Judge Joseph F. Crater disappeared, without any explanation, on August 6, 1930, in New York City.

Judge Crater, born January 5, 1889, in Easton, Pennsylvania, had pursued a varied career in law and teaching and was active in the New York City Democratic Party. On April 8, 1930, New York State Governor Franklin D. Roosevelt appointed Crater to the New York State Supreme Court.

On the morning of August 6, 1930, Crater went to his office at the county court house on Foley Square in lower Manhattan. He placed some papers into two briefcases and five cardboard portfolios. He asked his court attendant to cash two checks, one for $3,000 and another for $2,150, against his accounts at two banks. He placed the cash, uncounted, in his pocket. Accompanied by his court attendant, Crater took the portfolios and briefcases to his apartment. Then, at noon, he dismissed the attendant, telling him that he was going up to Westchester County, New York, north of New York City, for a swim.

Early in the evening, Crater appeared at a New York City ticket agency, seeking a ticket for that evening's performance of a comedy. The agent did

Mrs. Stella Crater Kunz, holding note left by the missing Judge Crater. (UPI photo.)

not have one, but promised that, should he be able to get one later, he would leave it at the box office. The agent subsequently left a ticket at the box office and it was picked up, but whether by Crater or someone else is not known.

Crater then proceeded to a restaurant where he met two friends. He told them he intended to go to Maine, where his wife was vacationing, before court reconvened on August 25. All three left the restaurant at 9:15 p.m., well after curtain time. Crater hailed a cab and, as far as is known, was never seen again.

It was not until January 21, 1931, that Crater's wife made a puzzling discovery in a bureau drawer. She found four manila envelopes with her initials and the word "personal" written in the judge's hand. One contained a will bequeathing all his property to her. The second contained $6,619 in cash and three checks for $500, $12, and $9. The third contained four life insurance policies totalling $30,000. The fourth and most mysterious contained a three-page memorandum in the Judge's handwriting. It contained a list, partially undecipherable, of twenty persons and companies to whom the judge owed money. The memorandum ended: "Am very weary. Love Joe. This is all confidential" (underscored).

It is generally thought that Crater was murdered for some unknown reason (See T. Meehan, "Case No. 13494", *New York Times Magazine*, August 7, 1960) and that the New York City Democratic Party was not anxious to have the case probed deeply. A thorough investigation of the Judge's activities may have proved embarrassing to highly placed associates such as Al Smith or Franklin D. Roosevelt. Therefore it was safer to leave the case unsolved and keep open the possibility that Crater was still alive.

For more information, see Stella Crater, with Oscar Fraley, *The Empty Robe* (Doubleday, 1961).

Jukes and Kallikaks

The Jukes and Kallikaks were two families with a supposedly high proportion of socially undesirable members. This phenomenon was hypothetically attributed to hereditary factors.

The Jukes—In 1874, Richard L. Dugdale discovered that six people who were in jail simultaneously were all related. Intrigued by this, Dugdale traced their ancestry back five or six generations to two brothers who married two sisters. He arbitrarily named all their descendants Jukes. Confining himself to Jukes in Ulster County, New York, the residence of the two brothers, he traced the lives of the family members from prison, court and poorhouse records, and interviews with older residents of the area. He discovered 709 people who were Jukes or married to Jukes: eighteen had kept brothels, seventy-six had been convicted of crimes, 128 were prostitutes, and 200 had been on relief.

Some forty years later, Arthur H. Estabrook, who was determined to demonstrate that socially undesirable traits were hereditary, did further research. He found that not a single Juke family was living in Ulster County by 1912 because the cement factory which had been the major employer in the area had shut down. He, however, traced another 2,111 Jukes, in addition to Dugdale's 709 in New York, Connecticut, New Jersey, and Minnesota. In nine generations, he found 131 who were feebleminded, 171 who were criminals, 175 who were prostitutes, 282 who were alcoholics and 366 who were adult paupers.

The Kallikaks—The study of the Kallikak (from the Greek words for good and bad) family began in 1897 when an eight-year-old girl was brought to the Training School for the feebleminded at Vineland, N.J. The results of the study, conducted by Elizabeth S. Kite, appeared in *The Kallikak Family* published in 1912 by Henry H. Goddard, the school's director.

The girl's great-great-great-grandfather, called Martin Kallikak, came of good family, and had an illegitimate son by a feeble-minded tavern maid. The son, known as "old Horror", had ten children of his own. Of his 480 descendants, 143 were feebleminded, eighy-three died in infancy, thirty-three were sexually immoral, twenty-six were illegitimate, twenty-four were alcoholics, three were criminals, and three were epileptics. However, Martin eventually married a woman of good family and their descendants were teachers, doctors, lawyers, judges—all pillars of the New Jersey establishment.

Today these studies, as attempts to correlate socially undesirable traits with hereditary factors, have been wholly discredited. The methods of data collection and evaluation were faulty. For instance, in the Dugdale and Estabrook studies, the breakdowns of socially undesirable individuals do not specify whether or not the people included in one group are counted in another group as well.

For more information, see: R. L. Dugdale, *The Jukes* (G. P. Putnam's Sons, 1877); A. H. Estabrook, *The Jukes in 1915* (Carnegie Institute, 1916); and H. H. Goddard, *The Kallikak Family*, (MacMillan, 1912).

LEGENDARY CREATURES

Amazons

According to Greek legend, the Amazons were a tribe of warrior women.

Mythology says the Amazons refused to acknowledge the existence of men except in the capacity of servile workers. Some legends state that they mutilated or even killed their male children and propagated their race through chance contacts with strange men. According to Plutarch, the Amazons met annually with Albanians for two-month intervals on the banks of the Thermodon River, but then withdrew to a celibate existence in their own country. Others state that the Amazons perpetuated their tribe by copulation, at intervals, with men of neighboring tribes, but that they raised only the females, either banishing the male children or mutilating and enslaving them.

War was the main passion of the tribe; their patron was the goddess, Artemis, the virgin huntress. According to Herodotus, the mythic hero Heracles (Hercules), through a misunderstanding, made war on the Amazons, who had been a friendly tribe. Many Amazons were killed and some were taken as prisoners. These prisoners, who were being transported to Greece in ships, rose up and massacred the crews, but, being unfamiliar with the handling of ships, they drifted until reaching the land of the Scythians, in the area north of the Black Sea. There, they seized horses and moved to the north, where they settled. They continued to hunt and make war, decreeing that no woman could marry until she had killed a man in battle.

Amazons. (19th century engraving, New York Public Library Picture Collection)

Other legends about the Amazons are varied, numerous, and often contradictory. For example, one of the labors of Heracles was to fetch the girdle of Hippolyta, the queen of the Amazons. Heracles fought the Amazons, killed Hippolyta, and seized the girdle, which was thought to bestow magic properties on its wearer. The great Athenian hero Theseus had joined Heracles on his expedition. As his share of the spoils, he received the Amazon, Antiope, by whom he sired Hippolytus. In revenge, the Amazons invaded Attica but were defeated by Theseus.

The Amazons fought on the side of the Trojans in the Trojan War. They were also associated with Dionysus, usually as opponents, and with the Centaurs, also as combatants.

The derivation of the name Amazon is unclear. Possibly it comes from the Greek words meaning "breastless," via a legend that the Amazons destroyed the right breast of their daughters, to prevent it from getting in the way of a bow-string or a javelin.

Another theory states that the Amazons were originally priestesses of Artemis, the moon goddess. One version of the etymology of Amazon traces it to a Caucasian word meaning "moon." It postulated that the Artemis priestesses cut off their breasts to represent the male ideal in the female sex.

Although early legends about Amazons are largely fictitious, they may have a kernel of truth, for it is a fact that the women of many early German tribes followed their men into battle, bringing food and encouragement. The Mongol armies of Ghenghis Khan were also accompanied by their families. It is possible, too, that in wars against the Greeks, tribal women joined in battle, giving rise to the legends. It is also possible that Greek travelers brought back tales of women who performed brave feats, and the takes were embellished until they gained mythical significance. It is unlikely, however, that there was ever a tribe of women warriors.

In the 16th century, the Spanish explorer, de Orellana, reported coming into conflict with "fighting women" in South America, possibly explaining why the Amazon River was so named.

For additional information, see: M. P. O. Morford and R. J. Lenardon, *Classical Mythology* (McKay, 1971) and M. Collignon, *Manual of Mythology* (Grent, 1899).

Unicorn

A unicorn is a legendary animal resembling a horse, deer, or kid, with a single prominent horn in the center of its forehead. The unicorn appears in the mythology and legends of Europe, the Near East, and China.

The legendary Chinese unicorn, the *ki-lin*, resembled a large deer, but with the tail of an ox and the hoove of a horse, and with a single short horn. It was believed to represent an incarnation of the five elements—fire, water, wood, metal, and earth. It was extremely gentle, lifting its feet high when it walked so as not to step on any living animal or plant. It did not eat grass, but only what was already dead and beyond injury.

The *ki-lin* appeared only fleetingly, from time to time, after its first appearance in the garden of the legendary emperor Huang Ti nearly 5,000 years ago. It would appear at the court of the emperors to signal the excellence of their rule, or as an omen of childbirth. The mother of Confucius was said to have seen a *ki-lin* before his birth. Through the centuries, the *ki-lin* came to be seen as a protector of sages and saints.

European ideas of the unicorn came mainly from the account of a Greek physician named Ctisias, who visited Persia in the 4th century BC. He recounted that in India there lived a variety of white ass the size of a horse, too swift for capture, with blue eyes and a single horn (*monokeros*) in the middle of its purple head. The horns were red, white, and black and had marvelous medicinal properties. They could also detect the presence of poison. In Latin, *monokeros* became *unicornis*.

Christian use of the motif derived in part from a mistaken belief that a Biblical Hebrew word, *re'em* (a wild ox with powerful horns) referred to the unicorn. The animal became a medieval symbol of Christ. Literary and artistic allegories were developed around the hunting and killing of the unicorn, a theme also represented in Chinese and Islamic art. According to some Christian versions, a unicorn could be subdued only by a virgin, whose scent attracted the beast. In general, unicorns were assumed in Europe to be fierce, solitary animals, gentle only at mating time. They could throw themselves from any height and land, unhurt, on their horns.

The horn was believed to have miraculous powers against poison. The rich had cups made of purported unicorn horns, the poor used tiny chips to test food. At one time, powdered horn was valued at ten times its weight in gold.

Unicorn; (New York Public Library Picture Collection)

There were several famous specimens; one was kept in a vault at St. Denis Cathedral in France, and was said to be so potent that water in which it was steeped could cure a sick person. Another, valued at 100,000 pounds, was kept at Windsor Castle in the time of Queen Elizabeth I.

The purported unicorn horns were, of course, fakes. They were generally made of ivory, while the powder usually consisted of ground-up horns or bones of domestic animals. But in the period between the end of the 14th century and the end of the 16th, few Europeans challenged the widespread belief that at least some of the horns and powders were genuine. Tests were devised to distinguish the genuine from the fake. True horns were thought to generate bubbles in water, to emit a sweet odor when burned, and to kill poisonous plants and animals placed nearby.

The unicorn was a believable "fabulous beast." There is nothing basically absurd about it. Some varieties of rhinoceros have only one horn. Various one-horned individuals in other species have been known, and they are usually prized. These are either mutations, or the results of special procedures.

Certain African tribes have been reported to possess the secret of producing one-horned animals. In a recent experiment conducted in the U.S., the normal horn buds of a young calf were grafted together and transplanted to the center of the forehead, where they grew as a single large horn. The bull grew exceptionally strong and became leader of the herd. At the same time, he developed such "unicorn traits" as gentleness and mildness.

Adding credence to the myth, Arctic sailors used to find spirally grooved horns believed to come from unicorns. Actually, they were ivory tusks of the narwhal, a small Northern whale.

For more information, see: O. Shepard, *The Lore of the Unicorn* (Unwin, 1930) and P. Lum, *Fabulous Beasts* (Pantheon, 1951).

Dragon

A dragon is an imaginary beast with a major role in the mythology and folklore of almost every culture in the world. In the Judeo-Christian scriptures, dragons are mentioned thirty-one times, and the best known dragon image is the serpent in the Garden of Eden. In Babylonian mythology, the prime female deity was a dragon named Tiamat whose ritual killing by Marduk each year marked the great flood of the Tigris-Euphrates river system and the beginning of the growing season. The myth of Tiamat and Marduk is probably the source of all the dragon and dragon-slayer stories in the world.

Dragons are usually pictured as huge, scaly, lizard- or serpent-like creatures, often bat-winged, and usually breathing fire or noxious fumes. Some dragons have seven or nine heads; others have the forelegs and head of a lion or an eagle hawk; some have horns and others have barbed tails. The dragon has been the recipient of all the terrible imaginings that storytellers could devise.

Dragons were usually associated with water and were thought to live in caves under lakes or in palaces on the ocean bottom. A fundamental element of the dragon's power is its control of water. In medieval tales, the dragon dried up rivers and caused drought, forcing the local inhabitants to pay an annual tribute of gold or fair maidens. Many heroes of mythology were dragon slayers: Marduk, Perseus, Hercules, Apollo, Siegfried, St. Michael, St. George, Beowulf, King Arthur, and Tristan.

It is the primordial force of chaos which the dragon most frequently represents. The multiplicity of forms, and in some cases the dragon's ability to change form, illustrates the threat of chaos. The water, which the dragon controlled, is still a prime Freudian image for the unformed, chaotic uncon-

Dragonel, a young dragon (*Pierre Belon, 1553*)

scious, just as the serpent is still the Freudian image of a sexual passion. The dragon Tiamat held the world enthralled, and the association of primitive chaotic forces with the dragon may derive from its close association with Mother Goddess myths. The story of the dragon slayer may reflect the replacement of female-centered religions with patriarchal organization.

The dragon's connection with evil and chaos, however, also brought it a reputation for great wisdom about the ways of the earth and remedies for sickness. To this day, the symbol of medicine in the West is a winged staff with two serpents entwined about it. In other stories, dragon's blood, one drop of which was usually thought to be lethal, was instead an elixir which conferred a knowledge of the language of birds, the messengers of the gods. The Chinese and Japanese image of the dragon has always been of a more beneficent creature than that of Westerners, and in taoism dragons symbolize the deified powers of nature. Taoism also uses water as the fundamental image, not of chaos, but of nature's power.

In spite of their reputation for wisdom and cunning, dragons have also been portrayed as naive and stupid. In the Middle Ages, the image of a dragon was often carried in processions to symbolize evil; it was stoned and kicked and soon became an object of good-humored scorn. In other cases, the dragon was portrayed as easily fooled by clever ruses or absurd excuses.

In one story the local dragon, instead of his usual dinner of Fair Maiden Tartare was tossed a dummy filled with pitch, sulphur, and nitre, a simple form of napalm. The dragon, no gourmet, downed the morsel in one gulp, bellowed in satisfaction and exploded into flame.

For more information, see: C. Clair, *Unusual History* (Abelard-Schumann, 1951); G. E. Smith *The Evolution of the Dragon* (Longmanns Green, 1919); and E. Ingersoll, *Dragons and Dragon Lore* (Playson and Clarke, 1928).

Gryphon

A gryphon (also spelled griffin or griffon) is a mythical animal, half mammal and half bird, associated with wealth and power.

The gryphon is usually depicted with the rear, tail, and hind paws of a lion, and the head, beak, and wings of a bird, usually an eagle. The forelegs end in bird's claws, and the head often has pointed, upright mammalian ears. Gryphons are sometimes shown with curly manes, crests or horns.

The beast was considered fierce, cunning, and rapacious, but was usually shown recumbent or on its haunches.

Gryphon motifs, common in the decorative arts of the Near East and Greece, were often found in sanctuaries and tombs. They were associated in ancient mythologies with eminent personages; they pulled the heavenly chariots of Jupiter, Apollo, and Nemesis, and, according to medieval legend, the chariot of Alexander the Great.

Other medieval accounts held that gryphons nested high in the mountains of India and Scythia (roughly the areas north and east of the Black Sea). There they guarded the wealth of the sun or of the Orient. Their nests were lined with so much gold that any one of them could make a person wealthy for life. But intruders would be torn to pieces by the gryphon's claws, each one as big as the horns of an antelope. In fact, purported gryphon horns, resembling antelope horns, were brought to Europe by travelers from the East. Cups made from them were highly prized.

Dante, referring to "the animal that is one single Person in two Natures," used the gryphon in his *Divine Comedy* as a symbol of the union of the human and divine in Jesus Christ.

Gryphons were much used in heraldry, and one of them appears on the coat of arms of the City of London.

Gryphon; (New York Public Library Picture Collection)

There is some evidence that the gryphon symbol may have originally arisen about four thousand years ago on the Eastern Mediterranean coast and spread within a few hundred years through western Asian and Greek territories. The *senmurv*, or dog bird of Persia, which, according to an old belief, was the only connecting link between heaven and earth, may bear some relation to the gryphon.

Some gryphon stories may have arisen from the discoveries of huge fossil bones in the gold-bearing regions of the East, suggesting the idea of a giant animal guarding a gold treasure.

For more imformation, see P. Lum, *Fabulous Beasts* (Pantheon, 1951).

Phoenix; (New York Public Library Picture Collection)

The Phoenix

The phoenix is a large, graceful and brilliantly colored bird of mythology, who, after a very long life, is consumed by flames and rises reborn from the ashes.

According to a myth very popular in classical times, the phoenix lived in a magical, utopian land in the East, often associated with India or Arabia, where the sun rose. The land was mountainous and thus had escaped the ravages of the great flood (itself an almost universal myth). Eternal spring and eternal daylight reigned; sorrow, hatred, hunger, and death were banished; and the fountain of youth had its source there.

In the midst of this paradise lived the phoenix, larger than an eagle, with scarlet head, breast, and back, gold or multicolored irridescent wings, and sea blue eyes. It lived on nothing but pure air.

Only one phoenix lived at a time, and its lifespan was a thousand years. When it felt its age coming upon it, the bird flew west, stopping in Arabia to gather perfume and spices, and then on to Phoenicia—the land that bore its name. There it built a nest in a tall palm tree (*phoenix* in Greek) with the spices it had gathered.

At dawn, the phoenix turned its eyes eastward and sang a hymn to the sun in an exquisitely beautiful voice. The sun heard, and reined in his golden horses to listen. At that moment, the universe stood still. But the sparks from the flaming hair that is the sun's rays set fire to the nest, and the bird was consumed. At once a new phoenix rose from the ashes of the old, to return to the distant paradise that would be its home for a millennium. But first it deposited the remains of the nest on the altar of the sun at Heliopolis, in Egypt.

Elements of the phoenix story were part of the folklore of several ancient cultures. In China, early legends similar to the burning of the phoenix nest were incorporated into a later myth of the phoenix (feng-huang), the female counterpart of the dragon and a symbol of brides. The feng-huang had a beautiful song of its own, and also enjoyed human music.

The Roman emperor Heliogabalus (A.D. 218–222) tried to achieve immortality by consuming food that contained a phoenix. He tasted all sorts of exotic birds hoping that one of them might be the legendary creature. At last he was brought a bird of paradise, which he was convinced was the true phoenix. He had it cooked and ate it. Shortly thereafter, he was murdered.

As a symbol of immortality, the phoenix was associated by many Romans with the permanence of their empire. Among Christians, it became a symbol of the death and resurrection of Christ. The phoenix was later commonly used in European heraldry.

For more information, see: P. Lum, *Fabulous Beasts* (Pantheon, 1951).

Golem

The golem was a legendary creature created by Rabbi Judah Loew of Prague to thwart a wave of anti-Semitism.

A golem is a creature, particularly a human being, made in an artificial way by virtue of a magic act, through the use of holy names.

According to legend, in the 16th century, the Jews of Prague in Czechoslovakia were sorely pressed by anti-Semitism, led by Thaddeus, a Catholic priest who was stirring the populace with scurrilous tales of ritual murder perpetrated by the Jews against the Christians. Rabbi Loew prayed for divine guidance, and in a dream received a message to "make a golem of clay" who would become a champion of the Jewish people. After elaborate procedures of purification and prayer, the rabbi, along with three wisemen, went to the river Moldau, found a bed of clay, and made the figure of a golem. Each of them walked around the golem seven times, reciting appropriate incantations, and finally Rabbi Loew himself walked around the clay figure and placed in its mouth a piece of parchment inscribed with the name of God. After further prayers and recitations, the golem came to life. They dressed him in the clothes of a sexton, and to all appearances he was exactly like an ordinary person, only lacking in the ability to talk.

Setting out to protect the Jewish population against their enemies, the golem, time and time again, uncovered and thwarted plots hatched by the wily Thaddeus, finally bringing about his discreditation and punishment. When the wave of anti-Semitism subsided, Rabbi Loew destroyed the golem using the same procedure he had used for creating him, but in reverse order.

The concept of the Golem, i.e., the creation of living beings, is widespread in the magic of many peoples. Among the Greeks and the Arabs, this concept is sometimes connected with astrological speculations related to the possibility of endowing lower beings with the spirituality of the stars. In Judaism, the idea of the Golem is associated with the Kabbalistic views of

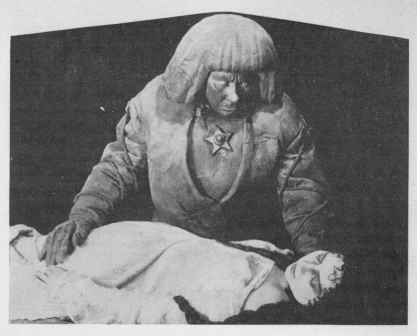

"Der Golem". (The Museum of Modern Art/Film Stills Archive)

creation and with the belief in the creative power of the letters of god's names
and the letters of the Torah in general.

The legend of the Golem of Prague has no historical basis in the life
of Rabbi Loew or in the era close to his lifetime. Originally, the legend was
attached to Rabbi Elijah of Chelm, and became connected with Rabbi Loew
at a relatively late date, probably the second half of the 18th century.

Rabbi Loew (1513–1609), born in Germany, was a famous Hebrew
scholar and Bible commentator, who preached a simple morality. As rabbi
of Prague, in order to end the enmity between Christians and Jews and to
unmask the baseless charges of ritual murder, he invited the cardinal of Prague
to a disputation on religious dogma and practice. The disputation, conducted
over a number of days and involving hundreds of churchmen, took the form
of questions submitted to the rabbi. The cardinal was so impressed with
Loew's astuteness and wisdom that he pledged his friendship and support.

For more information, see: C. Bloch, *The Golem Mystical Tales from
the Ghetto of Prague* (Steiner, 1972) and J. Trachtenberg, *Jewish Magic and
Superstition: A Study in Folk Religion* (Atheneum, 1970).

331

Zombies

A zombie is the body of a dead person that has been reanimated by a voodoo sorcerer and is subject to the sorcerer's will.

Haitian folklore cites many cases of people whose deaths were recorded and burials witnessed, but who were found after an interval of time to be alive (after a fashion) existing under the complete control of a *boko*, or practitioner of black magic. It is believed that the boko had reanimated the corpse in order to use it as a slave for benign or evil purposes.

The word comes from *zombi*, a term apparently deriving from various African languages, in which it signified a god or a good-luck fetish. The Haitian zombi can move, eat, hear, and, some say, even speak, but it has no memory and no knowledge of its condition.

Some Haitians believe that the boko uses certain drugs, which induce a profound state of lethargy indistinguishable from death. After burial, the boko recovers the body, which has in the process been deprived of its soul and reduced to a zombi. The zombi can return to the grave only when the time decreed for its natural death has been reached.

Relatives of a deceased Haitian are reported to have administered poison, or even knife wounds, to a corpse, to make certain that it is completely dead. Others bury the corpse face down with a dagger in his hand, so it may stab any sorcerer who disturbs its rest. Since a corpse can only be raised if it answers to its name, the mouths of the dead are sometimes sewn shut.

If a zombie is fed salt, a popular legend maintains, it will come to a realization of its condition, seek out its grave, and die, but not, according to some, before killing its master and destroying his property.

The late President Francois Duvalier's private army was said to have included zombies in its ranks.

Educated Haitians and other observers often assert that a zombi is merely a victim of a potent drug that incapacitates part of the brain, inhibiting speech and willpower but allowing motion. The secret of the drug is said to have been brought by early slaves from Africa. Hypnosis and suggestion could be used to complement the drug; however, no detailed medical explanation has been offered.

Other purported zombies may in reality be severely retarded or brain-damaged individuals, who may turn up in villages where they are unknown and therefore be mistaken for long-dead persons. Some cases are probably frauds. One magistrate is said to have discovered an air-pipe leading from a coffin to the surface of the ground, after witnessing the supposed reanimation of a buried corpse.

One interesting theory suggests that the zombi figure is a reminiscence of plantation days, when slaves learned the benefits of playing dumb before their master. Or, the zombi is seen as the ultimate slave's nightmare—a denial of the release from servitude that death otherwise promised.

One macabre item of zombi lore may have led to the charge that human flesh is sometimes sold in the marketplaces of Haiti. A zombi, it is said, may be transformed into an animal and sold in that form. Thus, ordinary animal meat may have at times been suspected by the superstitious of being human flesh.

For additional information, see: A. Metraux, *Voodoo in Haiti* (Schocken Books, 1972); F. Huxley, *The Invisibles: Voodoo Gods in Haiti* (McGraw-Hill, 1966); and D. Cohen, *Voodoo, Devils, and the New Invisible World* (Dodd, Mead and Co., 1972).